DISABILITY AND THE DILEMMAS OF EDUCATION AND JUSTICE

DISABILITY AND THE DILEMMAS OF EDUCATION AND JUSTICE

Edited by
Carol Christensen and Fazal Rizvi

Open University Press
Buckingham · Philadelphia

Open University Press
Celtic Court
22 Ballmoor
Buckingham
MK18 1XW

and
1900 Frost Road, Suite 101
Bristol, PA 19007, USA

First Published 1996

A catalogue record of this book is available from the British Library

ISBN   0 335 19584 9 (hb)   0 335 19583 0 (pb)

Library of Congress Cataloging-in-Publication Data
Disability and the dilemmas of education and justice / edited by Carol Christensen
    and Fazal Rizvi.
        p.   cm.
    Includes bibliographical references and index.
    ISBN 0-335-19584-9(hb.). — ISBN 0-335-19583-0 (pbk.)
    1. Handicapped—Social conditions.   2. Handicapped—Education.
3. Special education.   4. Social justice.   I. Christensen, Carol, 1949–   .
II. Rizvi, Fazal, 1950–   .
HV1568.D567   1996
371.9—dc20   96-11907
                                                                              CIP

Typeset by Type Study, Scarborough
Printed in Great Britain by St Edmundsbury Press Ltd, Bury St Edmunds, Suffolk

In memory of Barry Troyna

Contents

List of contributors

Carol Christensen is a senior lecturer in educational psychology at The University of Queensland. Her research interests include cognitive psychology and the social construction of disability. She has written on the social contexts of special education as well as student thinking and learning.

Alan Gartner is dean for Research and University Programs, and a professor of The Graduate School and University Centre, The City University of New York. He is a leading authority on inclusive education and has published widely on this topic and issues related to the rights of persons with disabilities.

Michael M. Gerber is a professor in the Graduate School of Education at the University of California, Santa Barbara. His research interests include cognitive approaches to learning disabilities and special education policy. He has written extensively on issues related to the education of students with disabilities and is one of the leading advocates of a cautious approach to inclusion.

Kenneth R. Howe is an associate professor in the School of Education at the University of Colorado at Boulder. He has written widely on the philosophy of education and ethics. He is one of the leading writers in the US in the area of ethical issues as they relate to special education. His book *Ethics of Special Education* (with Ofelia Miramontes) is one of the seminal works in the field.

Peter Isaacs is a senior lecturer in the Centre for Applied Ethics at Queensland University of Technology. His research focuses on the ways in which ethical perspectives help inform professional practice. He has written a number of papers critiquing a variety of educational and social practices.

Andrew Jakubowicz is professor of sociology at the University of Technology, Sydney. He is one of Australia's leading writers on multiculturalism and cultural policy. His most recent work examined issues of representations of race, ethnicity and disability in the media and popular cultural texts. He has recently published *Ethnicity, Racism and Media*.

Dorothy Kerzner Lipsky is director, National Center on Educational Restructuring and Inclusion, The Graduate School and University Center, The City University of New York. Together with Alan Gartner, she is editor of *Beyond Separate Education: Quality Education for All* and author of *Supporting Families with a Child with a Disability: an International Outlook.*

Bob Lingard is an associate professor in education at The University of Queensland, Australia. He is a sociologist of education who has written extensively on theories of the state and equity policies in education. He is a coeditor with John Knight and Paige Porter of *Schooling Reform in Hard Times.*

Genée Marks obtained her Ph.D from Deakin University on the implementation of the Victorian (Australia) policy on integration of students with disabilities. She is currently an educational policy adviser with the New South Wales Technical and Further Education System. She has written on gender and disability and the problems with policies of integration.

Helen Meekosha is a senior lecturer in social work at the University of New South Wales. She has written extensively in the areas of sociology of migration, ethnic affairs and issues of public policy development and implementation.

Fazal Rizvi is a professor in educational policy at Monash University. He is a philosopher of education whose research interests include theories of social justice and educational policy. He has published widely on issues of racism, the politics of multicultural education and the problems of democratic reform in education.

Roger Slee is professor of educational policy at Goldsmiths' College, University of London. He has written extensively on the sociology of special education, particularly related to issues of policy and integration of students with disabilities.

Sally Tomlinson is professor of educational policy at Goldsmiths' College, University of London. She is a leading British writer on issues of racism, multicultural education and the sociology and politics of special education. She is the author of the acclaimed text, *Sociology of Special Education.*

Until his untimely death in February 1996, *Barry Troyna* was a professor of education at Warwick University in the UK. He was a prolific writer in the area of racism and education, with ten published books. His research interests included politics of difference, educational policy research and ethical issues in educational research.

Carol Vincent is senior research fellow at Warwick University. She has written on parent participation education reforms in England and Wales, racism and disability, and policy sociology.

Fazal Rizvi and Carol Christensen

Introduction

In 1966 Burton Blatt and Fred Kaplan published *Christmas in Purgatory: A Photographic Essay*. In it, they captured the day-to-day lives at the time of thousands of intellectually disabled children and adults who were institutionalized. The images portrayed were as horrifying as any that had emerged from World War II death camps. Skeletal inmates, many of them naked, were found huddled in corners and on benches, faeces smeared on walls, dormitories so crowded that it was impossible to walk from one corner of the room to the other without clambering over beds, windows and doors barred, children bound to furniture by rags and lying helpless in straitjackets. The overall picture was one of unspeakable human suffering and deprivation. Many of the captions attached to the photographs were originally written in the eighteenth and nineteenth centuries. Yet they were as appropriate to the conditions in institutions in 1966 as they were when first penned.

In many cases conditions of incarceration for people with disabilities were far more terrible than those which existed for people with criminal convictions. Yet, these people had committed no offence against society. They suffered such degrading and inhumane treatment simply because they were disabled. In most western societies, babies who were born in some way 'defective' – physically or intellectually – were routinely incarcerated in large institutions for their entire lives. Blatt and Kaplan's photographs were enormously revealing of such institutions. They brought to attention ethical issues that society had conveniently pushed behind institutional bars. They pointed to the gross injustices suffered by the people with disabilities.

Outside institutions, the discrimination faced by children and adults with disabilities was no less disturbing. In schools children with disabilities were regularly placed in segregated settings. In many ways, such segregation institutionalized a system of unequal education. Students with disabilities were excluded from the right to participate in normal educational processes open to all other children. They were marginalized and excluded in ways that would not have been tolerated by any other social group.

In the late 1960s, Blatt and Kaplan's graphic depiction of institutional life was only one of many works protesting at the treatment of people with disabilities. The book was part of an emerging social movement asserting the rights of people with disabilities. Governments had to take note. The avalanche of protests, critique and litigation that was unleashed during the 1960s resulted in widespread legislative mandates and reform of practices in the 1970s and 80s. The unfettered incarceration of 'imperfect' babies and the warehousing of children and adults in massive state-run institutions were curtailed. Institutions that previously housed thousands of children and adults were emptied.

Many children with physical, sensory and intellectual disabilities are now educated in their community schools along with their non-disabled peers. Much has clearly changed since the publication of *Christmas in Purgatory*. But for many critics much has also remained the same. Despite far-reaching reforms, criticism and critique has continued, informed not only by new policy contingencies but also new theoretical insights pertaining to both ethical theory and educational practice. For example, poststructural insights have raised new issues for curriculum and pedagogy that might be more responsive to the postmodern politics of difference. And the nature of politics itself has changed within which moral claims concerning the rights of people with disabilities must now be expressed. Increasingly, governments across the world are withdrawing the commitment they have had since the 1960s to ameliorate social disadvantage through the use of public funds. Many of the welfare services that were once taken for granted are now being privatized – left either to the mercy of the markets or to the good will of the charitable institutions. The 'user-pays' principle has enormous implications for those with disabilities.

We stand at the crossroads in reform of the educational treatment of people with disabilities. This book is located at this junction. It is based on the view that while notions of justice have always been implicit in the discussion of the theoretical, policy and practical issues concerning the education of people with disabilities, these notions are seldom made explicit and subjected to sustained analysis. As a result, much rhetoric may be found in the literature. So, while there is widespread recognition that as a group people with disabilities have been subjected to social practices which are fundamentally unjust, there is a lack of clarity on what constitutes injustice and what would constitute a socially just community for people with disabilities. Clearly, justice is a highly contested term which can be used in a variety of ways to suit a variety of political interests. This book is based on the conviction that while it is impossible to explicate a definitive definition of social justice, it is nonetheless important to look at the various ways in which considerations of justice relate to the practice of education.

Many of the early reformers advocated more humane treatment and care of people with disabilities. Thus, non-disabled advocates argued that the way in which people with disabilities were treated in society was a violation of their human rights. For example, in their essay, Blatt and Kaplan (1966) included a chapter titled 'The Promised Land' in which smiling, well-fed and well-dressed children and adults were captured at work and play. Children were seen being rocked in the arms of their carers. Institutions were clean, brightly decorated and full of human activity. Here was a norm of a socially just, caring and compassionate society. Wolfensberger (1972), another leading advocate for 'the disabled', called for 'normalization'. Normalization required that people with disabilities should have access to the same rights and social resources as 'normal' people. The view of justice assumed here was thus located within a logic of welfare which stressed the notions of equality of access and treatment. Yet the 'normal' itself was not made problematic. The focus thus was on individual rights rather than institutions.

This view of justice is consistent with a Rawlsian theory of justice which sees social justice as being based on a fair and just distribution of social goods. In his highly influential book, *A Theory of Justice*, Rawls argues that there are two basic principles in maintaining socially just practices. First, that each person 'is to have the most extensive basic liberty compatible with similar liberty for others' (1971: 61). Second, that primary social goods should be distributed equally, with the exception of an unequal distribution which favoured those who were socially disadvantaged. The distributive view of social justice regards it a responsibility of the state to provide for the needs of disabled students. Thus, initial reforms in the education of students with disabilities often focused on providing a fairer educational opportunity based on individual needs. In Britain students were referred to as having special educational needs while in the US each 'handicapped' student was provided with an individual education plan which documented his or her specific needs.

Fairness of distribution was often articulated as access to 'normal' environments. Thus, a range of policies were implemented, from deinstitutionalization to education in the least restrictive environment to provide access to the physical, social and educational environments available to everyone else in the community. The current language of integration and inclusion has emerged out of these 'normalization' initiatives. Yet there is now ample evidence to suggest that these policies have not produced the kind of changes envisaged. Nor have they satisfied the disability rights movement which has interpreted these changes as not only piecemeal but also limited. They are regarded as piecemeal because there are insufficient resources to accommodate students with disabilities in regular classrooms. And they are limited because they focus attention on the individual child and not on the educational system that perpetuates and sometimes produces disadvantage.

What is becoming increasingly clear is that the distributive notions underpinning many of the recent reforms in special education are insufficient to take account of the cultural economic and political relations that define people's lives in schools and society. In other words, distributive solutions to social injustice fail to recognize power relationships which shape and sustain injustice. People with disabilities continue to be culturally oppressed and socially marginalized while their interests are still defined by advocates acting on their behalf. People with disabilities continue to demand the right to define what is in their own best interests.

These considerations suggest a need for social justice in education to be rethought, going beyond the limited welfarist distributive model to a model which recognizes the multiple voices of people with disabilities. The essays in this book grapple with the challenge of rearticulating the idea of social justice in education. They suggest that we need a language of social justice that highlights notions of recognition, rights and empowerment of people with disabilities. Such a task requires discussion of the issues of representation of disability and its articulation with gender, sexuality, race, class and other categories of social difference. As well as analysing the theoretical nuances of social justice, we need to examine the ways in which injustices are expressed in practices related to integration and inclusion in schools, and the dilemmas of professional practice in education. Such an agenda demands that analyses not be located within a single disciplinary frame, but draw upon a variety of disciplines, including philosophy, sociology, psychology and history. This book is therefore an interdisciplinary one, committed to a systematic analysis of the issues and not necessarily to any particular ideological position.

In the opening chapter, Rizvi and Lingard put the notion of social justice in the spotlight. They suggest that social justice is a highly contested concept which has been interpreted in a variety of ways to serve a variety of interests. Most definitions of social justice have variously focused on issues of fairness, desert and need. These views compete for political ascendancy. In recent years, social justice has increasingly become associated with the idea of property rights and an individualism that undermines the collective ethos of education. Furthermore, Rizvi and Lingard maintain that each of the dominant views of social justice is located within a distributive logic that cannot adequately account for a contemporary politics of difference which takes into account the complex realities of the lives of people with disabilities. They conclude that distribution on its own is insufficient and that a politics of recognition is a necessary component of a more comprehensive view of educational justice.

The theme of the contested nature of social justice is also central to Peter Isaacs's chapter. According to Isaacs, however, the idea of educational justice should be located within a moral form of life that presupposes a particular view of persons. Shared collective practices such as education must respect that persons are self-aware social beings who are active and self-creative; and that if people with disabilities are recognized as persons then they are entitled not only to self-respect and autonomy but also to opportunities that enable them to realize their full potential. In so far as the traditional practices of special education are not necessarily embedded in such moral imperatives, they cannot claim to be committed to educational justice. Isaacs goes on to argue that we need to realize that disability is a social construction, and that special education needs to be reconstituted in ways that reorganize the power relations which have traditionally defined the ways in which students with disabilities have been treated in education.

Like Isaacs, Kenneth Howe is also concerned with issues of ethical practice in relation to children with disability. Howe's analysis is located within the framework of a current philosophical debate between those theories of justice which emphasize systems of principles and those which focus more upon communitarian practice and social relationships. Howe argues that we cannot afford to do away with either – and that we need to address systems of principles as well as community and relationships. He illustrates this argument by examining the principle of equality of educational opportunity, suggesting that in itself it is insufficient for the realization of educational justice and needs to be supplemented with a communitarian ethic. Applying this philosophical analysis to the concerns of special education, Howe argues that by the nature and severity of some disabilities, certain students cannot enjoy equality of educational opportunity; and that a rationale for educating such children must therefore reside within a broader concern for caring, community and belonging. This suggests that we need to create institutions which are not only based on the principle of inclusion but also meaningful educational participation.

Howe's reference to degrees of disability, and their relevance or otherwise to the principles of educational justice, highlights the need to examine the idea of disability itself. Carol Christensen's chapter examines the ways in which traditional special education has 'named' disability. She argues that the medical model which still dominates special education relates disability to notions of personal disease, pathology, disorder or deficit; but in doing so it often acts as a mechanism of social and cultural oppression. The model itself assumes that it is neutral in relation to particular political agendas but it can be shown historically to have marginalized and disempowered students with disabilities. The recognition that disability is a social construction leads us to the realization that real and enduring reforms in special education can only be achieved by addressing the power relationships that are embedded within the pedagogy, curriculum and organization of schools. Educational justice thus requires an explicit examination of the politics of representation.

The chapter by Meekosha and Jakubowicz examines this politics, with the conviction that any analysis of social justice in relation to disability needs to address the structural issues of representation and participation. Disability, they maintain, is a socially constituted and reproduced set of relationships through which people with disabilities experience society in a variety of complex but unequal ways. Various educational practices in special education, for example, assume categorizations which can have the effect of dividing and separating people with disabilities into mutually antagonistic blocs. Many of these practices emphasize the importance of managing and controlling disability within an ideology of normalization, but such a perspective often overlooks the barriers that people with disabilities have in accessing 'normal' institutions. It does not acknowledge the ways in which the ideology of normalization constitutes disability within a logic of deficit. In view of the rise of the disability movement along with the wider social mobilization around identity politics, practices of normalization which undermine the rights of people with disabilities to participate fully in defining their own social and educational futures can no longer be justified.

Meekosha and Jakubowicz's chapter highlights the importance of meaningful participation of the people with disabilities in determining the ways in which they would like to see themselves represented in all their diversity and complexity. Roger Slee's chapter takes up the challenge of exploring the complex relationship between disability, class and poverty. The issue of disablement, he maintains, speaks both to complex structural relationships as well as to the politics of identity and representation. No single theoretical narrative, Slee argues, is sufficient to explain the structural realities of the political economy of disability. The disproportionate level of homelessness among people with mental illness, discriminatory employment practices and flawed assumptions concerning the productive capacities of people with disabilities serve to show the complex ways in which issues of disability and class articulate with each other, and the manner in which disablement restricts student options and reinforces existing class hierarchies. Slee suggests that many of the recent reforms in special education have floundered because they have not always attended to issues concerning the ways in which the classed context of schooling helps determine distributive patterns in society. The focus of many of these reforms has been on individual disadvantage abstracted from its history and its cultural and social context. Educational reform agendas that do not consider the issues of how disability is defined and by whom are unlikely to produce socially just educational practices.

The theme of 'who may speak for whom?' is central to Genée Marks's chapter, which seeks to explore the manner in which issues of gender and sexuality articulate with each other. Marks suggests that fear and myths about sexuality are projected on to people with disabilities, who are variously framed either as asexual or oversexed, but these representations are not the only way in which girls and women with disabilities are oppressed. Drawing upon three different examples, Marks shows how sexual and gendered discrimination impacts on people with disabilities. First, she considers issues concerning marriage and parenting, something which is frequently denied to women with disability. Second, she draws attention to patterns of discrimination that women with disabilities face in relation to work, which is often either unwaged or underpaid. Third, Marks explores specific problems that gay women with disabilities confront in being able to express their sexuality. This analysis leads Marks to conclude that the contemporary politics of difference must accept the reality of difference and diversity among the various groups whose rights have been championed by various emanicipatory movements. This requires an inclusive politics of voice and representation rather than a policy rhetoric of inclusion that leaves structures of domination unchallenged.

It is in the policy field that the notions of inclusion and integration have been widely utilized to put forward an alternative to the traditional deficit language of special education. Despite this reform, the field of special education has remained, as Troyna and Vincent point out in their chapter, dominated by what they refer to as 'ideology of expertism'. It is an ideology which depoliticizes issues of educational reform, converting many political issues into technical ones, leaving much of the power of decision-making in the hands of a few 'experts'. Drawing a parallel with some of the limitations of mainstream reforms in addressing the problems of racism in schools instituted in local education authorities in England, Troyna and Vincent view the fullest participation of people with disabilities in the decision-making processes that affect their lives as an imperative that cannot be overlooked. They suggest that collective action that is premised on a politics of difference is needed to subvert the ideology of 'expertism' which has left people with disabilities without both voice and representation.

These concerns highlight the issue of participation which is central to the chapters by both Lipsky and Gartner, and Gerber, though their chapters take different positions on the policy of inclusion of the students with disabilities within the regular classrooms. Lipsky and Gartner argue that despite legislative reform, nearly 10 per cent of the school-age population in the US remain in some form of segregated special education. They suggest that this state of affairs is inherently unjust. In order to honour the fundamental rights of students with disabilities, they must have the opportunity to participate fully in the mainstream of the education system; all children should be placed in regular classroom settings alongside all their peers. Additional resources must be made available so that children receive disability-effective educational provision. Lipsky and Gartner suggest that the presence of students with disabilities, including students with severe disabilities, in regular classrooms would provide the necessary impetus for necessary structural reforms of regular education. While the option of segregating some students remains, the fundamental structure of education will remain intact, continuing injustice.

Gerber's chapter, on the other hand, insists that such a principle of full inclusion is too absolutist. He prefers a gradualist and contingent approach. Gerber argues that in the United States, current debates are rooted in the contradictory pressures which resulted in the establishment of special education at the turn of the century. These contradictory pressures persist, and that a generalized strategy of inclusion may be counterproductive. The social injustices faced by disabled learners are quite distinct from those faced by other socially oppressed groups. By virtue of their disability, these students cannot be expected to compete with other students. To place them in regular classrooms without fundamentally restructuring the current meritocratic system will simply perpetuate their disadvantage.

Gerber highlights some of the complexities faced by school administrators, teachers and parents as they negotiate the legislative, judicial and policy mandates while at the same time attempting to cater for the diverse social-emotional and educational needs of their students. Tomlinson continues with the theme of the dilemmas faced by professionals working in the field of special education. She suggests that professionalism has become an ideology through which power relations are instantiated in schools. Professionalism creates a mystique so that the decisions about the lives of students are surrounded by a sense of infallible authority. Earlier notions of professionalism were predicated upon the ideals of autonomy and service. However, professionals are becoming increasingly engulfed in a bureaucratic rationality as more and more professionals are employed by the state. Tomlinson discusses a range of dilemmas that emerge from the contradictory pressure of cultur of autonomy, ideals of service, interprofessional rivalries and political bureaucratic demands. As a result, the provision of services to students with disabilities becomes fragmented and students' interests are subordinated to the interests of the state and its bureaucracy.

Tomlinson's analysis returns the discussion to the issue of the role that people with disabilities must themselves play in making decisions that affect their lives. Collectively, the essays in this book have served to illustrate the limitations of the distributive views of social justice as they relate to the education of people with disabilities. The essays have shown the need to take issues of difference, representation and recognition seriously, because it is around these ideas that the dilemmas of educational justice must be addressed and perhaps resolved.

References

Blatt, B. and Kaplan, F. (1966) *Christmas in Purgatory: A Photographic Essay.* Boston, MA: Allyn and Bacon.
Rawls, J. (1971) *A Theory of Justice.* Cambridge, MA: Belknap Press.
Wolfensberger, W. (1972) *The Principles of Normalisation in Human Services.* Toronto: National Institute on Mental Retardation.

Fazal Rizvi and Bob Lingard

Disability, education and the discourses of justice

Introduction

Although academic interest in the education of children with disabilities can be traced back to the nineteenth century, in most western countries it was not until the early twentieth century that special education became established as a distinctive field of study. A number of factors contributed to its development. In countries where legislation had made education compulsory, students with disabilities posed special problems. Educators knew very little about these problems and about the educational provisions appropriate for these students. This void in knowledge, it was argued, could only be filled by more systematic research. Research was needed in order to determine how students with disabilities could be managed more effectively. At the same time, the new century had ushered in great moral optimism and belief in human improvement, together with an emerging concern for the 'weaker' members of human society.

The search for a better knowledge base and an implicit moral commitment to the welfare of students with disabilities have thus been the basic tenets of special education. Yet the field itself is surprisingly devoid of an explicit examination of its moral premises. As Solity (1992: 4) has observed,

> The fact that the earliest forms of special education were those with physical and sensory difficulties, which were seen to be clearly identifiable medical conditions, gave the medical model (that is, that difficulties arise due to the characteristics of the child and that there is therefore something wrong with the child) considerable currency in special education.

The medical model viewed disability as a problem with associated signs and symptoms which could either be remedied or whose impact could be minimized or managed with appropriate treatment. Such a view was however based on a range of normative assumptions about what constituted a perfectly healthy person. But those working with the medical model seldom questioned the moral constitution of such assumptions. Nor did they consider issues of treatment in ethical terms. Special education thus developed as a *technical* field, located within a positivist framework, concerned with issues of diagnosis, assessment and causes of disability and appropriate forms of treatment.

So dominant has been the medical model that responsibility for the education of students with disabilities has been shared between health departments and educational authorities. In England and Wales, for example, it was the 1944 Education Act which placed the special educational needs of 'handicapped' pupils firmly within the general responsibilities of local education authorities. And in the US, despite many court cases aimed at obliging regular schools to admit children with disabilities, it was not until 1975 with the passage of the Education of All Handicapped Children's Act that the federal government recognized the rights of all students with disabilities to mainstream public education (Pijl 1994). This recognition was, of course, part of a broader political struggle for justice led in the 1960s by feminist and civil rights leaders. But for educators and parents of students with disabilities the language of equal opportunity was to prove highly effective. It enabled them increasingly to question the provision of segregated special education and call for the integration of students with disabilities into regular classrooms.

In Australia, a similar equal opportunity agenda in relation to students with disabilities was recognized by the federal Labor government's Karmel Report, published in 1973. But it was not until the early 1980s that integration as a principle became a policy reality. In Victoria, for example, integration was given a firm legislative authority by a Labor government in 1984 (Fulcher 1989). The idea of integration was a simple one: children with disabilities were to be educated in regular schools provided certain conditions were met, and when in regular schools they were to engage in activities of the school alongside other students to the greatest extent possible. The rationale for the policy of integration was both educational as well as moral, grounded in a social justice strategy that stressed equality of access and opportunity for all. However, the nature of the relationship between this political commitment to social justice and the dilemmas of educational practice was seldom examined. As a result, practices of integration varied a great deal from school to school, and segregation and integration continued to exist alongside each other (Fulcher 1989). Nor did, as Slee (1993) has argued, the medical model disappear entirely – those working with positivist assumptions simply appropriated the language of social justice to continue to pursue their research, persisting with the idea of individual deficit.

Most researchers in special education remain reluctant to undertake any systematic examination of what justice might mean, and how it might relate to the construction of their research questions and the uses of research findings. The dominant assumption appears to be that a concern for equal educational opportunities provides sufficient justification for the conduct of research, but that this value commitment must not be allowed to 'contaminate' research. The relationship between value and research is thus believed to be an *instrumental* one. The consequences of this instrumentalism for the practices of special education, and of integration, have been significant because practice must somehow seek to integrate values and research in ways that researchers are not required to do. As Meijer, Pijl and Hegarty (1994: 136) have observed, in each of the six countries they surveyed, there is 'a lack of clarity about the goals of integration and means to achieve them'. In this chapter, we suggest that part of the problem may lie in the fact that there are competing definitions of social justice operating in special education, that unless issues of ethics and politics of education are addressed explicitly, the field will continue to leave many educators, parents and students confused and bewildered, and that many reform initiatives will continue to flounder. We argue that educators cannot hope to tackle the dilemmas of educational practice adequately unless they appreciate that issues of justice are central to their work, and that the idea of justice itself is a site of much contestation. Our discussion in this chapter will focus largely on Australia, though we will make more general remarks wherever applicable.

The idea of justice

The immediate difficulty one confronts when examining the idea of social justice is that it does not have a single essential meaning – it represents discourses that are historically constituted and it is a site of conflicting and divergent political endeavours. Social justice does not refer to a single set of primary or basic goods, conceivable across all moral and material domains. Its social meaning, as Walzer (1983) has pointed out, is historical in character. Having said this, however, it needs to be acknowledged that injustice does have a material reality that is readily recognized by those who are subjected to it. Those who are hungry or poor or homeless or physically impaired do not need abstract definitions in order to be able to recognize their plight. In policy discourse, the idea of social justice has practical significance, and needs therefore to be articulated in terms of particular values, which while not fixed across time and space, nevertheless have to be given specific content in particular struggles for reform.

In the Australian context, MacIntyre (1985) has provided ample evidence to show how the political ideal of social justice has expressed itself in different forms at different times over the past two hundred years. He has shown the ideal to be essentially contested. He has argued further that 'the search for social justice arises from the meeting of a particular kind of authority with particular aspirations that are located in particular historical circumstances' (p. 112). Tracing its Australian genealogy, MacIntyre has demonstrated how over the past decade the idea of social justice has been rearticulated by a federal Labor government increasingly unclear about how to achieve the social democratic goals to which it has been traditionally committed. Consequently, its symbolic commitment to justice has become trapped within its wider concern with the restructuring of the Australian state towards a more market-driven political economy. It has sought to develop an organizational structure that is responsive to market considerations, is efficient and effective, and is able to compete effectively within an increasingly globalized economy. However, to a much greater extent than is the case in Britain and in New Zealand, concerns of equity and social justice are still stressed in Australian public policy, but they have clearly been rearticulated.

The restructuring of the Australian state has had a number of implications for the provision of services to people labelled as 'disabled'. The structure of many welfare services has changed as levels of funding have been reduced. There has been a greater reliance on 'user-pays' principles, and new managerial practices have been developed which have made access to services difficult. But beyond these, more significant have been the ideological changes that have changed the form in which the state now expresses its responsibility to people. The market logic intervenes to change citizens into clients − with their social relations with the state now increasingly mediated by concerns of their productivity and their contribution to the national economy. Nowhere are these cultural changes more significant than in education, as education impacts on the development of people's sense of social worth. In what follows, we want to discuss these ideological changes in the notion of social justice, especially as they relate to recent policy practices in special education.

Of course, these ideological shifts, away from a social democratic settlement to a market-driven definition of the relationship between the state and people, are not restricted to Australia. They can also be found in other western countries. Indeed, it was in Thatcher's Britain and Reagan's America that market considerations were first applied in the social policy arena, where marketization of education was first institutionalized. But what makes the Australian situation particularly interesting is that in Australia these changes have taken place under a Labor government committed to the principles of equity and social justice. It is a government that has had to reconcile its determination to restructure the Australian state with its social justice credentials. Thus, it has had to promote social justice while instituting organizational practices which at the same time have the potential of undermining it. The ideological shifts that have occurred in Australia are thus much more complex and equivocal than elsewhere (see Fitzclarence and Kenway 1993, and Lingard *et al.* 1993). Similar tensions are also manifest in the Blair-led Labour policy manifesto in Britain.

Shifts in ideology

The idea of social justice has always played an important role in the myths Australia has had about its social character. 'Fair go' has long been a popular sentiment in Australia, but it was not until the 1960s and 70s that this sentiment was translated into an educational settlement that justified an expansion of educational provision and expenditure. It was the Karmel Report (1973) that forcefully articulated a strong definition of equality of opportunity, acknowledging the limitations of the longstanding meritocratic objectives of education. Karmel (1973: 13) argued that 'the equal valuing of people based on their common humanity might lead to a quite different interpretation of equality of opportunity' from the one that had prevailed in the past. As indeed it did, leading to the creation of a range of federally funded specific purpose programs, including the Disadvantaged Schools Program and the Commonwealth Schools Commission's Special Education Program, aimed at achieving more equal outcomes from schooling and giving greater voice to the previously marginalized groups.

The end of the postwar economic boom in the mid-1970s, however, led to a shift in this ideology. During this period, successive Liberal and Labor governments spoke of a new context of austerity, a changed economic context in which Australia had to become more competitive internationally. It is within this context that Labor's attempts at redefining social justice must be viewed. It should be noted, however, that the notion of 'context' is not a simple one; rather, it is an ideological notion which serves to highlight only some of the circumstances in ways that serve to support some political purposes better than others. What is regarded as 'the context', and the constraints it is believed to imply for various policy options, is thus a matter for considerable political debate (Seddon 1994). So, it is against a particular interpretation of the social and economic conditions facing Australia that Labor's social justice approach has been formulated.

Thus, while in the 1970s Labor was guided by a social welfare reformism, predicated upon a deep concern for the disadvantaged and a belief in the capacity of the state to promote social justice through judicious intervention-ist programs, the current approach proposes to work towards social justice within the framework of an economic rationalist understanding of Aus-tralia's 'economic context'. The government has effectively assumed that progress on social issues can only be achieved through unrestrained capital growth, the free market, economic individualism, the minimalist state and private property as the basis of individual freedom (see Pusey 1991). Within the framework of these assumptions, it has called for a Thatcherite rolling back of the state, and in particular cutting back on so-called 'unproductive' welfare spending. Further, the government's decision to deregulate the market has effectively reduced its policy options, leaving it exposed to the often intemperate judgements of the international money markets. However, given that Labor cannot afford electorally to abandon its social democratic rhetoric, its conception of social justice has had to be rearticulated in terms which are consistent with the neoclassical economic postulates which it has now accepted.

Related to this philosophical orientation has been the government's managerialism. According to Considine (1988), public policy and programs are now developed in an economistic culture which views the business of public administration in corporate terms, as a more or less effective and efficient instrument for producing goods and services. The economistic criterion of cost-efficiency has become paramount, regardless of the actual character of these goods and services. However, since there is no market in the public sector, cutbacks have frequently been viewed as necessarily resulting in more efficient performance. Competition within and across the public sector is encouraged, and wherever possible, agencies are permitted, if not encouraged, to cross-charge each other for their services, and to commercialize their services in the open market (Yeatman 1990). There is considerable pressure on public agencies, including schools, to 'achieve more with less'.

This managerialism has resulted in a redefinition of citizens as consumers of publicly provided goods. Public administrators are thus encouraged to place emphasis on the consumer's right to 'choose' from the range of services provided. But as Yeatman argues:

> The effect of this reasoning is that 'consumers' of public goods and services are atomised in relation to each other, and the assumption is made that they can understand and express their preferences independent of any collectively oriented and/or political dialogue about how best to explore, express, and meet their needs in relation to publicly provided goods and services. They are no longer members of a public community of citizens, but become instead private self-interested actors.
>
> (Yeatman 1990: 2)

Such a view has major implications for the discourse of social justice and for thinking about the education of students with disabilities. To begin with, it has the effect of 'privatizing' persons. It implies that social relations are somehow irrelevant to public policy. Since autonomous actors are thought to be both the primary category of social analysis and the object of the provision of public goods and services, any reference to the background of individuals, as well as to their capacity, is rendered irrelevant to policy-making. This is an ideological position which creates major dilemmas for those responsible for the provision of educational and other social services to people with disabilities. This is so, because as Carpenter (1993: 185) has argued, 'Services are no longer regarded as a civic or human right but as commodity for consumers. People become consumers, services focus on consumer outcomes and human rights are narrowly redefined as consumer rights.'

The dilemmas faced by service providers are further accentuated by the pressures to cut back on services or privatize them. In maintaining its commitment to develop a system of administration that is fiscally efficient and responsible, federal Labor's successive budgets have restrained public sector activity through staff cuts, program rationalization, increasingly tight welfare targeting and privatization of services. Many of these managerialist 'reforms' have been implemented in the name of efficiency and strategic necessity, but whether these reforms disproportionately affect particular people is an issue that is often overlooked. The government's deregulation and privatization strategy has clearly rested within a business rather than a service framework, with the assumption that there is no place in the public sector for independent agencies that do not have the potential to raise revenue. It is not surprising therefore that those unable to pay, the poor and those with disabilities among them, have had to carry the greatest burden of the government's program of managerial 'reforms'.

To overcome some of the negative consequences of managerial reforms upon the disadvantaged, the government's social justice strategy has sought to reconcile them by rearticulating the idea of social justice into a weaker form, making it largely synonymous with a notion of fairness for each individual. As Rizvi (1993: 120) suggests, social justice is no longer 'seen as linked to past group oppression and disadvantage' judged historically, but represented simply as a matter of guaranteeing individual choice under the conditions of a 'free market'. This redefinition is clearly evident in reports and reviews produced by the Disability Advisory Council of Australia (DACA), established in 1984 to examine disability services, particularly those provided by the Department of Social Security, but also by other departments such as Education (Carpenter 1993). What is interesting about the work of DACA is that although it maintains the principles of human rights and participation, it nonetheless repositions its administrative ethos towards a narrowly focused behaviourist and technocratic discourse which requires services to be judged in terms of efficiency and effectiveness, against a set of abstract norms. In this way, its social justice rhetoric conflicts with its thinking about administrative norms on the basis of which it seeks to implement policies and deliver services. It also demonstrates conflicting views of social justice at work.

Traditions of social justice

As we have already noted, the idea of social justice is a highly contested one. It does not represent a timeless or static category. It has been interpreted in a variety of ways to reflect changing social and economic conditions. Indeed, the Australian Labor Party (ALP) does not have, and never has had, a uniform understanding of the idea of social justice. It is, for example, possible to identify, within the ALP, a number of traditions which underpin its thinking about the meaning and significance of social justice. Throughout its one hundred years of history, these traditions have struggled for supremacy. Indeed, it may plausibly be argued that it is this differing understanding of the notion of social justice that is the basis of the formation of the various factions within the ALP (MacIntyre 1985). The current policy debates simply represent the triumph of one particular understanding over others, for it is only within the framework of the currently dominant understanding that it is possible to reconcile the competing discourses of social justice and economic rationalism.

The three main traditions of thinking about social justice can be identified as *liberal-democratic* or *liberal-individualist, market-individualist*, and *social democratic*. The *liberal-individualist* view conceptualizes social justice variously in terms of either desert or fairness. In recent philosophical literature, perhaps the most outstanding contemporary advocate of the view of social justice that emphasizes justice as fairness is John Rawls (1972). To derive his principles of justice, Rawls constructed a hypothetical state of ignorance in which people do not know of the social position they might occupy in the future – with regard, for instance, to their income, status and power, and also to their natural abilities, intelligence, strength, etc. In such a state, Rawls argued, people, acting in their own self-interest, would inevitably select principles that are likely to do them least harm and maximize their chances of happiness. From this 'veil of ignorance', as Rawls called it, people will want to cover themselves from the various possibilities of misfortunes.

This philosophical projection led Rawls to suggest two principles: each person was to have the most extensive basic liberty compatible with similar liberty for others; and there should be equal distribution of primary social goods – unless unequal distribution was to the advantage of the least favoured. The first principle implied individual freedom, while the second principle suggested that the state had a special responsibility to create policy initiatives and programs directed towards 'removing barriers, arising from unequal power relations and preventing equity, access and participation' (Rawls 1972: 60).

Rawls's theory of social justice has been enormously influential in most western countries. During the 1960s and 70s, it led to a social democratic settlement of the 1970s, which included programs of affirmative action, as well as some, though not as many as some imagine, redistributive policies. In the 1990s, Rawls's views are still promoted by a section of the ALP, most notably by Andrew Theophanous, a leading parliamentarian in Australia, whose book, *Understanding Social Justice* (1993) uses Rawls to provide a blueprint to steer the government's social justice strategy towards a liberal-democratic definition. What Theophanous's analysis does not make clear, however, is how his government's economic rationalism can be reconciled with the Rawlsian redistributive philosophy he promotes.

In opposition to Rawls's view, Nozick (1976) has presented a view of social justice based on a *market-individualism* that emphasizes desert. Writing in the tradition of Locke and Sidgwick, Nozick argued that Rawls's theory focused on the issues of distribution and ignored the issue of people's entitlements to what they produce. Most theories of social justice, he pointed out, focus only on the end distribution of holdings; they pay little attention to the processes by which holdings were acquired. Nozick suggested that it is the justice of the competition – that is, the way competition is carried on and not its outcome – that counts. Nozick argued for a minimal state, limited to its functions of protection against force, theft, fraud, entitlement of contracts and so on – that is, protection of individuals to exercise their liberty. He thus rejected redistributive notions of social and economic justice. His entitlement theory suggested that it was unjust for the state to transfer property that belonged to individuals. Now while the differences between Rawls and Nozick are considerable, they both assume that people always act in their own self-interest. They both consider individualistic liberty as a value prior to any consideration of distribution. And they both assume community to be simply a sum of the individuals who reside in it.

The other tradition of thinking about social justice within the ALP – the *social democratic* tradition – is based on a very different set of assumptions. It is derived from Marx and stresses the idea of needs. As Beilharz (1989: 94) has pointed out, 'it is qualitatively different to the preceding understandings, in that need is viewed as a primary rather than a residual category, and it is this which sets this view off from the charity-based arguments about the "needy" which are compatible with either the "desert" or the "fairness" principles.' This 'needs' tradition highlights a more collectivist and cooperative image of society. It is important to note thus that liberal-individualist and social democratic traditions rest on very different understandings about the nature of the relationship between social justice and the market. The liberal-individualist regards the market as the most basic provider of social justice, of employment, services and welfare. The state is seen simply as a vehicle for promoting the activities of the market, and it is assumed that the market, if left to operate freely, will be able to deliver distributive fairness on its accord. According to the social democratic view, on the other hand, as Agnes Heller (1987) has pointed out, the idea of social justice may not necessarily be incompatible with markets, but it is unlikely to be achieved unless the market is controlled in sufficiently rigorous ways. State activity is thus seen as 'market-replacing' (Heller 1987), correcting its excesses, and minimizing the costs of its arbitrary exercise.

In Australia, as in other western countries, the market-individualist view of social justice, and more particularly the view of social justice as desert, has become increasingly dominant over the past decade or so. Thus, as

Beilharz argued, the Victorian Labor Government's social justice strategy was based on the hope

> that the economy itself can be steered in the direction of 'social justice' – a non-sequitur outside the logic of markets, necessarily introducing residual welfare mechanisms in order to buoy up the human flotsam which cannot negotiate justice for itself through the market. To argue in this way is necessarily to introduce the logic of charity, and the language of the 'needy', for there are citizens, and there are those outside the city gates, who are deserving compassion.
>
> (Beilharz 1989: 92–3)

These assumptions necessarily introduce deficit considerations, with women, migrants, people with disabilities and the poor, and especially the unemployed, becoming the disadvantaged to whom the market, through its agency, the state, has a special compensatory responsibility. Beilharz suggested further that social justice understood in this way thus became not so much a universal ethical principle as an administrative principle, the practical symbol of which is targeting of funds to ameliorate the most harmful consequences of market activity.

In Australia, the federal Labor government's social justice strategy seems to rest on similar assumptions. It suggests that freedom, prosperity and equity can only be delivered by the expansion of markets. With such a reliance on the market, the government's major responsibility becomes that of 'good management' of the social and cultural conditions necessary for capital accumulation. Labor's restructuring program may be seen in this light. Among the assumptions that lie behind the restructuring is the belief that the less the state is involved in market operations the better. Thus, tariffs have been cut, controls on the conduct of the market have been reduced, controls over banking and finance have been removed, tax breaks have been given to speculators to borrow abroad, new concentrations of wealth and media have been permitted, and a program of the sale of public enterprises has been started. And all this has often been justified on the grounds that free association of buyers and sellers in an open market will in the end bring a fair and equitable exchange. Moreover, it is assumed that with an expanding economy, it will be possible to do more for the disadvantaged.

Problems with market-individualism

What is clear then is that a conception of social justice has now been found by Labor which is consistent with the requirements of capital accumulation and gives markets a freer reign. Social and educational policies and programs are now subjected to this piece of ideology. The view of social justice now emerging in the form of a consensus is a contradictory amalgam of Rawlsian redistributive principles and Nozickian entitlement theory. In Australia, it seems that while the Nozickian ideological framework has not yet been totally accepted, at least to the extent it has been in Britain and the United States, it nevertheless has gained considerable policy ascendancy.

In the United States, Michael Apple (1988) has argued that there is now a recurrent conflict between property rights and person rights. A property right, he suggests, vests in individuals the power to enter into social relationships on the basis and extent of their property, while person rights are based on simple membership in their social collectivity. Person rights involve equal treatment of citizens, freedom and expression of movement, equal access to participation in decision-making in social institutions, and reciprocity in relations of power and authority. These rights achieved, in the 1960s, according to Apple, have been under sustained attack. In the process, the meaning of what it is to have the social goal of equity has changed. He argues:

> The citizen as 'free' consumer has replaced the previously emerging citizen as situated in structurally generated relations of domination. Thus the common good is now to be regulated exclusively by the laws of the market, free competition, private ownership and profitability. In a sense the definitions of freedom and equality are no longer democratic but *commercial*.
>
> (Apple 1988: 11)

While it would indeed be an overstatement to suggest the triumph of property rights over person rights in Australia, a great deal has already happened to raise the issue of what is wrong with the Nozickian view of social justice, why it should concern educators and how its logic might be confronted.

Nozick's view of social justice is located in the processes of acquisition and production, rather than redistribution. Its moral consequences should be disturbing to all educators because as Barry (1973: 17) has noted, a market view of social justice eliminates all transfer payments through the state, leaving 'the sick, the old, the disabled, the mothers with young children and no breadwinner and so on, to the tender mercies of private charity, given at the whim and pleasure of the donors and on any terms they choose to impose'. The freedom a market conception guarantees benefits the privileged in a disproportionate way.

Market-individualism refuses to supply social goals for economic allocation, substituting for them procedural criteria for the proper acquisition of income and wealth. But such a view individualizes the processes of production and acquisition. The activity of production in modern industrial societies is more social in character than Nozick appears to assume. All economic activity depends upon a network of cooperative relations between individuals. It is the social dimension of acquisition which makes distribution problematic in ways Nozick does not acknowledge. What seems also to be assumed by Nozick is that equality in respect of acquisition of material wealth is somehow unrelated to equality in respect of power. As Norman (1988: 97) has pointed out, 'trapped as he is within his individualistic assumptions, he [Nozick] still seems to think in terms of individuals being forced to put their individual property into a social pot. He ignores the possibility that what goes into the pot may be, from the start, socially produced and socially owned.'

What these arguments show is that market criteria are insufficient for determining social and educational policy, and that solely procedural criteria are insufficient for achieving social justice. To do so is to privilege the economic, and to view it as somehow unconnected to the cultural and the social. It is the social in the notion of social justice that we need to stress. The moral idea of social suggests above all the need to develop a sense of cooperative community in which rewards are not determined simply on the basis of productive contribution, but also on broader considerations of need and the human right everyone has to participate in social life to the best of her or his ability. A community that is not genuinely cooperative cannot be just.

In cooperative communities everyone benefits from participating in activities and in social institutions that are collectively productive. One can have a more productive life if one shares one's energies with others, in relations of open trust which enable one to see others as allies rather than competitors. Cooperation broadens one's interests and enlarges people's practical outlook by sharing the concerns of others. Beyond the benefits to individuals, these same considerations can be formulated as contributing to the general welfare of society, leading to general happiness. Market-individualism, on the other hand, favours those who are already advantaged. For people with disabilities, the market view of social justice can often mean no justice at all.

Beyond access and integration

What these considerations indicate is that market-individualism has a number of disastrous consequences for education generally, but for the education of people with disabilities in particular. In our view those researchers in special education who are reluctant to engage in discussions of social justice, and who prefer to view their research as being divorced from issues of politics, risk becoming co-opted within the ideology of market-individualism which has gained considerable hegemonic ascendancy in Australia and elsewhere in recent years. They need to recognize that the language of justice is highly contested, and that their research in relation to students with disabilities cannot be effective unless it includes some understanding of the ways in which the dominant expressions of market-individualism in education work against the interests of people with disabilities.

Recent reforms in special education have been linked to issues of access and equity. But what has become increasingly clear is that these distributive concerns are not sufficient to account adequately for either contemporary politics of difference, or the various complex ways in which exclusion and discrimination are now practised, in both their individual and institutional forms. Nor do they respond effectively to the calls by the disability rights movement to have voices of the people with disabilities themselves heard in processes of decision-making that affect their lives. A distributive politics is clearly necessary but not sufficient. This is so because while access and equity policies enable individuals to gain entry into mainstream institutions, they often leave the institutions themselves unaltered. In the case of students with disabilities, while many are allowed access, by and large the social conditions they experience have remained much the same, leading to their frustration and inability to cope. A broader view of justice is therefore required.

Such a view must entail the creation of conditions which encourage the maximum degree of cooperation between individual students in schools. These must include access to teachers' time and to all of the facilities which schools have to offer. But if genuine cooperation is to be achieved, then participation of all students in schools must be more than 'happiness therapy' – simply their retention in regular schools. It must move beyond questions of relevant curricula to a broadening of curriculum choice and pedagogical practice. We would want also to emphasize performance as a concomitant of participation, a point particularly pertinent to considerations of the increased number of students who now have access into regular schools. It is not sufficient for these students simply to have access – their *engaged* participation is necessary; it should be not merely symbolic but real.

A strong commitment to social justice understood in a socially cooperative sense is required at each of the system, school and classroom levels. Each is important in its own way. Certainly strong central policy commitment to social justice is important to support classroom teachers in their work with respect to equity concerns. Schools and teachers need symbolic and material support for equity policies and practices. That is particularly true within devolved systems, where integration is a legislative requirement. In our view, the recent restructuring of administration in most western countries, with its simultaneous centralization of policy formulation and devolution of policy implementation, has weakened the capacity of the state to support social justice initiatives at the local level. At the school level therefore teacher commitment to integration is required, because without such a commitment integration of students with disabilities risks becoming counterproductive. We need robust, caring and participatory schools to ensure social justice outcomes.

The idea of integration itself needs to be understood within this broader framework. As numerous educational advisers in the UK (see Adams 1986) have pointed out, while the policy of integration is progressive and egalitarian, it contains a number of inherent dangers for students with disabilities, especially in times of reduced state resources for schools. The integration argument suggests that on the grounds of human and educational rights, everyone should have access to regular schools and classrooms. However, when this strategy is invoked to suggest that the needs of everyone could be catered for through the same generalized services, it simply becomes an instrument of the drive for efficiency, rather than a moral idea designed to promote social justice. Moreover, access itself does not guarantee either full participation or more equal outcomes. Without adequate levels of funding and professional support, the access simply becomes an administrative rather than an ethical initiative. In a system which does not have an adequate financial and support base, the needs of students with disabilities often become marginal, even with the best intentions of teachers. Genuine social justice, on the other hand, requires that teachers and schools be given the capacity to cater adequately for difference.

From distribution to recognition

In his book, *Spheres of Justice*, Walzer (1983) has posed an issue that is critical to our attempt to work towards the articulation of a new model for securing social justice in education: how should educational policy and practice best respond to a society that is both heterogeneous and, it is to be hoped, committed to social justice and democracy. In a complex society, asserts Walzer, the idea of 'simple equality' – that everyone gets access to the same thing in the same form – is neither achievable nor desirable. It is not achievable because people do not have the same means and capacities, and it is not desirable because people do not have the same needs. This has been historically demonstrated in Australia and elsewhere in that centralized uniformity of educational provision was always insufficient for achieving social justice. Consequently, a system that encourages integration of 'special needs' students should not continue to work on the assumptions of uniformity. Relevant differences in relative power, capacities and aspirations of students and parents must be acknowledged without risk to the notion of social justice.

Taking into account such heterogeneity, Walzer argues for a 'complex equality', which involves the distribution of different social goods according to different criteria. But this involves the old Aristotelian problem of how to determine what counts as 'relevant difference' that might require different treatment for a just situation to ensue. Clearly, criteria of justice are required that reflect the specificity of goods, their social significance and the variety in interests and capacities of the recipients. So rather than invoking the normative principles that would apply in all cases, from either the rights of individuals or the promise of universal emancipation, what is required is an organizational structure that enables the widest possible participation in order to develop context-specific meanings and criteria appropriate to particular spheres. This means that systems should generate general principles of social justice which are broad enough to allow for specific adaptation in different contexts, including schools and classrooms.

Walzer's is a significant step forward in its recognition of the contemporary politics of difference, in the diversity of inflections that can found within the category 'people with disabilities', as well as the diversity of interests they represent. In this, Walzer takes the political claims of the contemporary social movements seriously. However, he does not recognize the extent to which social movements have changed both the conception and the politics of social justice. As Nancy Fraser points out,

> the struggle for recognition is fast becoming the paradigmatic form of political conflict in the late twentieth century. Heterogeneity and pluralism are now regarded as the norms against which demands for justice are now articulated. Demands for 'recognition of difference' fuel struggles of groups mobilised under the banners of nationality, ethnicity, race, gender and sexuality. Group identity has supplanted class conflict as the chief medium of political mobilisation. Cultural domination has supplanted economic exploitation as the fundamental injustice. And cultural recognition has displaced social-economic redistribution as the remedy for injustice and the goal of political struggle.
>
> (Fraser 1995: 68)

Of course, material inequality has not disappeared but is now seen as articulated with demands for recognition of difference. What is also clear is that the distributive paradigm, as Iris Marion Young (1990) calls it, within which the major traditions of thinking about social justice are expressed, is no longer (if it ever was) sufficient to capture the complexities of injustice. This observation is consistent with the analysis presented above of the limitations of the policies of access and equity, be they in the form of integration or any other.

The distributive paradigm is concerned with the morally proper distribution of benefits and burdens among society's numbers. Paramount among these are wealth, income and other material resources. This definition, however, is often also stretched to include non-material goods such as rights, opportunity, power and self-respect. These are treated as if they were material entities subject to the similar logic to zero-sum games. So what marks the distributive paradigm is a tendency to conceive social justice and distribution as coextensive concepts. Young has identified two major problems with this way of thinking about social justice. First, she has argued that it tends to ignore, at the same time as it often presupposes, the institutional context that determines material distribution. Its focus is on consumption, rather than on mode of production. As a consequence, it cannot account for those injustices that occur in the processes of social exchange and cultural formation. Second, in treating non-material goods like power, values and respect as if these were commodities, the distributive paradigm tends to misrepresent them. It obscures issues of decision-making power and procedures, as well as of divisions of power and culture which can often lead to the perpetuation of gross injustices.

With the work of feminist scholars like Nancy Fraser and Iris Marion Young, a new mode of thinking about social justice is clearly emerging. While the distributive paradigm was associated with concepts like interest, exploitation and redistribution, this new paradigm is concerned to focus attention also on issues of identity, difference, culture domination and recognition. The distributive paradigm saw injustice as being rooted in the political-economic structure of society which results in economic marginalization, exploitation, denial of access and equity, and often inadequate material standards of living. The remedy was assumed to require political-economic restructuring for greater access and equity. The recognition paradigm does not dismiss these concerns as irrelevant, but suggests that they do not exhaust the range of injustices that occur in human societies. Chief among these is the injustice resulting from cultural disrespect. Fraser (1995) argues that injustice can also be rooted in social patterns of representation, interpretation and communication, which result in cultural domination, non-recognition and disrespect.

The semiotic issues of representation, interpretation and communication are highly relevant to the concerns for justice in the education of students with disabilities because it is in education that students learn to develop their sense of self-worth and acceptable modes of social communication. As we have already pointed out, the practices of integration have only promoted access for students with disabilities; they have done very little in changing the culture of schooling so that those with disabilities feel recognized and valued. This situation has been exacerbated by the reality of restraint and cuts in educational expenditure. Pedagogic and curriculum practices have remained largely unchanged with respect to the need to cater for the wide range of differences which are now acknowledged to exist in schools. Schools are still based on the assumptions of homogeneity and uniformity. They still require conformity and obedience to rules that are based on the requirements of administrative convenience rather than moral principles.

For there to be genuine integration, located within the widest possible definition of social justice, cultural and symbolic changes to the ways schools are structured are clearly needed. According to Fraser (1995), the politics of recognition require social transformation in ways that would change *everybody's* sense of self. But the most significant insight that has emerged from this discussion is that reform for educational justice is complex, and requires attention not only to issues of the political economy of schooling – concerns of access and equity – but also to issues of the culture of schooling; that is, the way things are named and represented, the manner in which difference is treated and the ways in which the values, significations and norms which govern life in schools are negotiated and established.

Conclusion

In this chapter we have tried to do a number of things. First, we have sought to argue that the field of special education is largely devoid of any discussion of the moral premises upon which it is based. It has used the notion of social justice to promote its research agenda, but has failed to consider how moral and political issues cannot be divorced from the ways in which it constructs its questions and suggests the utilization of its findings. Often, policies of integration have been promoted which are based on a narrow conception of social justice defined simply as a matter of the rights of students with disabilities to have access to regular schools. Issues concerning the ways in which schools must be restructured in order to achieve the full benefits of integration have not been tackled. Second, we have argued that the concept of social justice is highly contested, and that in recent years, it is the view of social justice based on the assumptions of market-individualism which has gained considerable policy ascendancy in most western countries. We have suggested that this ideology has a number of disastrous consequences for the education of students with disabilities. It has the potential of sidelining once again those individuals who are assumed to be 'economically unproductive'. Third, we have contended that most traditional theories of social justice have focused attention on the issues of distribution; but that this has now been shown to be insufficient to account for the politics of recognition which call for major cultural changes in the ways difference is represented and catered for in institutions such as schools. There are real political difficulties here: the struggle for social justice policies and practices which recognize the need to overcome both cultural and economic domination has to be pursued by a new managerialist state which demands that services be delivered more cheaply; this state has a weakened capacity to resist such globally dominant market-individualist ideology. The integration of students with disabilities resulted, in the first instance, from the joining of a 'simple equality' construction of justice with a weak recognition of cultural rights. What is required now is a 'complex equality' construction with a strong recognition of cultural rights within a broad redistributive framework. There are very real political and educational challenges here for all educators and all educational researchers.

Of course, the discussion in this opening chapter has been necessarily brief. We hope, however, that we have opened up a range of issues that will be addressed in more detail in the chapters that follow.

References

Adams, F. (ed.) (1986) *Special Education*. London: Longman.

Apple, M. (1988) Equality and the politics of commonsense, in W. Secada (ed.) *Equity in Education*. London: Falmer Press.

Barry, B. (1973) *The Liberal Theory of Justice*. Oxford: Clarendon Press.

Beilharz, P. (1989) Social democracy and social justice, *The Australian and New Zealand Journal of Sociology*, 25(1): 85–99.

Carpenter, C. (1993) Corporate restructuring of the Australian disability field, in R. Lingard, J. Knight and P. Porter (eds) *Schooling Reform in Hard Times*. London: Falmer, pp. 176–92.

Considine, M. (1988) Corporate management as an administrative science, *Australian Journal of Public Administration*, 47(1): 4–19.

Fitzclarence, L. and Kenway, J. (1993) Education and social justice in the postmodern age, in R. Lingard, J. Knight and P. Porter (eds) *Schooling Reform in Hard Times*. London: Falmer, pp. 90–105.

Fraser, N. (1995) From redistribution to recognition: dilemmas of justice in a 'post-socialist' society, *New Left Review*, July–August: 68–93.

Fulcher, G. (1989) *Disabling Policies*. London: Falmer Press.

Heller, A. (1987) *A Theory of Needs*. Cambridge: Polity Press.

Karmel, P. (1973) *Schools in Australia*: Canberra: Australian Government Printing Service.

Lingard, R., Knight, J. and Porter, P. (eds) (1993) *Schooling Reform in Hard Times*. London: Falmer.

MacIntyre, S. (1985) *Winners and Losers*. Sydney: Allen and Unwin.

Meijer, C., Pijl, S. and Hegarty, S. (eds) (1994) *New Perspectives in Special Education: a Six-country Study of Integration*. London: Routledge.

Norman, R. (1988) *Free and Equal*. Oxford: Oxford University Press.

Nozick, R. (1976) *Anarchy, State and Utopia*. Oxford: Blackwell.

Pijl, S. (1994) United States, in C. Meijer, S. Pijl and S. Hegarty (eds) *New Perspectives in Special Education: a Six-country Study of Integration*. London: Routledge, pp. 55–78.

Pusey, M. (1991) *Economic Rationalism in Canberra*. Cambridge: Cambridge University Press.

Rawls, J. (1972) *A Theory of Justice*. Oxford: Clarendon Press.

Rizvi, F. (1993) Multiculturalism, social justice and the restructuring of the Australian state, in R. Lingard, J. Knight and P. Porter (eds) *Schooling Reform in Hard Times*. London: Falmer, pp. 120–38.

Seddon, T. (1994) *Beyond Context*. London: Falmer.

Slee, R. (1993) The politics of integration: a critical analysis of professional culture and school organisation, *Disability, Handicap and Society*, 8(4): 351–60.

Solity, J. (1992) *Special Education*. London: Cassell.

Theophanous, A. (1993) *Understanding Social Justice*. Melbourne: Elikia Press.

Walzer, M. (1983) *Spheres of Justice*. Oxford: Blackwell.

Yeatman, A. (1990) *Bureaucrats, Technocrats and Femocrats*. Sydney: Allen and Unwin.

Young, I. M. (1990) *Justice and the Politics of Difference*. Princeton, NJ: Princeton University Press.

Disability and the education of persons

The human condition is an interpreted one. What we see in the world, the act of perception, is an act of interpretation reflecting both what is out there in reality and the conceptual frameworks and interests which we as perceivers bring to the perceptive act (Arbib and Hesse 1986). How we choose to act in the world is also an interpretive engagement since our choices will reflect how we see our situation, what we see as desirable and achievable goals, and what we see as appropriate strategies for achievement. Similarly, shared collective practices, such as the practice of education, are also interpretive since the practice is constituted by ways of seeing and ways of acting which provide an authoritative guiding framework for those engaged in that practice (Langford 1985). This applies to the education of all children including those with disabilities. The ways of seeing which guide the practice of special education incorporate explicit assumptions about disability and education. They also incorporate, perhaps implicitly rather than explicitly, assumptions about persons and the requirements concerning the moral form of life.

In this chapter I wish to explore how contemporary accounts regarding the nature of persons might better inform our understanding of special education and of the challenges which emerge when we come to see that practice as an ethical engagement. The chapter seeks to develop this understanding by drawing together four areas of concern. In the first section a view of persons is advanced which draws from contemporary philosophical discussions. This view presents a richer and more complex account of persons than the simple mind–body account which has tended to influence much of modern thought and has permeated past perceptions of disability. One significant feature of persons which emerges from this account is their modality as social beings – as persons they are necessarily embedded within relationships with other persons – and this feature raises the question of what kinds of relationships between persons are conducive to enhancing, or limiting, the good life as experienced at both the individual and collective levels. Thus the discussion in the second section moves to a consideration of persons and the moral form of life. In the third section the links between persons and education are considered. The discussion here draws specifically from the writings of the English philosopher, Glenn Langford, and gives particular attention to the question of education as an ethical engagement. The fourth and final section focuses on the area of disability and education and suggests that the understandings developed in the previous sections challenge us to respond to a number of ethical and political imperatives which now emerge in the continuing provision of special education.

The approach taken in this chapter is broadly philosophical. More specifically the method followed is drawn from descriptive metaphysics, an approach which seeks 'to lay bare the most general features of our conceptual structure' (Strawson 1959: 9). Such an approach provides a holistic contrast to the piecemeal analytical approaches familiar in much recent English-speaking philosophy and philosophy of education.

The nature of persons

A familiar and traditional view of the human individual sees that individual as composed of two quite distinct parts, a body and a mind (or spirit). This dualistic picture of the human individual has had a profound influence on western thinking, influencing religious thought, philosophy, the sciences, the social sciences, medicine and education. It has encouraged an emphasis on rationality as the distinctive feature of the human individual and supported an individualistic or atomistic account of social reality. Its strong affiliation to the biomedical model of health care, as well as its broader cultural dominance, has allowed it to significantly shape our thinking about disability, especially the view that disability is a biological disorder signalling a lack or deficit in the one who is disabled.

In contemporary philosophy there is emerging a growing literature which rejects the mind–body dualism and proposes instead a more complex picture of the human individual with emphasis on the nature of human individuals as persons as a central motif. The origins of this literature are varied and the discussions are complex (e.g. MacIntyre 1984; Langford 1985; Glover 1988; Langford 1991; Ricoeur 1992). It draws from philosophical criticisms of the metaphysical assumptions implicit in dualism. It draws from the long traditions of social philosophy and philosophical anthropology found in European thought. It reflects, as well, people's experience of the human social condition especially as discussed by sociologists and anthropologists drawing on phenomenological approaches. For the purposes of this discussion we might note seven themes in this literature which emerge as distinctive characteristics of the nature of human beings as persons.

First, persons are seen as embodied beings who posses a biological dimension. Persons experience the world through their bodies and are identified by others in the world through their bodies. They are also members of a biological species, *homo sapiens*, through which they are related in an evolutionary way to other animal species. Because they are embodied biological beings persons are subject to the natural laws which govern the natural world. Thus they have needs relating to sustenance, shelter, procreation and good health, they are vulnerable to injury and disease, and, as with all individual living things they are mortal – they are born, they live and they die.

Second, persons possess what Glenn Langford has termed a psychological dimension (see Langford 1991: 23). Persons' perceptions of their world are mediated through conceptual schema which provide the basis for beliefs and actions. Conceptual schema allow persons to form beliefs about their present experiences: what is the case. However, given the facility of memory, such present beliefs might be linked to recollections of what was the case (the past), and further linked, through the facility of imagination, to anticipations of what might be the case (the future). Such beliefs allow persons to frame intentions to change what is the case, a short-term intention, or to frame intentions that will guide future actions over an extended period of time, as in longer-term purposes or extended projects. Thus conceptual schema provide the basis for beliefs about what has been, what is, and what might be, and provide, as well, the epistemological basis for action and change. Accordingly, we see the behaviour of persons as purposive, both guided by beliefs of how things are and directed by intentions regarding those changes which persons see as desirable.

Third, persons are temporal beings, they possess a temporal dimension. As indicated in the previous paragraph, persons are able to form both tensed beliefs and tensed intentions. Thus persons' experiences of the present are linked to a network of beliefs or recollections about the past, and they see themselves as having an identity stretching back into the past. As Langford notes, persons 'may be said to possess histories, whereas other animals have only life spans and physical objects have only pasts' (p. 25). Persons also look towards a future. They can adopt purposes, projects or commitments which structure more immediate actions and activities and serve to give shape and direction to their lives. Significant here is the notion of a life plan, that consciously chosen and distinctive set of commitments and achievements whereby each person seeks to give shape, direction and meaning to his/her life. Persons have both histories and futures and their sense of who they are includes a sense of where they have come from and what they might aspire to.

Fourth, persons are social beings, indeed, inasmuch as they are persons they are necessarily social beings. At birth the human individual enters both a natural world and a social world and it is the presence of this responsive world of others combined with the open-ended nature of human learning which allows the infant human to grow as a person. This world of others –

mother, family, peers, community, society – provides an evolving and increasingly complex web of relationships whereby the individual comes to see himself/herself as a person among other persons. The nature of these relationships, especially significant ones like those of child to parent, and the kind of society that the individual is born into, significantly shape the kind of person that the individual might become.

Fifth, persons are self-aware beings. Persons are aware that their awareness is always now, at this point of time. The notion of *be-ing* captures the pervading 'presentness' of persons' awareness in that the act of awareness, of consciousness, is always predicated in the present. However, this sense of self-awareness also incorporates a 'here' inasmuch as it signifies the point or place of awareness. The possession of conceptual schema not only provides for perception, intention and action, but also allows persons to situate themselves in a sophisticated spatio-temporal framework of beliefs and relationships with their own subjectivity, their own reflexive sense of 'I, myself' as occupying the central point of reference. Persons can view other persons, events or relationships as here or there or as now, then or maybe (in the sense of possibly coming about in the future). They can structure their *be-ing* in the world according to a unitary spatio-temporal framework with themselves at the centre. In terms of their social world, that world in which they see themselves as a self among other persons, persons can see themselves at the centre of a complex relational framework which radiates out from close relationships of intimacy, to those of kin and near friends, to those of acquaintances and colleagues, to those of community and nation and so on. Thus persons see themselves as occupying 'the point of reference' for the world which they encounter. They are able to identify *where* they are in the world, whether spatially or temporally, and they are able to identify *who* they are in the world in terms of their relationships to others. In terms of their identification of where they are in the world as spatially and temporally structured, persons can experience a sense of 'being at home' as against 'being lost'. And in terms of their identification with others persons can experience a sense of 'being at ease', as sharing a reciprocal sense of acceptance, as against 'being an outsider' or 'being a stranger'. Given, too, the significance of others in shaping one's sense of self, there is a sense in which structured and enduring sets of relationship are seen as shaping distinctive features of the self as an identity. Hence, writers speak of one's *identity*, family identity, vocational identity, political identity, ethnic identity, moral identity and so on.

Sixth, persons are active beings. Persons are able to act in and on their world, a characteristic foreshadowed in the previous discussions of persons as possessing a psychological dimension and as possessing a temporal dimension. Persons as individuals can seek to bring about change through short-term actions or pursue a longer-term activity or project in which a number of actions are structured and given direction over time by the overall goal or purpose of the activity. But persons can also participate with other persons in social practices which both exhibit certain distinctive logical features and provide outcomes which could not be individually attained. Social practices depend for their existence and identity on the overall purpose which the members of that practice share and are reciprocally aware of sharing (Langford 1991). Social practices are also extended in time, their temporal continuity being structured by a tradition, the way of seeing and the way of acting distinctive of that practice (Langford 1985). Social practices have significantly contributed to our present expectations regarding the good life since they provide a context for both individual achievement and community advancement (Taylor 1992b). Because social practices are social in an internal sense, persons are aware of the practice and its tradition and, as well, are reciprocally aware of each other as practitioners in the practice. An individual person can neither establish a practice by himself/herself nor discover an established practice from the outside. Social practices are learned from others and necessarily involve a process of induction.

Seventh, persons are self-creative beings; they are beings who are continuously open to a process of *be-coming*. This creative potential has two dimensions. Persons can seek to create themselves in the light of the future, some anticipated achievement, goal or ideal. In pursuing such a future persons can also re-create themselves in the light of the past. They can seek to overcome a flaw in their character or transcend some impediment or vicissitude which circumstances may have bequeathed them. Persons can change and expand themselves over time through developing new and worthwhile understandings, new and fulfilling relationships or new and challenging experiences. It is in this context that we respect personal autonomy, we acknowledge the significance of a person's life plan and we value the good life as one of flourishing.

While discussion of the seven characteristics above may help us to appreciate more fully the complexity of the nature of persons, it would be misleading to infer that what are conceptual distinctions made for the sake of enhancing understanding reflect distinctions in fact. Nothing could be further from the truth, for ontologically, that is, at the level of *be-ing*, these modalities interrelate in shaping the being of the integrated self. However, this is not to suggest that each modality has equal significance in shaping the substantive nature of the self. As we shall see, the modality of persons as social beings has a significant impact on shaping the kind of person we substantively become.

Persons and the moral form of life

Given that persons are social beings, persons are aware from an early age that relationships with other persons are different from relationships with mere things or objects, and that these relationships carry with them considerations and obligations of a special, reciprocal kind. From an early age the infant person begins to learn that one needs to consider how one's actions affect other persons, that one must accept responsibility for one's actions, that some actions are praiseworthy while others are blameworthy, and that certain dispositions and related character traits are esteemed and admired while others are disapproved of and condemned. Thus persons as they grow learn to relate to other persons as mutual members of a distinctive, shared form of life, which we term the moral form of life, and which is characterized by its own distinctive discourse and related beliefs, ideals, prescriptions, dispositions, sentiments and modes of decision-making and justification.

How does our understanding of the nature of persons shape our understanding of the moral form of life? At a general level we could suggest that persons are central to moral discourse and moral action since it is only inasmuch as individuals display the characteristics of persons that they are seen as the subjects of such discourse and action. Since persons are self-aware and self-creative beings they possess the status of being ends-in-themselves. They have a value in and for themselves which non-persons do not possess. Non-persons may have value for another. They may have an instrumental value relative to the self-regarding values of another, however, they cannot have value in and for themselves. The moral form of life is simply that which endeavours to build and enhance relationships between persons on the basis of continuing reciprocal awareness, continuing reciprocal respect, and continuing reciprocal treatment of the other as first and foremost a person. Hence the moral form of life seeks to cultivate a shared life which is both self- and other-regarding, which accords all persons dignity and respect, which acknowledges that the interests of all persons ought to be taken into account where they might be seriously affected by social decisions, and which encourages the flourishing of every person provided such flourishing is not at the expense of others.

A fuller account of the link between our understanding of the nature of persons and the moral form of life might emerge if we consider the implications of the moral ideal of personal autonomy which is strongly grounded within contemporary society. The *idea* that persons are self-creative beings is an ontological claim. It reflects the nature of persons as the kind of beings that they are. However, the *ideal* that persons ought to be able to create themselves as they see fit and not as nature, tradition, society or others might ordain is a moral ideal with significant ethical, political and educational implications. Charles Taylor has pointed out that this moral ideal is relatively recent in western thought, emerging only at the end of the eighteenth century and reflecting both the collapse of a hierarchical social order and the emergence of the ideal of authenticity, the notion that each individual is challenged to discover and realize his/her own original way of being (Taylor 1992a). This emphasis on the ideal of self-realization is clearly linked to the contemporary moral notion of personal autonomy with its concomitant emphasis on the necessity of certain social conditions of freedom if autonomy is to be exercised. The reference to social conditions of freedom, which is particularly emphasized in liberal moral and political theory, recognizes that self-realization is a creative possibility which in actuality may be frustrated, stifled or suppressed by others. These conditions of freedom can be appreciated better if we look again at those characteristics which define the modality of one's being as a person and note the extent to which they can be socially constrained.

However, an overemphasis on autonomy, freedom and constraint can easily suggest a metaphysics of individualism and an atomistic view of social reality. Yet a significant thread running through the account given of persons is the modality of persons as necessarily social; this logically implies that the individual ideal of self-realization needs to be complemented by social ideals which seek to articulate those values which will sustain for individuals a society which is cohesive, compassionate, just and nurturing. Accordingly, both communitarian and feminist commentators argue that the moral form of life posits both individual and collective ideals and has both an individual/ethical and a social/political dimension. Thus social conditions which, from the individual's vantage point of pursuing self-realization, appear as external and stubborn constraints, may appear, from the vantage point of life as collectively shared, as challenges for change whereby society might further nurture and enhance the good life for its members. These conditions might be elaborated by extending the discussion of the first four modalities regarding the nature of persons referred to in the previous sections.

First, the conditions of material embodiment and of biological life set limits to the process of self-realization. Self-awareness and a degree of mobility are necessary for self-realization, as are the necessities of air, sustenance, shelter and health. These basic needs have to be satisfied to guarantee survival and provide that security of temporal continuity within which a sense of the future is meaningful and within which planning towards the future points to a realizable reality. What is realizable will also be shaped by a person's genetic constitution with its inherited capacity to be either adaptive to certain natural conditions or vulnerable to others. However, a person's ability to plan their life within the limits of their biological constitution can be enhanced through both an understanding of their biological nature and of the situations of harm or risk that prevail in the surrounding environment. A general understanding of what constitutes good diet, hygienic practices and positive exercise and an appreciation of what constitutes potential harm or risk, allows a person to be more protective of their life at the biological level. More specific understanding of one's biological profile and genetic dispositions may allow a person to plan his/her life within safe limits and to modify the eventuality of certain outcomes through changes in lifestyle or appropriate medical intervention. Even where certain debilitating features of a person's physical constitution are irreversible, the delimiting effect of those features may be minimized through the use of drugs, artificial aids and prosthetics. What emerges from these reflections is that although the conditions of embodiment and of biological life are limiting, they can be minimized and even circumvented through the social provision of adequate material standards of living and the application of appropriate social understandings, practices, interventions and technologies. This is a feature of life in societies such as ours which often are characterized as advanced societies. Yet these provisions and applications, which are social constructs, might only be selectively available to those who possess the restricted means of accessing them, such as knowledge, power or wealth. Hence, in such advanced societies the boundaries between nature and culture, between biological inevitability and social neglect or selectivity, fuse with each other, and the debilitating feature can be justifiably characterized as a social construction albeit one constructed from biological reality.

Second, a person can be constrained at the psychological level. In terms of belief a person's life can be narrowed in that he/she is restricted to an impoverished conceptual schema and can form only a limited understanding of their world and of their opportunities in it. Wittgenstein's well-known aphorism that 'the limits of my language mean the limits of my world' (1974: 56) draws attention to the fact that our conceptual schema, which are provided through language, limit the beliefs we might form, the intentions we might shape and the actions we might pursue. A person's life can also be constrained by a lack of imagination or by a lack of motivation, since these limit the possibilities of choice or the actualization of choice. Thus in terms of self-realization that person's life will be richer where social conditions prevail which provide for knowledge and understanding, and support creativity and purposiveness. In the previous paragraph it was noted how appropriate understandings can further the quality of life at the biological level, but since belief, with its cognates of knowledge and understanding, is a modality of the being of persons, there is a link between knowledge and individual quality of life which pervades the whole of a person's life and their being in the world.

Third, persons can be constrained in those situations where their sense of being-in-time is threatened. This is most clearly the case where a person loses a sense of the future as a time of challenge and opportunity and comes to view the future as threatening, foreboding or futile or becomes resigned to a view of the future as an inevitable extension of an unchangeable present. This loss of a sense of hope in the future can generate destructive symptoms of apathy, anxiety, suffering and despair since it threatens the ongoing integrity of the self as self-actualizing (Cassell 1991). The self can also be threatened by the lack or loss of a sense of the past, the destruction of one's own personal history. This is understandable given that the question 'who am I?' is tied to answers to a previous question of 'where have I come from?'. More correctly the 'I' who seeks to answer the question 'who am I?' is a subject whose identity has been formed from a past of relationships, situations, choices, aspirations and challenges, and the loss of past identity here may be experienced as a loss of self-identity as a distinctive individual (Sacks 1985), or as a loss of self-identity as a member of a distinctive social group (Kundera 1982).

Fourth, persons can be constrained by their social situation, by the others who constitute that web of relationships to which each person sees himself/herself as tied. Already the influence of the social has been foreshadowed in the modalities of constraint already discussed; it is desirable that discussion of that influence now be widened. Clearly autonomy requires certain social conditions of, and for, freedom, access to certain primary social goods as demanded by justice in a free and fair society. John Rawls has argued that 'the chief primary goods at the disposition of society are rights and liberties, powers and opportunities, income and wealth . . . These are the social primary goods. Other primary goods such as health and vigor, intelligence and imagination, are natural goods; although their possession is influenced by the basic structure, they are not so directly under its control' (Rawls 1971: 62). Primary goods would include such benefits as health, shelter, some form of education, an adequate income, freedom of association and freedom of speech. Rawls also draws attention to self-respect or a sense of one's own worth as a primary social good. A full account of the rights and liberties, powers and opportunities which theorists such as Rawls envisage is not possible here, but discussion of two of these is apposite. These are the freedom of association and the primary good of self-respect or sense of one's own worth.

As we have seen, there are aspects of the good life which only emerge within social practices, and access to such social practices is contingent upon a process of induction. An example already given is that of the importance of traditions of knowledge and understanding in contributing to an individual's quality of life. Hence, an important extension to the primary good of free association is the open access that persons might enjoy to those social practices which are constitutive of their good as they desire it. In commenting on the context such practices provide to human action, Alasdair MacIntyre has written:

> Now I must emphasize that what the agent is able to do and say intelligibly as an actor is deeply affected by the fact that we are never more (and sometimes less) than the co-authors of our own narrative. Only in fantasy do we live what story we please. In life, as both Aristotle and Engels noted, we are always under certain constraints. We enter upon a stage which we did not design and we find ourselves part of an action that was not of our making. Each of us being a main character in his own drama plays subordinate parts in the dramas of others, and each drama constrains the others . . . Each of our dramas exerts constraints on each others, making the whole different from the parts, but still dramatic.
> (MacIntyre 1982: 213).

MacIntyre's comments illustrate well how interdependent our lives are. We might also note the ambiguity of the term 'character' with its implicit allusions both to a scripted role and to the personality of the individual who might play that role (akin to the moral character of the individual player). Thus the support given or the constraints imposed by others can originate either in the character as role or the character as individual personality. An enabling social role can be extended by a generous person but corrupted by a narcissistic or authoritarian person and, equally, an enabling person can be constrained and defeated by a hierarchical or authoritarian setting while, within such a setting, the narcissistic or authoritarian person may flourish.

The most obvious social mechanism of constraint is that of exclusion, denying certain persons access to participation in a social practice. Such discrimination may be direct in that clear rules of exclusion exist or it may be indirect in that exclusion results as a denial of access to those resources which serve as a prerequisite for entry. To extend MacIntyre's scenario we can see that certain individuals or groups may be barred from certain scripted roles because of a *politics of discrimination*. We are quite familiar with this in those social settings where some are directly discriminated against on grounds of race, class or gender, or there is indirect discrimination based on a lack of economic resources. Clearly, such forms of discrimination can also apply to those whose lives are challenged by disability.

Rawls's identification of self-respect, of the sense of one's own worth, as a primary social good indicates how the lack of such self-respect can be damaging and emphasizes that such a lack can be a matter of social treatment. The possibility that others can shape one's sense of self-respect reflects the fact which we have noted already, that social relations are internal and conceptual, they arise within relations of reciprocal self-awareness. Thus a person's behaviour to and with others is shaped by how those others see that person and how that person himself sees those perceptions (Langford 1991). In terms of MacIntyre's stage scenario, one's life is shaped not only by the nature of one's own character, but also of one's perceptions of the character of others, and, further, by one's perception of the others' perception of one's character, and so on. Thus one's perception of oneself and one's perception of one's abilities can be shaped by the beliefs of others with whom one shares these relationships of reciprocal self-awareness. Others can exert power over another through this social process of mutual self-awareness, of mutual recognition. Hence in understanding the dynamics between the self and others we need also to acknowledge the reality of a *politics of recognition*. Taylor has characterized this reality as follows:

> The thesis is that our identity is partly shaped by recognition or its abuse, often by the misrecognition of others, and so a person or group of people can suffer real damage, real distortion, if the people or society around them mirror back to them a confirming or demeaning or

contemptible picture of themselves. Non-recognition or misrecognition can inflict harm, can be a form of oppression, imprisoning someone in a false, distorted, and reduced mode of being.

(Taylor 1992a: 25)

It follows from the preceding discussions that the modern ethical ideal of self-realization needs also to acknowledge the ontological position of the actualizing or creative self as a person among other persons, as a person who can be either considerably constrained and conditioned by these others or considerably enhanced by them. Thus the moral form of life needs to acknowledge that the good life is one of *freedom within community*, is one of interdependence rather than isolated independence, is one which strives constantly to balance the demands imposed by individual respect and autonomy with communitarian needs for society to be cohesive, nurturing, just and inclusive (Gutman 1992; Taylor 1992b). This would suggest that the moral form of life is essentially one of creative tension, dialogue and politics.

The moral form of life is one of creative tension, a tension which flows in two ways. There is the tension between present reality and possible (future) ideal; and there is the tension between the possibilities inherent in individual self-realization or self-interest and the requirements of sustaining a cohesive, harmonious and just community. The moral form of life is one of dialogue since it involves negotiation between those who seek to be and those others who seek to determine what they can be. Negotiation is appropriate since the ideal of self-realization can only be articulated by the self in question. Here, another cannot reliably speak for oneself. The moral form of life is one of power since social life raises questions about who has power over whom, who has power to shape the social conditions of life, and who has power to access the goods which are communally produced. It is also about power since, given the politics of recognition, all social relationships are power relationships. Wendy Seymour neatly characterizes some of this tension with the following sociological description:

> We do have the potential to be creative, but only within the limitations of our socially created selves. Our selves are created in interaction with others in a social context. The self is thus constrained by the dimensions of the context from which it arises, and by the forces of socialisation influencing other individuals with whom we interact. . . Thus choice can never be free of the constraints inherent in our social being. Individual decisions and actions are prescribed by such structural considerations.
>
> (Seymour 1989: 22–3)

Persons and education

In modern societies education is one social context, if not *the* social context, wherein the tension, the dialogue and the politics of the self and others unfolds. The role that education plays in socialization, in citizenship formation, in making available the intellectual, cultural and recreational heritage of a society, in the provision of the resources of social imagination and creativity, and in enhancing one's vocational opportunities all point to the significance of education in shaping both the self and society. Conceptually, there is an inexorable logical link between persons, education and society, and in this section I shall seek to delineate the nature of this link. In his extensive writings in the philosophy of education, Langford has sought to explore the framework of our thinking about education and his writings provide for us a helpful point of departure.

Langford has been critical of the analytical approach that has dominated much English-speaking philosophy of education and of the ontological or metaphysical assumptions implicit in that approach. He has characterized his own approach as follows:

> I have not felt obliged to address any one philosophical method. I do not consider the traditional empiricist metaphysics of atomism adequate for an understanding of the nature of social phenomena nor, therefore, the method of analysis associated with it particularly suitable. The method I have adopted would therefore be better described as descriptive or phenomenological rather than analytic.
>
> (Langford 1978: 1)

Consistent with this phenomenological approach, Langford has argued that education typically refers to an activity that is carried on in schools, colleges and universities. More strictly, he refers to this activity as formal education since 'two parties may be distinguished, one of whom, the teacher, accepts responsibility for the education of the other, the pupil' (Langford 1973: 3). He acknowledges that we can also speak of informal education, education which may come about independently of the structured social practice of formal education, but our reflections on education should begin from that social practice which is primarily carried out by teachers in formal institutions such as schools, colleges and universities.

As already suggested, social practices display a unity and direction which is conferred by the overall goal or purpose which the practice pursues. Responsibility for education rests primarily with teachers and the practice of teaching has as its overall purpose the promotion of education. Hence, Langford proposes that an understanding of education can be accessed through an account of teaching as a social practice. The strategy adopted has been that of starting with the activities of teachers – that is, at what might be called the phenomenological level – and raising the relatively abstract question of the nature of education only after the correct context for it has been established (Langford 1978: 77). Langford's account of teaching as a social practice presupposes an account of social phenomena, an account which in turn rests on an account of the nature of persons. Hence, the first logical link between education, persons and society is that which emerges from a phenomenological awareness of teaching as a social practice constituted by persons.

Within the context of teaching as a social practice, Langford suggests that the question 'what is education?' is ambiguous as between a particular question or questions, which in turn have either a descriptive or prescriptive form, and a more general philosophical question (Langford 1978: 77). The question 'what is education?' assumes a particular form when it arises within the context of, and is directed towards, a particular educational (teaching) tradition or practice. As a descriptive question it invites an account of the educational practice concerned and its historical development. As a prescriptive question it invites consideration of what form the practice ought to take in the future. The linguistic turn which moves from a focus on what is the case to a focus on what ought to be the case presupposes the possibility of change to the established practice and invites reasons or grounds as to why the proposed change should be seen as desirable and justified. Inasmuch as such considerations seek to promote or prescribe what form the practice should take in the future, they are prescriptive (pp. 78–80). However, such planned adaptation and change is not a necessary feature of social practices. A distinction can be made between critical social practices which constantly seek to appraise and to improve a practice and conservative or traditional practices which discourage change (Langford 1985). The possibility of change within any practice will reflect a number of factors including the practitioners' own perceptions of their practice, the expectations of the wider community within which the practice is situated, and changing understandings of the overall point or purpose of the practice.

What account might be given of the question 'what is education?' when interpreted as a general philosophical question? Langford suggests that this is a question which arises when we move beyond our own education tradition and recognize the presence of other education traditions at different times and in different places: 'accordingly, the question "what is education?" may be a request for the principle of identity according to which we recognise different educational traditions as instances of the same kind of thing. It is when understood in this way that the question becomes philosophical' (Langford 1978: 80).

Since the answer to this question involves the indentification of social phenomena which are crosscultural and across time, the answer provided can only be of a very general kind. Here, Langford provides the following pithy account: 'My own view is that a social tradition is educational if its overall purpose is that others should become educated; and that to become educated is to learn to be a person' (p. 84).

This account achieves a crosscultural and historical generality since it reflects certain features of the human condition grounded in the nature of persons. These features are that persons are initially born merely as human beings, they become persons over time, the kind of person they become reflects significantly the community of other persons they are born into, and this process of becoming reflects both the open-ended nature of human learning and the nature of human societies as constituted by shared relationships structured by shared social traditions or practices. Langford comments on these features as follows:

> Human learning . . . is characteristically open-ended. What men learn depends not so much on innate dispositions which display themselves during a single lifetime as on the circumstances, especially the social circumstances, in which they find themselves. To put it another way, what they learn depends on the particular society into which they are born. Above all, they learn the ways of looking at things and behaving which are characteristic of that society; and in the course of doing so acquire also the shared concepts which make those ways of seeing things and behaving possible . . . If we are prepared to talk of societies other than our own . . . we will also have to insist that, although the members of other societies are persons like ourselves, the kind of person they are will depend on the social traditions of the society to which they belong and to which they were introduced by a process of learning . . . Finally, although it is true that the members of any society have to learn to become persons, it does not follow that there will be a group of people in every society whose job it is to help them to do so. In a simple society unplanned face-to-face contacts may suffice. Explicit, formal educational provision, with teachers accepting responsibility for the education of others, is a feature only of relatively large, complex societies like our own.
>
> (Langford 1978: 84–5)

Here we see a second logical link between education, persons and society; the link emerges from the place of persons as learners within education. The content of their learning will reflect those ways of seeing and ways of acting which are held to be desirable in that society and will provide the significant pathways whereby each individual learner might actualize his/her sense of self.

Langford's descriptive account suggests a number of further and important points. First, there are no substantive a priori or transcendental values constitutive of education. Rather, values in education are socially constructed, and those responsible for education must see themselves as bearing responsibility for the values which prevail: 'the view that there are educational or any other values which can be discovered *a priori* by philosophers of education or educational theorists or, indeed, by any one else, and which must therefore be accepted by all, has already been rejected. Values exist only in being held' (Langford 1978: 50). Second, given that the values which do obtain are socially constructed and exist only insofar as they are maintained, there is no guarantee that existing values will survive through time. Educational practices are projects and, as such, are always liable to fail in terms of sustaining a given set of values. Hence, in our society the emergence and preservation of educational practice as a rational and an ethical practice which reflects certain critical and moral values will depend on the enduring commitment of those, such as teachers, responsible for education and on the continuing acceptance of such values by the broader community.

Given the socio-cultural context of our own society as a liberal-democratic and capitalist society three further reflections follow. First, given the extent to which our understanding of persons and society has been shaped by moral traditions, and given the place of education in providing to individuals opportunities to pursue the good life, fidelity to these moral traditions and the moral nature of the educational enterprise require us to see education as an ongoing moral project. Education is unavoidably a moral project since it is tied to questions related to what kind of society do we desire and what kind of persons do we want as citizens. And since education is itself a social good, it is also a moral project in that it necessarily gives rise to questions related to who will have access to this good. Second, given the nature of our society as open to the adoption of other value systems, such as instrumental and narcissistic value systems which can corrupt the moral agenda, then values in education must be seen as contestable, with the survival and importance of moral values within education being itself an ongoing political struggle. There is an unavoidable moral tension between the ethical ideals inherent in the liberal-democratic tradition and the self-serving and materialist ideals inherent in the capitalist economic tradition. From this perspective, education as an ongoing moral project is also a political project. Third, where those responsible for education see themselves as having a degree of autonomous social responsibility for the practice of education (which is an ideal encapsulated in the notion of teaching as a profession) and resist the view that they are merely intermediaries, then the exercise of that responsibility requires a high level of integrity and moral and political commitment.

Disability and education

From the preceding discussion a number of observations might be drawn pertinent to the provision of education for people with disabilities. First, if we see disability as a social construction, albeit one constructed from biological reality, then we need to reject traditional assumptions that the misfortunes of people with disabilities reflect non-human causes, and reflect certain biological givens. Thus, we must deconstruct that practice, that way of seeing and that way of acting, based on the impoverished medical deficit model of special education with its limited ontology of personhood and its exagerrated legitimation of the 'normal'.

Second, if we adopt a fuller account of persons which recognizes the distinctiveness of each individual person, which values his/her unique aspirations towards self-realization and which acknowledges the power of the social to create conditions which may either enhance or constrain individual flourishing, then we need to reconstruct a new practice of special education, a new way of seeing and of acting, which places the person at the centre and adopts an ethical framework, rather than a medical one, as the fundamental basis for understanding and responding to all students, including those with disabilities and their needs. Such an ethical response requires that we recognize the demands placed on us by the requirements of justice, for as Judith Shklar has noted,

> the difference between misfortune and injustice frequently involves our willingness and our capacity to act or not to act on behalf of the victims, to blame or to absolve, to help, mitigate, and compensate, or to just turn away. The notion that there is a simple and stable rule to separate the two is a demand for moral security, which like so many others, cannot be satisfied . . . we must recognize that the line of separation between injustice and misfortune is a political choice, not a simple rule that can be taken as given.
>
> (Shklar 1990: 2, 5)

Third, and as Shklar has indicated, the ethical demands of justice have political implications. The reconstruction of the practice of special education along lines required by responsive concern and justice requires a deconstruction of the culture and concomitant power relations associated with the established tradition. This is consistent with Rawls's argument (1971) that the creation of the just society involves a developmental process of social transformation and not merely the adoption of a social justice goal, principle or perspective. The creation of a just society requires first the creation of those social preconditions which provide the necessary fertile ground for the full principles of social justice to flourish. Hence, the justice perspective demands not only changes at the macro level of institutions, such as changes in policy, but also changes at the micro level, such as changes at the everyday level of interaction between people with disabilities and those others who surround them. The politics of discrimination need to be vigorously countered at the systemic level of educational provision. But they also need to be vigorously countered at the level of the everyday established culture of each institution and each local community (see Wolfensberger 1991).

It is relevant to note here that the commitment required is not to any justice perspective but to a *specific* justice perspective. In the sixth century Justinian had argued that 'justice is the constant and perpetual will to render to everyone their due' and, although there is an alluring simplicity in Justinian's definition, the ambiguity of the notion of 'due' introduces a vexatious note which has plagued discussion of the concept of justice since those early centuries. What constitutes one's due depends on whether one argues from a perspective of rights, desert or need; so what we have is not a justice perspective but different and contesting justice perspectives. As David Miller (1976: 25) puts it, 'there is a tension in our thinking about justice . . . the different principles of justice find their natural home in conflicting ways of looking at society'. In terms of the account provided of the nature of persons it could be argued that what is required in this educative context is an emancipative justice perspective which seeks actively both to create conditions which will nurture the individual and to critique conditions which sustain injustice.

To adopt an emancipative justice perspective is to adopt a perspective which is firstly responsive to the specific concerns and specific contexts of each individual person rather than a perspective which seeks only to focus on broad, systemic procedures. What is desired is an ethic of care which is responsive to the individual, as well as the collective, needs of people with disabilities, and which ultimately allows them to name their own reality and to shape their own futures as active and autonomous participants in society. This requires that we seek to transform existing power relationships from those in which people with disabilities remained dependent to those in which people with disabilities, along with those who are not disabled, can exercise relationships of independence and interdependence.

The possibilities open to people with disabilities will depend on both opportunity and the responsiveness of others. The former requires that we address the politics of discrimination while the latter requires that we address the politics of recognition. As we have seen, social relations are expressions of ways of seeing, and a significant social dynamic of disempowerment is mediated through the ways in which the individual person is disparagingly viewed as 'the other'. Given the pervasiveness of traditional disempowering social notions of disability, what is required is an educative strategy which encompasses not only those working within the field of special education, or even those working within education, but extends to the total community and seeks to critique all areas of the culture where negative connotations of disability still prevail.

The educational response being proposed is one which empowers people with disabilities in themselves and for themselves. This has implications for teachers as professionals within the practice of special education, for it challenges them to recognize that concern for 'the other' and advocacy on behalf of 'the other' can easily veil a paternalistic response to 'the other', well meaning but disempowering all the same. If we are to move beyond a culture of uniformity, of selective 'normality', to a politics of difference, what we need is a culture which values and celebrates difference, a culture which responds energetically to diversity. In such a culture what would be valued would be the richness and diversity of human experience and the creative capacity of each individual person. Such a culture can only emerge where there exists a profound respect for each person, no matter how individual their *be-ing*, and a profound commitment to enabling each person to realize his/her unique self within social conditions of cohesiveness, nurture, justice and inclusiveness.

Conclusion

In this chapter I have argued that our way of seeing the practice of education for people with disabilities needs to recognize a fuller account of the nature of persons. Such an account also suggests that education in general, and special education in particular, inevitably involves moral and political commitments, commitments which demand a response from all in society and especially from those, such as educators and teachers, who accept social responsibility for the practice of education. What has been proposed here is a way of seeing. It is for those committed to the practice of special education to evaluate whether and how such a way of seeing is best translated into a way of acting.

References

Arbib, M. A. and Hesse, M. B. (1986) *The Construction of Reality*. Cambridge: Cambridge University Press.

Cassell, E. J. (1991) *The Nature of Suffering*. Oxford: Oxford University Press.

Glover, J. (1988) *I: the Philosophy and Psychology of Personal Identity*. Harmondsworth: Penguin.

Gutman, A. (1992) Communitarian critics of liberalism, in S. Avineri and A. De-Shalit (eds) *Communitarianism and Individualism*. Oxford: Oxford University Press.

Kundera, M. (1982) *The Book of Laughter and Forgetting*. London: Faber and Faber.

Langford, G. (1973) The concept of education, in G. Langford and D. J. O'Connor (eds) *New Essays in the Philosophy of Education*. London: Routledge and Kegan Paul.

Langford, G. (1978) *Teaching as a Profession*. Manchester: Manchester University Press.

Langford, G. (1985) *Education, Persons and Society: a Philosophical Enquiry*. London: Macmillan.

Langford, G. (1991) Teaching and the idea of a social practice, in W. Carr (ed.) *Quality in Teaching*. London: Falmer Press.

MacIntyre, A. (1984) *After Virtue*, 2nd edn. Notre Dame, IN: University of Notre Dame Press.

Miller, D. (1976) *Social Justice*. Oxford: Clarendon Press.

Rawls, J. (1971) *A Theory of Justice*. Cambridge, MA: Belknap Press.

Ricoeur, P. (1992) *Oneself as Another*. Chicago: University of Chicago Press.

Sacks, O. (1985) *The Man Who Mistook his Wife for a Hat*. London: Duckworth.

Seymour, W. (1989) *Bodily Alterations*. Sydney: Allen and Unwin.

Shklar, J. N. (1990) *The Faces of Injustice*. New Haven, CT: Yale University Press.

Strawson, P. F. (1959) *Individuals: an Essay in Descriptive Metaphysics*. London: Methuen.

Taylor, C. (1992a) The politics of recognition, in A. Gutman (ed.) *Multiculturalism and 'The Politics of Recognition'*. Princeton, NJ: Princeton University Press.

Taylor, C. (1992b) Atomism, in S. Avineri and A. De-Shalit (eds) *Communitarianism and Individualism*. Oxford: Oxford University Press.

Wittgenstein, L. (1974) *Tractatus Logico-Philosophicus*. London: Routledge and Kegan Paul.

Wolfensberger, W. (1991) *A Brief Introduction to Social Role Valorization as a High-order Concept for Structuring Human Services*. Syracuse, NY: Training Institute for Human Service Planning, Leadership and Change Agency (Syracuse University).

3 Kenneth R. Howe

Educational ethics, social justice and children with disabilities

Special education has its own constellation of ethical problems that have grown out of its own history and mission. This does not mean, however, that ethics in special education can be understood apart from the larger set of ethical issues pertaining to schooling more generally or, in turn, from the still larger issue of schooling's role in shaping and sustaining a democratic society. To complicate matters, a burgeoning philosophical controversy currently exists about how best to characterize and approach ethics in education – especially regarding how much emphasis to place on equality and justice – on the one hand, versus community and personal relationships on the other (see, for example, Strike and Ternasky 1993, Part I).

Theories that emphasize equality and justice typically elaborate and defend systems of principles. By contrast, theories that emphasize community and relationship typically find principles of quite limited use. Going somewhat against the tide perhaps, I will argue that much would be lost if the principle-based approach were abandoned, and that theories which emphasize community and relationship suffer from serious difficulties of their own, particularly with respect to justice. I will suggest that some way of accommodating both kinds of general theories is required.

Next, I provide a general analysis of the principle of equality of educational opportunity, the principle that has been at the centre of liberal educational policy in the second half of the twentieth century (at least in the west) and that it is thoroughly implicated in social justice. I then apply this general analysis to a peculiar difficulty that special education presents: by the nature and severity of their disabilities, certain special education students are precluded from enjoying equality of educational opportunity. I suggest that the rationale for educating such students, accordingly, must differ from the equality of educational opportunity rationale, but that it may, nonetheless, be grounded in the broader requirements of social justice.

I conclude with a few observations about the discouraging direction in which educational policy seems to be headed *vis-à-vis* social justice and the education of children with disabilities.

The view from nowhere, from here, and from places in between

Thomas Nagel (1986) coined the phrase 'the view from nowhere' to refer to the objective point of view, the point of view from which personal interests and partiality have no place. In ethics this corresponds to the point of view of equality, the point of view from which everyone's interests count the same. This general idea is to be found in one form or another in various political theories. (It underlies the idea of 'undistorted communication', for instance, in the Habermasian brand of critical theory.) But sorting out the intricacies of political theory on this point is beyond the scope of this chapter. I shall take a specifically liberal approach.

Liberal political theorists have fleshed out this general idea in three primary ways: libertarian, utilitarian, and liberal-egalitarian. Libertarianism identifies equality with respecting individuals' autonomy to the greatest degree possible, and justice with intervening to the least degree possible in the kinds of social and economic arrangements to which autonomous individuals freely agree. Utilitarianism identifies equality with treating all individuals the same in calculating the benefits associated with social and economic arrangements, and justice with social and economic arrangements that maximize benefits.

The third view, liberal-egalitarianism, is the most recent, and has dominated liberal political theory (perhaps western political theory in general) since the publication of John Rawls's celebrated *A Theory of Justice* (1971). Like libertarians, Rawls identifies equality with respect for autonomy. But, unlike them, he sanctions more pervasive intervention in social and economic arrangements to mitigate the effects of the natural and social 'lotteries' – whether one is disabled and who one's parents happen to be, for instance – to help ensure 'fair equality of opportunity'. Like utilitarians, then, Rawls seeks to manipulate the distribution of social benefits. But, unlike them, he places several constraints on the principle of maximization. One, already mentioned, is fair equality of opportunity. The second is an egalitarian principle of distribution. The basic idea is that distributing away from the more advantaged toward the less advantaged is required in the name of justice (Nagel 1991). This principle governs the *shape* of distributions so that they tend toward equality over time. Neither utilitarianism nor libertarianism has a similar egalitarian requirement.

Despite important differences, these theories nonetheless share an important defect, or so certain critics maintain. Locating the standards of ethical deliberation in abstract principles such as equality and impartiality – the 'view from nowhere' – divorces ethical deliberation from the standards to be found in tradition, community, and personal and family relationships – the 'view from here'. 'Communitarianism' and 'care theory' are two influential perspectives from which this criticism has been advanced.

Communitarians often trace their roots to Aristotle, who locates the standard of ethical deliberation in community practices and norms that define the virtuous person (e.g. MacIntyre 1981; Bricker 1993). Aristotle distinguished the particularistic 'practical reasoning' he associated with ethics from the universalistic principle-based reasoning he associated with science. For him, because ethical difficulties are concrete and often unique, principles are typically of little avail. The adequacy of ethical decision-making, accordingly, is to be judged in terms of the performance of the deliberator – the virtues she or he exhibits – rather than in terms of the application of principles. According to this view, evaluating an ethical decision is much more like evaluating a sculptor's transformation of a unique piece of stone, with its peculiar shape, colour, marbling and faults, than like evaluating a geometer's application of theorems.

Contemporary communitarians have built upon Aristotle's view in various ways, sometimes quite directly and sometimes less so, to further undermine liberalism's commitment to principles. One criticism is that lacking any exemplars of the ethically good person, liberalism provides only a 'proceduralist ethics' that has nothing to say about the validity of the various moral claims among which it merely referees (Taylor 1989). The result is a form of special interests politics – 'emotivism' – one in which no question arises as to whose moral perspective is indeed correct; the only question is who has the power and resources to work things to their advantage (MacIntyre 1981). A related criticism is that lacking any recognition of the way in which personal identity is 'discovered', any recognition of the way in which identity is bound up with and shaped by pre-existing communal relationships, liberalism presupposes an altogether individualistic and impoverished conception of the self (Sandel 1982).

Like communitarianism, care theory locates the standard of ethical deliberation in concrete human relationships (Noddings 1984). Accordingly, and for much the same reason, it is also highly critical of the appeal in liberal theory to the reliance on general principles, and to its putative individualist conception of the self. But care theory is much more closely allied with feminism than with Aristotelianism. Thus, whereas communitarianism is often sympathetic to traditional arrangements, care theory is often hostile to them. Particularly in so far as girls and women are oppressed by traditional roles, care theory is an instrument of change.[1]

But setting aside the question of how these differences might be worked out, communitarian and care theory critics of liberalism share the dubious assumption that a general ethical theory must be consistently dedicated *either* to some version of the view from nowhere *or* to some version of the view from here.

By saying this is dubious I do not mean to suggest that tensions do not exist. Indeed, stark ethical choices can arise in which the view from nowhere and the view from here are irremediably at odds. Nel Noddings illustrates this in dramatic fashion with the example of Manlius's punishment of his son:

> Manlius [was] a Roman commander who laid down harsh rules for the conduct of his legions. One of the first to disobey a rule about leaving camp to engage in individual combat was his own son. In compliance with the rules, Manlius ordered the execution of his son. A principle had been violated; for this violation, X must be executed. That 'X' was replaced by 'my son' gave Manlius no release from obedience to the principle.
>
> (Noddings 1984: 44)

Noddings's example is designed to question the principles of impartiality and equality associated with liberal theories of justice, principles that require treating everyone the same regardless of the concrete personal relationships that exist. Thus, it is not simply Manlius's rules that are at issue here (which, no doubt, might be criticized as generally too harsh) but that he was not swayed by the fact that it was his son to whom they were indifferently applied.

Noddings's general point may be illustrated with less dramatic examples, and one specifically from special education is relevant. Consider, then, the Amy Rowley case.

> Amy Rowley was a hearing-impaired first-grader. Consistent with the requirements of the Education for All Handicapped Children Act (PL 94–142), an individualized educational program (IEP) was devised for Amy that provided her with a hearing aid and instruction in sign language and lip reading. Against the protests of Amy's parents, however, the district special education office refused to provide an interpreter for Amy to translate spoken language in the classroom. The district reasoned that because Amy 'was achieving educationally, academically, and socially' (she was above average in each case) and was a 'remarkably well-adjusted child', it had no obligation to try to improve her performance further ... The Rowleys ultimately sued to obtain an interpreter for Amy and a lower court decided in their favor. However, the Supreme Court overturned the lower court, resting its reasoning largely on how Congress intended the expression 'free appropriate education,' mandated by PL 94–142, to be interpreted. The Court decided that Congress intended no 'substantive educational standard' by this expression and, in particular, that it did not intend the standard to be 'strict equality of opportunity or services' ...
>
> (Howe and Miramontes 1992: 5–7)

Now, it is perfectly appropriate for the Rowleys to behave as advocates for their daughter and to refuse to endorse the Court's decision. Indeed, it would be odd, if not objectionable, for them casually to assume the view from nowhere such that Amy's interests would be counted the same as anyone else's, as just another 'X', the way Manlius treated his son. It is by no means clear, however, that it is inappropriate for the Supreme Court to adopt this impartial perspective. On the contrary, it would be objectionable for a justice of the Supreme Court to show partiality toward Amy. One who knew the Rowleys personally, for instance, would be expected to withdraw from the case.

In this vein, it is important to observe that much of the sting would be taken out of Noddings's criticism of Manlius if he had withdrawn himself from the decision regarding the punishment of his son, particularly if he had gone on to advocate leniency. The general point here is that the degree to which it is morally appropriate (as well as psychologically possible) to assume an impartial perspective depends on the position that a person occupies within existing relationships. It does not follow from the fact that it is sometimes morally inappropriate to adopt an impartial perspective that it is always inappropriate.

Consider the consequences of completely jettisoning the demands of impartiality in favour of the demands of concrete community and personal relationships. The result can only be a blinkered moral perspective. In the case of care theory, because it is very difficult to make sense of moral obligations to strangers without appeal to some measure of impartial concern, strangers outside the orbit of established relationships are effectively excluded from consideration. In the case of communitarianism, because the predominant community values that serve as the final arbiter on moral matters must meet no standards other than their own, communities are free to treat their members as they see fit.

The history of special education in the US provides a concrete illustration of the safeguard that the view from nowhere provides. Reliance on the view from here – on local communities and concrete relationships – proved woefully inadequate. Special needs students were pervasively denied access to an adequate public education if not denied access to any public education whatsoever. In response, a series of federal court decisions and legislation were required to ensure that disabled children were provided with a free public education, just as other children are. The principle of equality of educational opportunity, particularly its requirement of non-discrimination, was taken to supersede community values, and was mandated in the face of marked resistance from local school districts.

So, it is a mistake to jettison the view from nowhere in favour of the view from here, for this is insensitive to the demands of justice. But it is no less of a mistake to do the reverse, for this is insensitive to the demands of concrete human relationships. What needs to be recognized is that there is no *solution* to the problem of the tension that exists between these two moral perspectives, that there is no comfortable 'moral harmony' (Hampshire

1983) to be had (see also Larmore 1987). This is not to suggest that the tension need reduce ethical deliberation to chaos. That it might be mitigated is implicit in certain practices that already exist. In particular, persons occupying certain roles – parents versus Supreme Court justices, for instance – are expected to deliberate in different ways *vis-à-vis* the view from here versus the view from nowhere. Amy Rowley's parents are expected to adopt the view from here, for instance, whereas Supreme Court justices are expected to adopt a view, if not from nowhere, and least from much farther away.

As it turns out, there are many places between the extremes of nowhere and here. Imagine a regular education teacher versus a special education teacher versus a principal versus a superintendent, all working in the same school district. Each would have different communities and different concrete relationships to command their loyalties, a different set of 'role-related obligations' (Howe and Miramontes 1992). The superintendent would be expected to take the most impartial view, taking into account the greatest number of individuals and being farthest removed from the interests and claims of particular students, parents, teachers, classrooms and schools. Next would come the principal, who would be an advocate for her or his school, but who would be expected to be impartial regarding matters within the school. Next would come the teachers, who would have a more particularized interest in their own students and classrooms. The special education teacher would also have a particularized commitment to the mission of special education that would put her or him in a unique position regarding loyalty to a community altogether outside the district. Of course, the variations on these perspectives and the relationships among them make for enormous complexity, and I shall not attempt to sort them out any further. Instead, I offer the general observation that how effectively conflicting perspectives and roles can be accommodated depends in no small way on the degree to which the context in which they must be negotiated exemplifies justice.

The extent to which citizens and educators can (should) forgo what they identify as their personal and community interests depends on the extent to which they can be confident that the burdens and benefits of doing so will be fairly applied to all. If they cannot be assured they will not be made worse off than others similarly situated by giving up something in the name of justice, why should they not scramble for all they can get? This observation helps to ground John Rawls's (1971: 3) basic premise: 'Justice is the first virtue of social institutions.'

For example, consider two schemes for distributing human livers for transplant, a dramatic case in which the demand for a resource far outstrips the supply. In plan 1, recipients must be medically suitable. After this pool is created, who gets the liver becomes a competition based on money, influence, getting on the talk shows, and so forth. In plan 2, recipients also must be medically suitable. But after the pool is created who gets the liver is determined by a lottery. I submit that plan 2 is more just than plan 1, and, that if agreed to, it would foster a much more cooperative set of social relationships. (I do not mean to suggest by this that the losers in the lottery can be criticized for not happily accepting their fate, though, speaking for myself, I would much prefer losing in this way to losing under plan 1.)

Now this, of course, is a dramatic case, and one of the things that makes it so is its all-or-none, life-or-death feature. More pervasive is the question of how to ensure a 'fair share' of social goods – income, medical care and education are among the most important – is had by all. In the next section I address the problem of what constitutes a fair share of education in terms of the principle of equality of educational opportunity. Subsequently I apply this analysis specifically to special education.

Equality of educational opportunity[2]

The concept of equal educational opportunity is a part of the conceptual apparatus of liberal-democratic tradition, functioning within a network of connected and mutually supporting concepts such as liberty, democracy, equality, choice, opportunity and justice. In general, the liberal-democratic tradition is not a strictly egalitarian one, because its interpretation of social justice does not require that the distribution of a society's goods be equalized unconditionally. Instead, equality is only a *prima facie* requirement; inequality is morally acceptable so long as individuals are provided with an equal opportunity to obtain society's goods.

Equal *educational* opportunity occupies a pivotal place in this tradition, especially in the wake of *Brown* v. *the Board of Education* (1954). Equality of educational opportunity is now recognized as an essential requirement of equality of opportunity more generally. It is an 'enabling good' in the sense that it is required to obtain other social goods such as income, employment and self-respect. But vast differences of viewpoint exist regarding what equality of educational opportunity requires – differences that have profound implications for educational policy. Three interpretations are in competition: formal, compensatory, and democratic.

The formal interpretation

The formal interpretation identifies equality of educational opportunity with the formal structure of educational institutions. In its purest form, it requires only the absence of formal barriers to participation based on morally irrelevant criteria such as race and gender. In a slightly stronger form, it also requires equalizing resources among schools, at least up to some floor. The formal interpretation can serve a progressive function, for banning legally sanctioned racial barriers to educational opportunity was surely a moral advance, and removing such barriers for persons with disabilities was an advance as well.

For the most part, however, the formal interpretation falls considerably short of the goal to which the principle of equal educational opportunity should aspire. It is often insensitive to the profound influence that social factors can have on educational opportunities, even when formal barriers are absent and resources such as funding are equalized. For example, the educational opportunities that a monolingual Chinese-speaking child enjoys in a school that is conducted exclusively in English are hardly equal to those that a monolingual English-speaking child enjoys. And this is precisely what the Supreme Court decided in the celebrated *Lau* v. *Nichols* (1974) case when it declared that the educational opportunities provided to Chinese children under these circumstances were not 'meaningful'. In order, then, for educational opportunities to be meaningful – to be worth wanting – they cannot be construed in terms of the formal features of educational institutions alone. Instead, they must be construed in terms of the interaction between these features and the characteristics that individuals bring to educational institutions.

The compensatory interpretation

The compensatory interpretation is sensitive to the importance of this interaction. Its goal is to help shape successful educational careers by compensating for characteristics of individuals that disadvantage them in educational institutions. For example, bilingual education is a means by which to compensate for the disadvantages of non-English-speaking children; Head Start is a means by which to compensate for economic disadvantages; and special education is a means by which to compensate for disabilities.

The compensatory interpretation is prominent in both liberal political theory and in the educational policy arena. It is the general kind of interpretation that is typically associated with both utilitarianism and liberal-egalitarianism, and it underlies much federal law as well (Salamone 1986). It has also increasingly become the target of criticism, from the right as well as the left.

Rightists include libertarians and conservative moralists who, although differing markedly with respect to civil liberties, both criticize the compensatory interpretation because of the governmental intervention it requires and because of the way in which it putatively places far too little emphasis on individual initiative and responsibility. Rightists are associated with a formalist interpretation of equality of educational opportunity, which I have already dismissed.

For their part, leftists have historically criticized the compensatory interpretation for being insensitive to sources of inequality that are found in underlying economic structures, particularly as related to social class (Bowles and Gintis 1976, 1989). Although these critics would be likely to concede that a compensatory interpretation is generally preferable to a formal interpretation, they are highly critical of both – indeed, of the principle of equality of educational opportunity *per se*. Focusing on equalizing educational opportunity diverts attention from the underlying structural sources of inequality associated with social class and, in the process, serves to legitimate and perpetuate vast inequality.

Over the last several decades liberal theory and policy has come under increasing criticism for also being insensitive to the effects of race and gender, in addition to class.[3] These groups have been historically excluded from negotiating the practices and curriculum of the public schools, and, as Janet Radcliff Richards observes, 'If a group is kept out of doing something long enough, it is overwhelmingly likely that activities . . . will develop in a way unsuited to the excluded group' (1980: 113–14). In this vein, current liberal society is characterized as being through-and-through a product and reflection of the historical dominance of white males, particularly those possessing economic power. Although various critics can substantially disagree, they all seem to converge on the following general conclusion: the liberal quest for equality is a sham because it merely serves to enshrine the *status quo*, rendering white males the standard of comparison and requiring disempowered groups to play by rules they had no part in formulating and whose interests such rules do not serve.

The democratic interpretation

One response to this challenge is to abandon the principle of equality of educational opportunity as a principle that inherently and irremediably legitimates dominance. Of late, several liberal-egalitarian theorists have marshalled a second response (Okin 1989; Kymlicka 1990, 1991). These theorists concede that the liberal tradition historically has been insensitive to the importance of factors such as culture, gender and disability, and that such insensitivity does indeed render it vulnerable to the charge of legitimating domination.[4] Rather than abandoning liberalism, however, these theorists call for a rethinking of what liberal principles demand, particularly the principle of equality.

Will Kymlicka (1991), for instance, contends that an adequate interpretation of equality is implicit in seminal liberal thinkers such as John Rawls and Ronald Dworkin, even if they do not themselves adequately articulate it. In particular, Kymlicka contends that Rawls's inclusion of 'self-respect' among the 'primary goods' that society must justly distribute opens the door to – indeed, requires – including a place for the effective expression and incorporation of diverse identities in the design of society's institutions. This is so because maintaining one's identity, and having what flows from it respected and taken seriously, is inextricably bound up with self-respect. In this general vein, Kymlicka (1991: 89) observes, 'it only makes sense to invite people to participate in politics (or for people to accept that invitation) if they are treated as equals . . . And that is incompatible with defining people in terms of roles they did not shape or endorse.'

The kind of view Kymlicka represents thus takes very seriously the objection that mere differential treatment in the name of responding to special needs, interests and capabilities – mere compensation for disadvantages – is insufficient or objectionable if it is not also rooted in equal respect for different views on what worthwhile needs, interests and capabilities are. Iris Marion Young echoes and extends this view (with major implications for educational institutions):

> Groups with different circumstances or forms of life should be able to participate together in public institutions without shedding their distinct identities or suffering disadvantage because of them. The goal is not to give special compensation to the deviant until they achieve normality, but rather to denormalize the way institutions formulate their rules by revealing the plural circumstances and needs that exist, or ought to exist, within them.
>
> (Young 1990a: 140)

This kind of general political framework yields the 'democratic interpretation' of equality of educational opportunity. Education remains an enabling good, but, in order to be morally defensible as well as effective, it must afford recognition to the diversity of backgrounds and life circumstances of the children it seeks to educate. By 'recognition' I mean something more than mere tolerance, more than merely putting up with those who are different. I mean including others on their own terms (Howe, forthcoming). Now, although this democratic interpretation requires the inclusion of a much wider spectrum of voices in negotiating the goals, curricula and practices of schooling than has historically been the case, it does not require abandoning wholesale the idea that some educational goals, curricula and practices should be shared. The idea that a democratic society must provide all of its citizens with a common education sufficient for them to participate effectively in democratic politics can be traced at least as far back as Thomas Jefferson. Jefferson's idea has recently been more fully articulated by Amy Gutmann, in her influential *Democratic Education* (1987), which I will discuss in the next section. Here I provide a brief description.

The key concept in Gutmann's theory is the 'democratic threshold', which she identifies with the type and amount of educational achievement required for citizens to be able to participate as equals in the democratic process. She equates the substance of the threshold with 'democratic character', which has two complementary dimensions: moral character and logical reasoning. These function together so that individuals are disposed to act as well as deliberate in moral (democratic) ways. For the deliberation to be effective, certain levels of knowledge and reasoning skills are required.

The threshold imposes a restriction on the discretion afforded individuals, families and communities – on the view from here – regarding the kind of educational arrangements that are politically and morally justified. In the name of democracy, all students who are capable must be educated up to the threshold (what to say about those who are not is an issue to be considered later). Educational resources must be distributed accordingly. In this way, Gutmann's threshold provides an egalitarian principle of distribution (described previously) that intimately links a fair share of education to participatory democracy.

Equality of educational opportunity and children with disabilities: the three interpretations revisited

In its purer forms, a formal interpretation of equality of educational opportunity is completely inadequate for children with disabilities. A wheelchair-bound child, for instance, will not find it very helpful that the school doors are open to everyone if the only way to the classroom is up a flight of stairs. To have any equalizing potential whatsoever, then, equality of educational opportunity requires removing physical barriers to access. This is obvious enough.

That merely removing physical barriers is insufficient is also obvious enough. Consider Amy Rowley once again. The fact that she is hearing-impaired entails that she requires additional – and different – instructional resources once she has gained physical access to the classroom, resources that mitigate her disability in order to equalize her educational opportunities.

Amy Rowley provides a paradigm case of the compensatory interpretation, and it is safe to say that this interpretation dominates policy and practice in special education today (though it often goes under the pejoratives of 'normalization', 'assimilation' and the 'deficit model'). How it works with respect to special education differs little from how it works with respect to other disadvantages: in the name of equality of educational opportunity, children with disabilities are to have their disadvantages mitigated as far as possible in order to have a fair chance of attaining the educational criteria deemed worthwhile.

In my earlier critique of the compensatory interpretation, I suggested that certain 'disadvantaged' groups might very well *not want* compensation because of the cost it exacts from them in terms of their identity. This criticism may be applied to compensating for disabilities as well, and there is a complication. Not only may persons with disabilities not want compensation. Compensation may also be fruitless, even where there is a willingness on the part of persons with disabilities to accept the cost that compensation can exact in terms of identity. As the activist Norman Kunc (1992) observes, no amount of therapy will enable a child with cerebral palsy to walk or talk normally (Kunc has cerebral palsy himself). To persist with compensation under such circumstances, Kunc says, is to condemn such a child to a 'life sentence' of marginalization.

How does the democratic interpretation fare in the context of special education? To answer this question, it will be useful to distinguish between two general kinds of cases: those in which there is a realistic chance of achieving the democratic threshold and those in which there is not.

The first kind of case (e.g. a child with a cerebral palsy, say, Norman Kunc as a child) is straightforward. All children who are capable of attaining the democratic threshold should be provided with educational effort and resources sufficient to achieve it, and different children will require different amounts. With respect to threshold, then, the democratic interpretation looks much like the compensatory interpretation.

There is no inconsistency here, for compensation is not inherently objectionable; whether it is depends on who determines needs and goals and whether they are controverted. In this connection, compensating Amy Rowley in the form of a hearing aid and training in lip reading toward the goal of improved communication seems uncontroverted enough. But there is a difference between this and insisting that her enunciation be perfect in order that she might be normal and whole. The chief complaint against the compensatory interpretation, broadly construed, is that it takes the traditional goals of schooling for granted, and, compensating as deemed necessary, applies them indifferently to all children.

Adopting the formation of democratic character as the overriding obligation of public schooling has specific implications for the practice of special education. Foremost among these is the strong support it provides for inclusion. Affording recognition and being recognized are reciprocal, and both are required to foster democratic character. There is no surer way of doing this than by providing face-to-face practice in deliberating with those who have different values, interests, talents and life circumstances. Inclusion is thus a necessary condition of fostering equality of educational opportunity under its democratic interpretation.

Inclusion is obviously not a sufficient condition. Mere inclusion, for instance, physically including children with disabilities in regular classrooms but otherwise excluding them from meaningful participation, can do little to promote equality of educational opportunity. Even when done right, however, inclusion still may not be sufficient. This leads to the second kind of case distinguished above, in which a child's disabilities give her or him no realistic chance of attaining the threshold, particularly because of its cognitive demands (e.g. a child with 'significantly limited intellectual capacity', SLIC).

One response is to adopt the goal of fostering a sense of 'belonging' rather than the goal of promoting equality of educational opportunity (Kunc 1992). This response squares with the considerations adduced by care theorists and communitarians and it also supports inclusion. I think it is basically correct, but I attach one important proviso: that it not be construed so as to reintroduce the forced choice between the view from nowhere and the view from here – between principles, social justice and equality of educational opportunity on the one hand, and caring, community and belonging, on the other.

Social justice is not identical with equality of educational opportunity. When equality of educational opportunity cannot be attained, as the kind of cases in question assume, social justice still makes demands, including educational ones. In this vein, the democratic interpretation has as one of its requirements that *all* persons be afforded recognition and have their self-respect secured, a requirement that can be met here. Rather than being goals separate from social justice, or actually at odds with it, fostering caring, community and a sense of belonging are its prerequisites.[5] Thus, an emphasis on caring, community and a sense of belonging should not be seen as *alternative* to an emphasis on social justice.

For the sake of completeness, I now consider a variant of cases of the second type, in which, arguably at least, not only the cognitive demands of the democratic threshold are out of reach, but so is a sense of belonging. These are truly tragic cases, in which a child's disabilities are so severe that the capacity for meaningful human interaction seems altogether absent. Consider Tommy, a 5-year-old, with such severe brain damage that his human interaction is limited to moving his head in the direction of people's voices (see the case, 'Pulling the plug on children with profound disabilities?' in Howe and Miramontes 1992: 37–41).

It is difficult to see how children like Tommy can themselves derive any benefits that are educational in any real sense from schooling. In turn, this makes it difficult to see how to apply the argument that social justice requires providing Tommy with his fair share of education. This is not to say that social justice is beside the point in cases like this. On the contrary, it requires that Tommy be cared for, both to serve his interests and the interests of his parents (who deserve the same freedom from day care responsibilities and its costs as any other parents). Rather, it is to say that there is no principled reason for schools *qua* schools to provide the kind of care Tommy needs. Social justice demands they do it because (in the US at least) no other options are available.

Conclusion

In this chapter I have tried to move social justice and equality of educational opportunity to centre stage (or perhaps back to centre stage). To be sure, libertarianism and utilitarianism are significantly flawed, and so are the formal and compensatory interpretations of equality of educational opportunity. But these are not the only ways to interpret liberalism, and liberal theorists have not gone to sleep in the face of an onslaught of criticisms – often warranted – inspired by communitarians and care theorists. In my view, liberal-egalitarianism combined with a democratic conception of equality of educational opportunity is able to meet these criticisms. What is more, it avoids some of the difficulties communitarians and care theorists encounter in providing an adequate conception of justice. This summarizes my philosophical reasons for keeping our attention focused on social justice in the ethics of education.

There are, for lack of a better term, also strategic reasons. It seems to me to be an especially bad time to be labelling the quest for social justice and for equality of educational opportunity as too abstract, too uncaring, too aloof from community. For this plays into the hands of the current attack on public education from the New Right, and opens the door to the alternatives it proposes.

For example, equality of educational opportunity has been identified as the chief culprit in 'dumbing down' the curriculum (Murray and Herrnstein 1994). In its place should be excellence, competition, and the same high standards and expectations for all. The implications for special education can only be bad. Of course, Noddings (1992), for one, would be staunchly opposed to competition and to sameness in standards and expectations, on the basis of her care theory. But (and here I set aside her questionable interpretation of equality) is it a promising strategy to combine opposition to these things with the argument that excellence ought to replace equality as the guiding educational ideal (Noddings 1993)?

Consider an even more threatening development: schools of choice. Schools of choice come in two general varieties: public and vouchers. The former, which takes many forms, keeps money and students within a given public school district; the latter permits public money to subsidize private schools. The basic idea is that parents should be afforded much greater discretion than they currently are to decide what schools their children will attend. Schools of choice place an immense trust in individual parents and communities – the view from here – a level of trust that seems altogether unwarranted in the light of the present political climate. For example, US presidential candidate Phil Gramm, a once serious contender for the nomination of the Republican Party, responded to worries about what choice means for special education with a question to the effect: do you think bureaucrats in Washington care more about handicapped children than people in local communities? Gramm then seemed to imply the wrong answer to his own question when he remarked that it would be perfectly alright with him to cut funding for special education (and increase it for the gifted) if communities chose to do so.[6]

Gramm's question should have been countered (it wasn't) with another: wasn't depending on local communities the *modus operandi* before the litigation and legislation of the 1970s required local communities to do much more to educate children with disabilities? For one thing, persons with disabilities are in an especially vulnerable position because they are such a small minority within individual communities (Gutmann 1987). For another, and to be quite candid, I really don't trust local communities to do the right thing. My reason is not that people are hopelessly callous and totally self-interested (though some clearly are). Rather, it is that justice can only be achieved under arrangements that take the broader community into account and prevent partiality from running amuck (recall the two plans for liver transplants).

But I am waxing philosophical again, and the claim that schools of choice will have dire consequences for special education need not be based on speculation. The much ballyhooed Milwaukee voucher plan, for instance, permits participating schools to exclude special education students, and the plan is currently under expansion (Lindsay 1995).[7] At the federal level, funding for portions of the Individuals with Disabilities Education Act (the successor legislation of the Education for All Handicapped Children Act, PL 94–142) is currently being held hostage to a national voucher plan (Pitsch 1995). In my own community a group of parents sought to establish an academically elite charter school (a form of public school choice) that would *de facto* exclude most special education students on the basis of inadequate test scores. (The attempt to establish the school failed, not for this reason, however, but because a suitable building was not available.)

In general, pressures to exclude special education students – under the banner of parental choice, community control and the abolition of 'unfunded mandates' – are increasing. The best (if not only) way to resist these pressures is by appeal to the requirements of justice – the first virtue of social institutions.

Notes

1 It should be observed here that care theory is also subject to the charge that, by celebrating the traditional roles of women, it, too, can reinforce the *status quo*. See, for example, Young (1990b).

2 This section is adapted from my forthcoming *Educational Opportunities Worth Wanting: A Radical Liberal Theory of Democracy, Justice and Schooling*.

3 The literature is truly massive here, but see Weis (1988) and Weis and Fine (1993) for several good overviews.

4 Although disability is not specifically included by thinkers such as Okin and Kymlicka, the general form of the arguments may be easily extended. Iris Marion Young (1990a), who doesn't view herself as a liberal, but with whom Kymlicka

(1995) broadly agrees, explicitly includes persons with disabilities among oppressed groups.
5 This is a plausible interpretation of both Kunc (1992) and Noddings (1992).
6 The *MacNeil Lehrer News Hour*, Thursday, 12/1/1995.
7 For a description and discussion, see Howe (forthcoming).

References

Bowles, S. and Gintis, H. (1976) *Schooling in Capitalist America*. New York: Basic
  Books.
Bowles, S. and Gintis, H. (1989) Can there be a liberal philosophy of education in a
  democratic society? in H. Giroux and P. McClaren (eds) *Critical Pedagogy, the
  State, and Cultural Struggle*. Albany, NY: State University of New York Press.
Bricker, D. (1993) Character and moral reasoning: an Aristotelian perspective, in K.
  Strike and L. Ternasky (eds) *Ethics for Professionals in Education*. New York:
  Teachers College Press.
Brown v. the Board of Education 347 US 483 (1954).
Gutmann, A. (1987) *Democratic Education*. Princeton, NJ: Princeton University
  Press.
Hampshire, S. (1983) *Morality and Conflict*. Cambridge, MA: Harvard University
  Press.
Howe, K. (forthcoming) *Educational Opportunities Worth Wanting: A Radical
  Liberal Theory of Democracy, Justice and Schooling*. New York: Teachers Col-
  lege Press.
Howe, K. and Miramontes, O. (1992) *The Ethics of Special Education*. New York:
  Teachers College Press.
Kunc, N. (1992) *The Importance of Belonging*, Lecture presented to St Vrain School
  District, Longmont, CO.
Kymlicka, W. (1990) *Contemporary Political Theory*. New York: Oxford Univer-
  sity Press.
Kymlicka, W. (1991) *Liberalism, Community, and Culture*. New York: Oxford
  University Press.
Kymlicka, W. (1995) *Multicultural Citizenship: a Liberal Theory of Minority
  Rights*. New York: Oxford University Press.
Larmore, C. (1987) *Patterns of Moral Complexity*. Cambridge: Cambridge Univer-
  sity Press.
Lau v. Nichols 414 US 563 (1974).
Lindsay, D. (1995) Wisconsin, Ohio back vouchers for private schools, *Education
  Week*, 12 July.
MacIntyre, A. (1981) *After Virtue*. Notre Dame, IN: University of Notre Dame
  Press.
Murray, C. and Herrnstein, R. J. (1994) *The Bell Curve*. New York: The Free Press.
Nagel, T. (1986) *The View from Nowhere*. New York: Oxford University Press.
Nagel, T. (1991) *Equality and Partiality*. New York: Oxford University Press.
Noddings, N. (1984) *Caring: a Feminine Approach to Ethics and Moral Education*.
  Berkeley, CA: University of California Press.

Noddings, N. (1992) *The Challenge to Care in Schools*. New York: Teachers College Press.

Noddings, N. (1993) Excellence as a guide to educational conversation, in H. A. Alexander (ed.) *Philosophy of Education 1992*. Urbana, IL: Philosophy of Education Society.

Okin, S. M. (1989) *Justice, Gender, and the Family*. New York: Basic Books.

Pitsch, M. (1995) Bill to push block grant for education, *Education Week*, 2 August.

Rawls, J. (1971) *A Theory of Justice*. Cambridge, MA: Belknap Press of Harvard University Press

Richards, J. R. (1980) *The Skeptical Feminist: a Philosophical Inquiry*. London: Routledge and Kegan Paul.

Salamone, R. (1986) *Equal Education Under Law*. New York: St Martin's Press.

Sandel, M. (1982) *Liberalism and the Limits of Justice*. New York: Cambridge University Press.

Strike, K. and Ternasky, L. (eds) (1993) *Ethics for Professionals in Education*. New York: Teachers College Press.

Taylor, C. (1989) *Sources of the Self: the Making of Modern Identity*. Cambridge, MA: Harvard University Press.

Weis, L. (ed.) (1988) *Class, Race, and Gender in American Education*. Albany, NY: State University of New York Press.

Weis, L. and Fine, M. (eds) (1993) *Beyond Silenced Voices: Class, Race, and Gender in United States Schools*. Albany, NY: State University of New York Press.

Young, I. M. (1990a) Polity and group difference: a critique of the ideal of universal citizenship, in C. Sunstein (ed.) *Feminism and Political Theory*. Chicago: University of Chicago Press.

Young, I. M. (1990b) Humanism, gynocentrism, and feminist politics, in *Throwing Like a Girl and Other Essays in Feminist Philosophy and Social Theory*. Bloomington, IN: Indiana University Press.

Disabled, handicapped or disordered: 'what's in a name?'

'tis but thy name that is my enemy
. . . O be some other name!
What's in a name? That which we call a rose
By any other name would smell as sweet.

(Juliet in *Romeo and Juliet* II. ii)

Although this sentiment is intuitively appealing, as Juliet was subsequently to discover, she may have understated the significance of names. In fact quite a lot can be in a name. Language reflects our perceptions, beliefs and understandings of our world. It also helps shape those perceptions. Thus language can exert a powerful influence on social processes which help shape human lives.

The role of language in political and social processes has been often stressed by groups concerned with social justice. Many socially oppressed groups have deliberately formulated an identity around a specific nomenclature. This nomenclature becomes one mechanism with which to challenge the dominant cultural expressions which serve to maintain social injustices. A notable example of this process is found in the fight for racial equality in the United States. Fraser (1995) argues that because of the dominant European culture, forms of expression have developed which valued and esteemed whiteness and disparaged and devalued blackness. Thus, the language of skin colour was a cultural mechanism by which specific racial groups were socially and politically marginalized. The battle for social justice required that aspects of cultural oppression be addressed. 'Black' was redefined in a way to valorize and recognize oppressed racial groups. Nomenclature of 'blackness' became a mechanism for anti-racist groups to combat the Eurocentric cultural hegemony.

Disability as cultural oppression

Disability is one of the most frequently forgotten forms of social, political and cultural oppression. As with other groups fighting for social justice, disabled groups have grasped the significance of language and sought to develop a nomenclature in which they control the definition of their own identity. The central issue, around which issues of social justice and the language of disability revolve, relates to notions of personal disease, pathology, disorder or deficit as mechanisms of social and cultural oppression. For much of this century the lives of people with disabilities have been dominated by the medical profession. As a group their identity was defined for them in terms of sickness, involving pathology or disorder. They were labelled as deaf, dumb, blind, mentally deficient, spastic. However, medical terminology inevitably intersected with social values and cultural norms of the time. In societies which valued youth, beauty, physical prowess and intellectual excellence, the medical language of disability soon became the social language of insult and disparagement. For example, medical terms used initially to classify people with intellectual disabilities included imbecile, moron and idiot. Similarly terms associated with physical disability such as cripple and spastic have lost their original medical connotations and become cultural tools to devalue and marginalize specific groups of people.

This process is of course not unique to disability. It has been repeated in relation to other socially oppressed groups, particularly minority racial groups. However, the intertwined nature of linkage between personal medical conditions and social functioning for people with disabilities has meant the nexus between language and social oppression has been particularly pernicious and intransigent in the face of pressure for social reform. During the 1960s and 70s those labelled 'disabled' sought to redefine their identity – and in the process, redefine the popular perceptions of the sources of their 'problems'. People with disabilities contested their identity as medical problems and challenged the personal tragedy view of disability which had underpinned much social policy to that point (Oliver 1986).

Personal tragedy, disability and educational reform

The personal tragedy concept of disability in education is problematic for a number of reasons. It is embedded in the notion that there are those in society who are able (or normal) and those who are not. This dualism segments society into two groups: those, the majority, who are whole; and those who are less than whole, who are imperfect and to be kept apart from the 'able'. As a result the 'disabled' are often portrayed in popular culture as either the 'courageous battler' or the 'pathetic cripple', but are rarely viewed or treated as 'normal people' (Gartner and Lipsky 1987).

Second, after being labelled as disabled or a category of disabled (e.g. blind, developmentally delayed or mentally deficient, emotionally disturbed, or physically impaired) the label tends to become the defining feature of the person. The person becomes 'the disabled' or 'blind' or 'cripple' rather than being viewed as a complex multifaceted, fully human person.

A third area of concern with the personal tragedy view of disability relates more specifically to educational systems and the manner in which they deal with difficulties, problems or failure. A disability or disorder is an inherent characteristic of the individual and consequently attributes student failure to a defect or inadequacy within the individual (Carrier 1983; Christensen *et al.* 1986). However, it can be argued that student disability results from organizational pathology rather than student pathology. Because disability locates the cause of failure within the individual student it masks the role educational systems play in creating and reproducing failure.

A disability implies a non-problematic pathological condition intrinsic to the individual; it fails to recognize that the concept of disability is socially constructed. Rather than being a real and non-problematic feature of the individual, it occurs as a consequence of diverse student characteristics interacting with the highly constraining demands of the classroom. This is particularly the case with 'mild' disabilities such as behaviour disorder, learning disability and intellectual disability. Many students are identified as disabled, stigmatized or excluded, not because their personal characteristics necessitate this but because schooling is structured in such a way that student diversity beyond very narrow prescribed limits cannot be accommodated. The lock-step, grade-based system of schooling requires a homogeneous school population to function efficiently (Skrtic 1991).

Thus, it can be argued that schooling is itself disabling, that its lack of flexibility in accommodating a diverse range of student attributes creates disabled students. However, because the manner in which schools function is taken for granted and seen as unproblematic, the source of students' difficulties is seen to reside in their disabilities or defects rather than the limitations and defects of schooling.

The central issue here concerns the ethics of school practices related to disability as a personal tragedy. It is suggested that ethical practice cannot occur unless there is a clear recognition of the role of both schooling practices and student characteristics in the identification of school failure. The use of concepts such as disability locates the cause of problems and failure in student deficit and thus serves to legitimate and mask the role of schooling in creating the problem. However, by doing so it also serves to obscure productive solutions to enduring and persistent problems.

Although this analysis seeks to reveal the role of previously covert institutional factors in the creation of disability, it is not sufficient as it fails to address the question of how these conditions arise. School practice is largely a result of the values of the people who engage in the practice (Skrtic 1991). Suggesting that school practice contributes to the construction of disabilities ignores the beliefs and values of practitioners which promote equity, justice and student success rather than failure. How is it then that school can simultaneously promote practices which disadvantage and stigmatize students while at the same time seeking to enhance their life opportunities. The answer to this question partially lies in the history and origins of special education. Initial special education programs were established at the conclusion of the last century and were based on a humanitarian ethic. They were designed to care for and educate people with sensory, intellectual or physical impairment who were likely to remain institutionalized without intervention. These programs were closely allied to medical interventions. For this reason and because of the clear physiological basis for many of the students' difficulties, special education practices were based on the personal tragedy view of disability and firmly embedded within the medical model.

Medical diagnosis and educational provision

This medical model assumes that the basic cause of an individual's symptoms is an underlying pathology or disease. The pathology requires appropriate diagnosis which determines the prescription of a treatment. The treatment should result in cure of the disease and the disappearance of the symptoms. In an educational context symptoms are generally based on the failure of an individual to function appropriately in a classroom. A broad range of categorial labels have been developed and used to describe various pathologies. These include sensory disabilities, physical disabilities, intellectual disabilities, emotional, attentional or behaviour disorders and learning difficulties or disabilities. According to the medical model, the diagnosis of the appropriate category of disability results in prescription of a treatment. In traditional special education, diagnosis occurred through an assessment, and treatment comprised placement in a categorially based segregated setting.

While special education was initially developed to assist a small group who had clear physiologically based conditions it grew rapidly during the first half of the twentieth century and increasingly has included students where no physical pathology, disorder, disability or impairment could be shown to exist (Gartner and Lipsky 1987). The rapid expansion and shift in the focus of special education commenced with and paralleled the introduction of compulsory education (Sarason and Doris 1979). Sarason and Doris provide a convincing argument that special education grew to meet the needs of a general education system required to accommodate a diverse range of sometimes recalcitrant and difficult students.

As a system, special education retained the assumptions of the medical model as a set of guiding principles. It also retained the humanitarian ideals which characterized its origins. However, in effect special education often functioned to provide a separate segregated system to contain those who because of their physical, emotional and intellectual characteristics did not fit the regular system. Thus, it served to relieve general education of the pressure to respond to diverse and sometimes resistant students.

While a quiet symbiosis seems to have existed between special and general education for some time, strident criticism of special education during the 1960s and 70s culminated in widespread reforms during the 1970s and 80s. One source of impetus for these reforms was the work of a number of researchers and scholars who demonstrated through empirical investigation that the assumptions of the medical model could not be sustained when applied to the practice of special education. Also, a large literature based on notions of social justice and fundamental human rights questioned the treatment of those labelled disabled. The objectives of the civil rights movement and women's movement articulated with those of the disability rights movement.

The medical model is founded on a logical link between pathology, diagnosis and treatment. In special education practice, this translated into a presumed pathology based on the assignment of a categorial label followed by placement in a categorially defined setting. The question of the role of a pathology in special education placement is a vexed one. First, definition and identification of a disability, disorder or impairment is often a matter of quantitative rather than qualitative deviation from the norm. For example, there is no clear distinction between when a person is a bit long- or short-sighted, or partially-sighted or seriously visually impaired or blind. This problem is even more pronounced with categories such as intellectual disability, behaviour or emotional disorder and learning disabilities, where the line between acceptable and unacceptable classroom behaviour and performance is extremely blurred.

Second, empirical investigation of various special education populations has shown that a number of labelled students demonstrate no detectable evidence of impairment, disorder or disability (Mercer 1973; Algozzine and Ysseldyke 1983). Rather than deviating from the norm on sensory, intellec-tual, physical or emotional dimensions, many special education students deviated on social, cultural, ethnic and economic dimensions. Special education, particularly for the 'mildly disabled' was shown to comprise disproportionately large numbers of students from poor or minority backgrounds.

Along with findings that many special education students failed to show a demonstratable pathology, assessment procedures designed to identify the pathology and therefore prescribe treatment have been found to be grossly inadequate (Coles 1978; Walker 1987). For example, Gartner and Lipsky (1987: 372) write that 'except for the case of physical disabilities assessment procedures are barely more accurate than a flip of the coin'. Thus, the link between assessment/diagnosis and instructional treatment assumed under the medical model did not hold when applied to assessment processes for special education. Rather assessment frequently served merely to locate the student within a disability category and consequently legitimate placement in special education (Wang *et al.* 1986; White and Calhoun 1987). In such cases assessment information did not provide useful information to guide instruction.

In addition to problems with definition and diagnosis, studies demonstrated that instruction based on categorial labels was not effective (Hallahan and Kauffman 1977) and that generally instruction which was effective for 'special education' students was fundamentally based on the same instructional techniques which have been shown to be effective for all students. Particularly disturbing were a series of studies which found that placement in segregated special education settings diminished rather than enhanced students' education success (Gartner and Lipsky 1987).

Taken together, these studies not only exposed the myth of the medical model which sustained and legitimated traditional special education practices based on student disability, they also raised serious questions about the humanitarian ethos which accompanied these practices. How could it be claimed that special education classes served to enhance and promote the interests of 'disabled' students if it could be shown that many students are better served by avoiding placement in special education?

Disability and the rights of students

During the period that these studies appeared in the literature a number of writers were raising a different set of concerns about special education based on issues of equity and social justice. They argued that exclusion of some children from any form of education based on an identifiable physical condition and the segregation of others in separate schools and classrooms violated their fundamental human rights (Wolfensberger 1972). They argued that these practices were stigmatizing and deleterious to students, and given the demonstrable lack of efficacy of segregated setting, indefensible in terms of serving students' interests.

These criticisms culminated in widespread reforms implemented during the 1970s and 80s. These reforms were international in scope, occurring in the US, Britain, Europe and Australia. Most significant of these reforms has been the trend towards mainstreaming or placement in 'less restrictive' environments. Unfortunately reports suggest that after approximately two decades of turmoil not only have the reforms failed to achieve their stated objectives but in some cases they have exacerbated the situation they were intended to remedy (Gartner and Lipsky 1987).

The reforms have failed because they failed to recognize and address the critical social function of special education and the personal tragedy theory of student disability in maintaining a relatively homogeneous and controllable population within general education. On a surface level there is an obviously incoherent logic in the removal of students from general education class-rooms for certification as 'disabled' only to restore them to the classroom with the additional stigma of the 'defective' label. At a more fundamental level,

> the objectification of school failure as student disability through the institutional practice of special education . . . prevents the field of general education from confronting the failures of its practices and thus acts to reproduce and extend these practices in the profession [of teaching] and institution of education.
>
> (Skrtic 1991: 44)

In other words social justice as it relates to disability and special education is embedded within the social institution of schooling and as such reflects broader social structures.

Society, justice and disability

Fraser (1995) argues that struggles for social justice can be theorized along two conceptually distinct dimensions. First is an economic-political dimension which is central to Rawls's (1971) distributive theory of social justice. Social injustice is viewed as primarily a result of the inequitable distribution of economic, social and political resources. According to this view, social justice is primarily an issue of socio-economic allocation, therefore the remedy to social injustice is to restructure the distributive system or develop *redistributive* solutions.

The second dimension of social justice is cultural in nature. According to Fraser:

> The second kind of injustice is cultural or symbolic. It is rooted in social patterns of representation, interpretation and communication. Examples include cultural domination (being subjected to patterns of interpretation and communication that are associated with another culture and are alien and/or hostile to one's own); nonrecognition (being rendered invisible via the authoritative representational, communicative and interpretative practices of one's culture); and disrespect (being routinely maligned or disparaged in stereotypic public cultural representations and/or in everyday life interactions).
>
> (Fraser 1995: 71)

Fraser suggests that socio-economic redistribution does not resolve issues of cultural injustice. Rather, cultural oppression is appropriately addressed through recognition and valorization of the oppressed group. Cultural injustice results from the devaluing, derision and degrading of particular groups because of their cultural practices. The solution is to respect and value these practices, which Fraser refers to as *recognition* remedies.

Fraser argues that while the two dimensions of social justice are obviously intertwined in practice, the solutions to these two forms of social injustice are to some extent contradictory. Redistributive solutions tend to blur social distinctions. As resources are allocated more equitably, differentiation according to economic-political affiliation becomes muted. Redistributive solutions to social injustice aim to undermine group differentiation. For example, redistributive solutions to economic inequity faced by some socio-economic groups aim at the abolition of the class structure. 'The task of the proletariat is not simply to cut itself a better deal, but to abolish itself as a class' (Fraser 1995: 76). In contrast to redistributive solutions, recognition solutions to social injustice emphasize the distinctiveness of social groups, thus increasing social differentiation.

Fraser suggests that most socially oppressed groups are *bivalent* in that they are both socio-economically disadvantaged and culturally marginalized. Thus, they require both socio-economic redistributive solutions and cultural recognition and validation. However, simultaneous pursuit of these contradictory solutions often results in the perpetuation of the inequities they were designed to resolve. Disability is an example of bivalent social injustice. People with disabilities suffer both socio-economic and cultural oppression. Both redistributive and recognition dimensions can be identified in recent policy reforms in disability and special education.

Redistribution, recognition and special education reform

In his distributive theory of social justice Rawls (1971: 6) suggests that socially just practices require 'equal distribution of primary social goods . . . unless unequal distribution is to the advantage of the less favoured'. Initial demands for reform of special education, particularly calls to integrate students with disabilities into regular classrooms (Wolfensberger 1972) reflected a Rawlsian redistributive approach to social justice. Thus, the issue of access to regular schools and classrooms for students with disabilities was interpreted as one of fairness of distribution of educational resources. For example, early arguments for mainstreaming referred to the process of 'normalization' (Wolfensberger 1972). This concept emphasized the intrinsic sameness of individuals and therefore the requirement for consistency and similarity of treatment of individuals. In other words, all students regardless of disability should be treated as 'normal' students.

The Rawlsian fairness view of social justice clearly appears in some aspects of the initial US legislation, PL 94–142, and subsequently the Individuals with Disabilities Education Act (IDEA), which prohibited the exclusion of children with disabilities from the provision of free, public education. PL 94–142 mandated that all children, regardless of disability, have access to a state-provided and publicly funded education in the same way that non-disabled students have access to public education. Also in keeping with the Rawlsian view, PL 94–142 mandated that all children should be educated in the least restrictive environment (LRE). This required that all students have access to the same (i.e. regular classroom) educational environments unless the magnitude of their disability indicated that they would be better served in a separate special education setting.

Despite the dramatic reforms mandated in PL 94–142 recent critiques have argued that pressures for change have not been successful in dramatically altering educational practice (Gartner 1986; Reynolds *et al.* 1987; Lipsky and Gartner 1989). After approximately two decades of turmoil, critics (such as Gartner and Lipsky 1987) charge that not only have the reforms failed to achieve their stated objectives, in some cases they have exacerbated the situation that they were intended to remedy. For example, Gartner and Lipsky argue that following PL 94–142 the identification of students with disabilities and segregated placement of children increased rather than diminished.

The reforms failed in part because they did not recognize the critical social function of special education. PL 94–142 did not address the prevailing place of disability labels in maintaining the legitimacy of school practices which result in an inequitable distribution of school failure. Schools in the United States have been able to comply with federal regulations without either changing the practices which make more students disabled in a school context than in broader society or without recognizing their own role in the academic and social difficulties of many students. Thus attempts at distributive solutions to social injustice which fail to address the personal tragedy construction of disability have led to contradictory outcomes for students in schools.

Oliver (1986) argued that the personal tragedy theory of disability is the root cause of much of the social injustice experienced by people with disabilities. He argues that the personal tragedy theory of disability is one variant of social theories centred on victim-blaming (Ryan 1971). Like other victim-blaming theories it has tended to *individualize* problems of disability and ignore the social and economic structures which serve to disadvantage people with disabilities. In terms of recent educational reforms as articulated in PL 94–142, the process of individualizing the problem was embedded in the individualized education plan (IEP). The IEP process was intended to ensure that decisions related to the curriculum content presented to students and the setting in which their education was delivered should be derived from each student's specific needs as documented by the IEP. The IEP was embedded in a notion of individual need focused on individual deficit or pathology. Thus distribution of educational resources was tied to individual 'needs' contingent upon the identification of a disability.

As with provision of education in the LRE, the IEP frequently failed to function in the way that it was intended. Ysseldyke *et al.* (1982) reported that IEP team decisions often did little more than verify the problems identified by the teacher. In a national US study, Algozzine *et al.* (1982) reported that 92 per cent of students who were referred for assessment for special education were tested and that 73 per cent of these students were subsequently declared eligible for special education services. Ysseldyke *et al.* (1982) suggested that the most potent influence in IEP decision-making was 'teacher squeak'. This was an index of the degree to which the teacher wanted the removal of the student from the classroom. Thus Reynolds (1984) referred to the IEP team decision meeting as a 'capitulation conference'. In his review of the literature Smith (1990: 6) suggested that the IEP was intended as

> an essential component of instructional design and delivery that enhances and accounts for students' learning and teachers' teaching. Yet, data support the contention that IEPs are not functioning as designed, including being inept at structuring specially designed instruction.

Moreover, he contended that 'despite overwhelming evidence that IEPs have failed to accomplish their mission, little has been done to rectify the situation' (p. 6).

Thus it appears that during the implementation process of the reforms posed by PL 94–142, the purpose and nature of the IEP process was transformed. As Smith (1990) argued, the original intent and spirit of PL 94–142 has been met with passive compliance or acquiescence. Rather than constituting a reasoned and compelling response to students' specific educational needs, IEPs tended to function as compliance documents in the process of referring students to special education. As with LRE, the IEP mandate has been transformed through practice to support distribution of resources based on individual pathology, deficit or disability.

Cultural recognition of disability

Oliver (1986) argued that real and enduring reform requires a reconceptualization of the notion of disability from an individual personal tragedy to an aspect of social oppression. Early advocates for 'the disabled' were often parents, members of the medical profession or charity organizations concerned with procuring additional resources for the care and treatment of individuals. These groups perpetuated the dependency relationship which was imposed on many people with disabilities. This is reflected by a commentary on policy by Topliss (1979) on a British policy related to economic provision for people with disabilities which suggested that 'sympathy for the handicapped has been translated into effective legislation' (p. 9). Similar attitudes prevailed in terms of educational provision. Vincent and Troyna (1995) quoted the Chair of the Education Committee's comments regarding an LEA's special needs services: 'In [this policy document] it says people who are vulnerable and in need, we should take care of them . . . the most vulnerable are the special needs' (p. 160).

The emergence of advocacy groups formed by and composed of people with disabilities has provided a forceful challenge to personal tragedy theory. In Britain the Union of the Physically Impaired Against Segregation (UPIAS) has been one strident and effective critic of the unreflective acceptance of disability as personal tragedy. In terms of Fraser's (1995) analysis, the shift from a personal tragedy view of disability to a social oppression theory reflects a shift from a focus on distributive solutions to cultural recognition solutions. The UPIAS set out to address the social marginalization, the perpetuation of dependency relationships and the cultural neglect of people with disabilities. The pervasive nature of cultural oppression of people with disabilities is perhaps best portrayed by Fraser herself. In her otherwise insightful analysis of social injustice she noted that cultural racism has resulted in the depreciation of people of colour which has been expressed through a number of 'demeaning, stereotypical depictions in the media as criminal, bestial, primitive, *stupid*, and so on' (p. 81, my emphasis); demeaning indeed for people with intellectual disabilities.

In 1976 the UPIAS promoted a radical approach to the definition of disability which explicitly located the problem within the social structures which served to marginalize and disempower people with disabilities. The UPIAS definition distinguished between *impairment* (which related to the physical attributes of individuals) and *disability* (which referred to the social structures responsible for cultural oppression).

According to the definitions, 'Impairment' is defined as lacking part of or all of a limb, or having a defective limb, organ or mechanism of the body. 'Disability' is the disadvantage or restriction of activity caused by a contemporary social organization which takes little or no account of people who have physical impairments and thus excludes them from participation in the mainstream of social activities.

While these definitions represented a radical departure from the dominant medical approach to disability, they have received support from a number of sources. For example, in 1981 the British Council of Organizations of Disabled People was formed and adopted the UPIAS definitions.

The acceptability of this redefined notion of disability in relation to nomenclature is reflected in the changed terminology in the US legislation. In 1975 the original legislation was identified as 'The Education for All *Handicapped* Children Act'. In 1990 the bill was reauthorized as 'The Individuals with *Disabilities* Act'. Nevertheless there has not been unanimous support for the revised definitions posed by UPIAS. In 1993 the UN General Assembly accepted new definitions of disability and handicap.

The term 'disability' summarizes a great number of different functional limitations occurring in any population in any country of the world. People may be disabled by physical, intellectual or sensory impairment, medical conditions or mental illness. Such impairments, conditions or illnesses may be permanent or transitory in nature.

The term 'handicap' means the loss or limitation of opportunities to take part in the life of the community on an equal level with others. It describes the encounter between the person with a disability and the environment. The purpose of this term is to emphasize the focus on the shortcomings in the environment and in many organized activities in society, for example, information, communication and education, which prevent persons with disabilities from participating on equal terms.

There are a number of examples of dispute around nomenclature in recent special education reform arising from the effort to combat the stigma of pathology, deficit or disorder. For example, Warnock (1978) coined the term 'students with special needs' in an effort to engender similar reforms in England and Wales to those mandated by PL 94–142 in the US. Warnock identified the concept of student disability as a legitimating factor in the inequitable treatment of students in special education. She attempted to transform the systemic conceptualization of special education and disabled students by transferring the locus of the problem from a disability within the child to inflexibility in the system of schooling. By suggesting that some students have 'special needs' she was attempting to encourage the notion that the educational system needed to change and become more responsive to particular student characteristics. Thus, the term 'student with special educational needs' was intended to locate the cause of the problem within the nature of schooling rather than within the nature of the student. This was a clear attempt to address the social and political aspects of the education of students with disabilities and challenged the role of individual deficit in legitimating the failure of diverse students.

However, rather than transforming the system of schooling, the concept of students with special needs was itself transformed by the system (Tomlinson 1982). Thus rather than identifying a child as *disabled* and therefore being inadequate for 'normal' schooling, teachers and administrators identified the child as 'special needs' and therefore inadequate. Dee and Corbett (1994) noted the repetition of this process in more recent attempts to change British nomenclature from 'special education need' to 'learning support'. They suggest that one category simply superseded the other. Rather than identifying specific learning support structures which the school needed to supply to students to ensure equity in educational experiences, schools continued to identify students with disabilities with labels such as 'The students are learning support' (p. 322). Similarly, Fulcher (1983) has documented a process where attempted reform based on educational responsiveness to students' education needs was reconstructed by teachers as resource allocation based on 'needy' students. To some extent these failures of nomenclature can be seen as failures of what Fraser (1995) terms the recognition remedy to social injustice. Rather than recognizing students as valued members of the school community, they were continually redefined as in some way disordered or deficient.

In addition to the distinction between economic-distributive and cultural-recognition approaches to social justice, Fraser distinguishes between *affirmation* and *transformation* strategies to achieve social justice. Affirmative and transformative strategies intersect with redistributive and recognition strategies. Fraser argues that affirmation strategies are aimed at addressing injustices without disturbing the fundamental social structures which generate injustices. Transformative strategies, on the other hand, seek to modify underlying social structures.

Fraser argues that transformative strategies can help the redistributive-recognition dilemma where actions to promote social justice result in contradictory outcomes. Thus for groups which experience bivalent injustice (i.e. both political-economic and cultural discrimination), transformative strategies can help simultaneously promote redistributive and recognition solutions. Students with disabilities clearly represent a bivalent social group. These students frequently fail to benefit from the level of educational resources available to most students. In order successfully to engage in schooling they require additional 'special' educational resources. Yet the provision of these resources has traditionally been tied to a process of social marginalization (segregation from peers) and personal devaluation (labelling as deficit, disordered or disabled).

While the US reform legislation sought to deliver more socially just practices to students, it did so by merely affirming disabled students' rights to educational services. Thus it failed to attack the fundamental perception of the locus of the problem and subsequently modify the outcomes that many students traditionally experience. For example, Nelson and Stevens (1981) argued that one of the major obstacles in developing teacher consultation models to deliver special education services in regular classrooms is the legislation itself. They see two aspects of the legislation as particularly counterproductive. First, provision of funding is based on the identification and labelling of a specific proportion of students. Second, provision of special education services was restricted to those children who were legally defined as 'handicapped'. Thus they suggested that

> the law itself provides a highly stigmatizing label which must be affixed
> to children before they can be served. This label is hardly conducive to

mainstreaming, in that regular classroom teachers resist working with 'mental health' problems. The refer-and-remove policy is consequently perpetuated.

(Nelson and Stevens 1981: 90)

Fraser argues that transformative strategies allow for the deconstruction of existing social categories in a way that transforms the identities of all participants. She notes that 'all axes of injustice intersect one another in ways that affect everyone's interests and identities'. For example, in examining gender equity Fraser argues that deconstruction challenges the hierarchical dichotomies (male vs. female, disabled vs. able) and allows them to be replaced by 'networks of multiple intersecting differences that are demassified and shifting' (Fraser 1995: 90).

Fraser argues – and the analysis of recent special education reforms suggests – that transformation of the social location and identity of one group (the dis-abled) will not occur if the social identity of the other group (the abled) remains intact. Fraser's notion of network of intersecting differences is a useful one. Most existing literature, including the literature which acknowledges and critiques the social construction of disability, has left intact the disabled–abled dichotomy. Yet the community of people with disabilities is not a large, homogeneous entity. People with disabilities reflect a diversity of human conditions, even in relation to the characteristics which have contributed to their identification as disabled. For example, many advocates within the deaf community reject the notion of inclusion in schools and wish to fight for recognition and affirmation as a distinct social and cultural group. Within the blind community there are tensions between people who are congenitally blind and those who are adventitiously blind. There are clear distinctions in the concerns and needs of those who are physically disabled and those who are intellectually disabled. Moreover, disability is only one facet of human functioning. Disability intersects with a vast array of other cultural, linguistic and social characteristics such as gender, race and socioeconomic background. Deconstruction of the notion of disability allows for flexible and generative analysis and policy formulation which can be responsive to these multiple, intersecting and constantly shifting interests.

In relation to education and disability, transformative strategies require a fundamental reformulation of the dualisms of special and regular education, of able and dis-able – in other words, transformation of the institution of schooling. The dualism of special and regular education has resulted from a form of traditional schooling which cannot accommodate diversity and so must screen it out. However, just as widespread segregation failed to deliver socially-just educational programs to many students with disabilities, the simple wholesale return of those students to regular classrooms without a basic transformation of those classrooms will similarly fail to provide social justice to all students.

If this dualism is to be transcended it seems inevitable that the nomenclature of disability itself will come under question. Whether it is used to designate an individual as in some way disordered, or is used to signify that social structures must be more responsive to individual needs, disability perpetuates the dualism. Real and enduring reforms need to be accompanied by fundamental restructuring of the culture and practice of schooling. This requires the development of a schooling which engenders an inclusive rather than exclusive form of educational practice. In such a practice students are not seen as disabled, defective or disordered. Rather, all students are seen as different, complex and whole. All students are recognized as reflecting a diversity of cultural, social, racial, physical and intellectual identities.

References

Algozzine, B., Christenson, S. and Ysseldyke, J. E. (1982) Probabilities associated with the referral to placement process, *Teacher Education and Special Education*, 5: 19–23.

Algozzine, B. and Ysseldyke, S. (1983) Learning disabilities as a subset of school failure: the oversophistication of a concept, *Exceptional Children*, 52: 242–6.

Carrier, J. G. (1983) Masking the social in educational knowledge: the case of learning disability theory, *American Journal of Sociology*, 39: 949–73.

Christensen, C. A., Gerber, M. M. and Everhart, R. B. (1986) Toward a sociological perspective on learning disabilities, *Educational Theory*, 36: 317–31.

Coles, G. S. (1978) The learning disabilities test battery: empirical and social issues, *Harvard Educational Review*, 48: 313–40.

Dee, L. and Corbett, J. (1994) Individual rights in further education: Lost, stolen or stayed?, *British Educational Research Journal*, 20: 319–25.

Fraser, N. (1995) From redistribution to recognition? Dilemmas of justice in a 'post-socialist' age, *New Left Review*, 212: 68–93.

Fulcher, G. (1983) *Disabling Policies? A Comparative Approach to Education Policy and Disability*. London: The Falmer Press.

Gartner, A. (1986) Disabling help: Special education at the crossroads, *Exceptional Children*, 53: 72–9.

Gartner, A. and Lipsky, K. (1987) Beyond special education: toward a quality system for all students, *Harvard Educational Review*, 57: 367–95.

Hallahan, D. P. and Kauffman, J. M. (1977) Labels, categories, behaviours: Ed., LD and EMR reconsidered, *Journal of Special Education*, 11: 139–49.

Lipsky, D. K. and Gartner, A. (1989) *Beyond Separate Education: Quality Education for All*. Baltimore: Paul H. Brookes.

Mercer, J. (1973) *Labelling the Mentally Retarded: Clinical and Social System Perspectives on Mental Retardation*. Berkeley, CA: University of California Press.

Nelson, C. M. and Stevens, K. B. (1981) An accountable consultation model for mainstreaming behaviorally disordered children, *Behavioral Disorders*, 6: 82–91.

Oliver, M. (1986) Social policy and disability: some theoretical issues, *Disability, Handicap and Society*, 1: 5–17.

Rawls, J. (1971) *A Theory of Social Justice*. Cambridge, MA: Belknap Press of the Harvard University Press.

Reynolds, M. C. (1984) Classification of students with handicaps, in E. W. Gordon (ed.) *Review of Research in Education* (Vol. 11 pp. 63–92). Washington, DC: American Educational Research Association.

Reynolds, M. C., Wang, M. C. and Walberg, H. J. (1987) The necessary restructuring of special and general education, *Exceptional Children*, 53: 391–8.

Ryan, W. (1971) *Blaming the Victim*. New York: Orbach and Chambers.

Sarason, S. and Doris, J. (1979) *Educational Handicap, Public Policy, and Social History*. New York: Free Press.

Skrtic, T. M. (1991) *Behind Special Education*. Denver, CO: Love.

Smith, S. W. (1990) Individualized education programs (IEPs) in special education – from intent to acquiescence, *Exceptional Children*, 57: 6–14.

Tomlinson, S. (1982) *A Sociology of Special Education*. London: Routledge and Kegan Paul.

Topliss, E. (1979) *Provision for the Disabled*. Oxford: Blackwell and Robertson.

Union of the Physically Impaired Against Segregation (1976) *Fundamental Principles of Disability*. London: Union of the Physically Impaired Against Segregation.

Vincent, C. and Troyna B. (1995) The discourses of social justice in education, *Discourse: Studies in the Cultural Politics of Education*, 16: 149–66.

Walker, L. J. (1987) Procedural rights in the wrong system. Special education is not enough, in A. Gartner and T. Joe (eds) *Images of the Disabled/Disabling Images*. New York: Praeger, pp. 98–102.

Wang, M. C., Reynolds, M. C. and Walberg, H. (1986) Rethinking special education, *Educational Leadership*, 44: 27.

Warnock, M. (1978) *Special Educational Needs*. London: Department of Education and Science.

White, R. and Calhoun, M. (1987) From referral to placement: teachers' perceptions of their responsibilities, *Exceptional Children*, 53: 467.

Wolfensberger, W. (1972) *The Principles of Normalization in Human Services*. Toronto: National Institute on Mental Retardation.

Ysseldyke, J. E., Algozzine, B., Richey, L. and Graden, J. (1982) Declaring students eligibility for learning disability services: Why bother with the data?, *Learning Disability Quarterly*, 5: 37–44.

Disability, participation, representation and social justice

Introduction

> In a society that is becoming increasingly reliant upon charitable organisations to satisfy a whole raft of demands which were once serviced by the State health services it is vital that the public understands the increased burden this places on the charity industry.
>
> (Needham 1993: 1)

Disability is a socially constituted and reproduced set of relationships within which impairment is given social meaning and people experience processes of power directed at their bodies. In societies which are organized around a capitalist mode of production (though not only in these, as experiences of disabled people in countries like China reveal), in which power relationships of gender and race are also active, disabled people experience society in complex ways which inscribe upon their bodies these social hierarchies. This chapter addresses these processes of inscription within an analysis of societies where cleavages of class, gender and race form the primary points of social inequality.

We would acknowledge, in opening, that the social constitution of the terminology of disability and its location within discourses of power are as embedded in the disability discourses of academia as in the wider public culture of society with its stereotypes and constructs. This book itself provides an example of the ways in which academic discourses contribute to perspectives on people with disabilities which then flow into an educational environment. Educational institutions then will influence the ways in which health, welfare and community professionals will perceive their roles and enact their responsibilities. In an apparent genuflection towards political correctness, we find chapters here which break the disabled into people who are 'racially identified', or people who are 'gendered' – yet we experience these categories as seamless parts of a total societal immersion.

The effect of these categorizations can be to divide and separate people into mutually antagonistic blocs, eroding solidarities which are crucial to the survival of individuals facing processes of atomization in the wider world. For one of the most powerful emotions experienced by people with disabilities who may also simultaneously be women, working class or Black, or carry a variety of identities, can be that of 'alone-ness', of isolation from the wider social interactions, as stigma and fear by the 'other' face them with rejection and exclusion.

In the wake of the International Year of the Disabled Person in 1981 and political movements seeking popular empowerment for people with disabilities in the United States, Canada, Europe and elsewhere in Asia, Africa and the Americas, there has emerged a new discourse to replace or at least in places supersede the traditions of rehabilitation and special education studies. The long-term institutional response to disability, with the incarceration of disabled people in factory-like disciplinary institutions, emerged during the early part of the Industrial Revolution and was developed through the mature phase of industrial capitalism. The model was based on an assessment of the likely productivity of people with disabilities, and their relegation to holding camps of various sorts if they were deemed to be unable to contribute economically to society. This institutional model carried with it a 'recreational' approach to managing the daily lives of disabled people, in which they were offered little emotional or creative stimulus and were often abandoned to lives of unutterable boredom and profound depression. In the worst cases these people were passively or actively eliminated in a form of state-sponsored murder (often labelled 'eugenics'), with authorities disguising the events or protecting the perpetrators.

By the late 1960s, initially in Scandinavia and then in the United States, a form of paternalistic reform emerged, albeit clothed in the language of a liberation movement. It was particularly focused around people with intellectual disabilities. Strongly influenced by emerging notions of individual rights, they reconceptualized people with disabilities as subjects in their own lives rather than simply as objects of medical and social regimes of control. This new discourse, which paralleled other innovations in the human services areas (for example in rehabilitative strategies in penology), argued for 'deinstitutionalization', and directly attacked the large factory model of containment. It proposed a 'training' model, in which disabled people would as far as possible be 'socially educated' to adopt patterns of behaviour which would allow them to be accepted in the wider community. This discourse recognized the level of community prejudice against many forms of disability, but argued that careful work with disabled people could reconstitute them in ways which would not offend against prejudice and minimize stigma; in the best-case scenario, it could actually erode prejudice and change social values to the benefit of disabled people (e.g. Wolfensberger 1995). Thus began the discourse of special and social education, with its crucial characteristic, the 'conservatism corollary', with its implications for adapting people with disabilities to survival in the wider class-, gender- and race-influenced dynamics of social inequality. So in every situation, the social learning would be to fit disabled people to a preordained place in an existing hierarchy, unchallenged and unchallenging. Disabled people were to be taught to play roles which would be acceptable to the others who might fear or reject them.

Social role valorization may well have been one of the influential ideological elements in the new discourses. Another important component was the academic institutional response to the development of a disability movement. This movement, with its demands for rights and participation, had greatest impact on the political and institutional scene in North America, where a number of pieces of legislation were enacted, even under conservative presidents, to give some recognition to the 'equality' demanded by activists and their supporters. In the USA the impact of thousands of Vietnam veterans returning with disabilities to an American society barely capable of coping with their existence, produced the federal Rehabilitation Act of 1973, followed by the Education of All Handicapped Children Act of 1975, renamed the Individuals with Disabilities Act in 1994. These acts prohibited discrimination against disabled people in federally funded programs, even where these programs were state run. They also sought to ensure children with disabilities were directed as far as possible into the free mainstream education system through a concern for the 'least restrictive environment', with complementary individualized education programs.

The Education Act was crucial for the new discourse of special education, for it confronted traditional and constraining ideologies of education with a demand for education which would enable participation. Even so, it was effectively created by the special education lobby, not by people with disabilities, and was said by some critics to reflect the interests of the special education industry in its drive for greater professional recognition and organizational influence, and to be concerned with mainstreaming the industry rather than guaranteeing rights to education (Woodward 1992). These American initiatives were also influential in gradually modifying thinking in the Australian environment. However the initiatives both in the US and Australia did little to affect the very real inequalities experienced by people with disabilities, which were particularly intensified for poorer women caught up in the systems which controlled disability and access to the scarce resources which existed (Meekosha 1986).

American research in the mid-1980s showed how discrimination continued to affect disabled people in their access to work, accommodation, transport, recreation and health care (Alexander 1995). Yet the earlier initiatives had started to improve the capacity of disabled people to take up opportunities had they been made available. A sustained campaign by many disability organizations focused on forcing through legislation, the Americans with Disabilities Act, which would prohibit discrimination in these areas

(Shapiro 1994). This sustained activism also began to influence the discourses on disability, as disabled people began to be seen as activists concerned with access rather than as 'courageous cripples' (Johnson 1991). Yet the underlying issues of social justice and their relation to the burgeoning literature of disability studies were left relatively untouched.

Approaching the political economy of disability

Any analysis of social justice in relation to disability needs to address the structural questions of representation and participation in the social constitution of the field. Thus a first crucial question must be the place that people with disabilities can take in formulating the agendas of education and social justice. While approaches to disability are changing under the impact of the disability movement and modernizing ideologies of normalization (both those referred to by Foucault (Bernauer and Mahon 1994: 143) in his analysis of the 'normalized subject' and that developed by Wolfensberger and his colleagues as part of the PASS and PASSING strategies (Wolfensberger 1970, 1995)) the structural opportunities are still very much constrained by the concerns for social control which exist within even these contemporary social technologies.

Disability is constituted as a field through economic, cultural and social forces. Thus one of the most crucial points of conflict has been around the relations of production. We have already noted the historic treatment of disability under capitalism, in which crude economic assessments determined life chances for those who survived medical intervention or the lack of it. In contemporary capitalist societies arguments about the economic 'value' of people with disabilities have formed a central component in social policy development. These arguments have emerged when economic rationalist ideologies have strongly influenced government thinking about social policy, and when trade union membership and power has been dramatically eroded.

Issues of participation and representation, and ideas of social justice (see John Rawls 1972, also 1993), have been identified as the heartland of pluralistic and democratic citizenship (Theophanous 1994). Government responses to these issues in Australia have been gradual; during the 1980s there have been a series of market-linked initiatives which have been designed to secure the greatest possible availability of disabled people for the employment market. The first move came in the late 1960s, as the stirrings of liberation movements were becoming influential in local discourses about social inequality. The period was marked by the withdrawal of the white Australia provisions in immigration policies, the recognition of Aboriginal rights to participate in the political life of society, the renewed identification of the rights of women, and the replacement of assimilation by integration in strategies on immigrant settlement. For people with disabilities, there was the provision of direct federal government support to sheltered workshops, places where the production of commodities under controlled environments could theoretically replace inertia and inactivity for institutionalized people.

Through the 1970s incremental moves were made to reflect changing discursive analyses, with direct federal support for 'handicapped' accommodation and an emphasis on training, both for closed employment and in social skills. A key moment in the refocusing of the discourse towards normalization (to use Wolfensberger's term) and integration into the community came from the Human Relationships Royal Commission (1977), with its stated commitment to deinstitutionalization. The Labor government after 1983 initiated a review of the handicapped persons programs, re-emphasizing this perspective and foreshadowing major reorientation towards labour market programs. The social security review followed this up by arguing that all Australians should be orientated towards the labour market unless otherwise proven incapable of work, and that disability should not mean automatic invalid status (and pension entitlements). The disability reform package and the related agreements with the states left the federal government with labour market responsibilities, and a number of projects rapidly emerged seeking to demonstrate to employers that people with disabilities would be loyal, grateful and responsive employees. In addition employers could receive salary support for them. Also new regulations allowed the payment of lower wages to workers who could not work at the same capacity of output as the 'able-bodied'.

While the right to work was clearly a major step forward for participation for many disabled people, liberating some of them from the controlling environment of sheltered workshops or chronic unemployment, at a period of generally high unemployment the unemployment rate for people with disabilities remained very high – expectations raised by training and the rhetoric of access were often shattered by the reality of the labour market.

The employment of disabled people is only one element of the political economy of disability. In contemporary Australia disability is big business. The Commonwealth programs are pumping millions of dollars each year into the human services industries, and the commodification of disability is a major outcome. With the privatization of many government services, the marketplace is awash with consultants and trainers anxious to utilize their skills to facilitate access to services. The disability reform package brought with it dozens of standards for assessing the quality of services, defining outcomes, monitoring effectiveness and implementing programs. Employment services sprang up around the country as community organizations found that their survival depended on them meeting the market-focused priorities of the bureaucracy.

Yet at the same time that a disability industry was emerging, so wider industry was creating disability. A major product of the industrial/commercial sector is disabled workers. Hundreds of thousands of industrial injuries occur every year; thousands of workers are permanently disabled. White-collar industries produce repetition strain injury as a significant contribution to the overall total – industrial deafness, muscular injuries, poisoning from toxic chemicals, cancers induced by exposure to unsafe materials, para- and quadriplegia from falls and employment-related motor accidents are all components of the personal and social costs of the right to work in a capitalist society. Associated with this dimension of disability is a huge workers' compensation, legal, medical, insurance and rehabilitation industry, its dynamics also determined by the logic of capitalist accumulation.

In 1992 the Commonwealth passed an Australian Disability Discrimination Act. Unlike the mass rights movement that had been so important in the US legislation, even under the conservative presidency of George Bush, the Australian legislation was very much the outcome of a bureaucratic and political agreement, supported by traditional service delivery agencies. It was legislation which claimed to be concerned with the rights of people with disabilities, but provided few resources to enable them to pursue their rights. Instead the great weight of resources went into codifying and regularizing the industry which would manage and control disability, emphasizing its normalizing role.

Michel Foucault and Wolf Wolfensberger have curiously opposite views of what 'normalization' means. As this word has tremendous importance in the whole issue of social justice for disabled people, it is worth exploring it for a moment here. Foucault's analysis of various social institutions covered both asylums and prisons, the public history of each he suggested was written as a march towards freedom and enlightenment. However, he argued that such genealogies were in effect myths, myths which disguised the processes through which claims to liberalism and progress (as in the growth of medical and psychiatric interventions in place of chains, cold baths and straitjackets) in fact produced individuals who were 'normalized' into a narrowing and impoverishment of human possibilities. It is the medical management of sexuality that lies at the heart of normalization, for normalization is concerned with the suppression of any attempt to transgress society's norms and practices (Bernauer and Mahon 1994: 150, 153). And yet the struggle by people with disabilities for their rights is a conscious transgression of the old order and its consignment of the disabled to lives of silence, inertia and penury.

Wolfensberger is a major figure in the integration movement. His position on social role valorization has become the new orthodoxy in Australia, and has been adopted as the central ideology underlying the disabled reform package and related assistance programs – it drives the performance agreements and underlies the push for standards in care provided by funded organizations. In addition it pervades the disability strategy adopted in 1994, which commits federal government agencies to full equality of opportunity for disabled people over a five-year period.

Wolfensberger (1970) has proposed that disabled people are devalued by society. This labelling has a severe impact on their self-esteem and is operationalized in their confinement and exclusion from society. Given this 'reality' the way forward is to revalorize them, by training them to behave in ways which don't threaten more powerful people, by building their own self-confidence through their learning to take more control over their immediate environment, and by changing wider social values through community education. They should be helped to become as near to the 'norm' of social behaviour as possible. They should not behave in transgressive ways, but rather be coaxed, led or otherwise pointed towards the most conservative social behaviour (the so-called conservatism corollary). They should be controlled into non-resistant socially passive participants. Wolfensberger has responded (1995) to this sort of criticism of his position by arguing that his technique has no political implications *per se* – it is the values of the commentators which are political.

The participation of people with disabilities in the agendas which constrain their lives has been determined in part through three key processes: the operation of charitable organizations through which many of the services they use are delivered, the public images of disability which affect attitudes (their own and that of others), and the activity of the disability movement as a political and cultural force.

The charitable nexus and social justice

The industry which is now involved in this normalization has adopted Wolfensberger's ideology but appears to be achieving Foucault's outcome. This dynamic lies at the human centre of the disability industry. Major organizations involved in this process of normalization have developed strategies to target the marketplace in which they operate. As New Right ideologies of welfare increasingly intrude into the business management of charitable sector organizations, we begin to see major programs geared towards the securing of charitable donations. These programs involve complex interlocking plans which are designed to stimulate fears, apprehensions or desires in order to unlock the scarce communal dollar.

In the United Kingdom one of the most controversial campaigns has been that created by the Multiple Sclerosis Society (see Needham 1993 for its advertising agency's rationale for the campaign). Over a period of more than eight years the society has aimed to become the most recognized charitable body and MS the most publicly identifiable disease. The campaign has been focused on two stages – an awareness stage ('Tear'), and a giving stage ('Glow'). The first part used images of naked bodies, in black and white, with segments torn from them as though they were sheets of paper. Thus one had lost her spine, another had his eyes torn out, and so on. The aim was to grab the attention of the viewers, to stun them by the graphic representation of loss, and then to force them to identify with the loss portrayed to the point of terror at the thought of it happening to themselves. They specifically targeted younger married women as the holders of the charity-giving purse strings in the household and as the group most likely to be affected by the images portrayed. The stark images allowed no softening or coloration, the ballet dancer bodies so perfect and 'beautiful', ripped apart by the disease. Or so it was made to appear.

Gilman has noted of the images and illustrations our society uses to communicate about the body and disease, that the healthy has come to be conflated with beauty and illness with ugliness. So our very aesthetics are interpenetrated by our sense of the politics of the body and our fears of pollution (Gilman 1995). The MS campaign utilizes this central confluence of societal body politics to generate the most effective outcomes recorded for a charitable campaign in Britain. It is important to recognize that this campaign was created during the apogee of Thatcherite Britain, a duration when society was said no longer to exist, and the individual was required to confront each other individual outside the family, through the market. Thus the beautiful, dynamic MS sufferer was epitomized as the Thatcherite hero/heroine, athletic, erotic, vibrant and successful due to their own strengths, suddenly slashed or ripped asunder through no fault of their own, shattered and left incapable of further autonomous action, aspirations wrecked and body (and therefore soul) damaged beyond repair, and thus abandoned. Except of course, by the MS Society.

Beauty converted in a moment to ugliness, health replaced by illness. For the woman with the torn spine, the text reads 'When this goes, everything else goes with it.' From posters on billboards across the country, lining the escalators that carried thousands of workers from the Underground in London to their streets and offices, these images spoke with the semiotics of desire to the fear of the aesthetic destruction that lay behind a thousand other advertisements for lipsticks and gymnasium memberships and makeup and diet drinks and pantyhose and babyfood ... As the campaign 'bit' MS became the most recognized (if misunderstood) disease in the country and the MS Society the single best-known charity (though all the cancer charities together still outweighed it in popular recognition). The UK debate over the validity of the campaign was short-lived. While some disabled activists condemned the campaign as exploitative and horrifying, misleading in terms of the real effects of MS, and so on, few people with MS were in a position to object. With most services delivered through the MS Society, with community services declining dramatically, the campaign had 'worked' to bring in donations when donations were crucial to the continuation of services. Indeed the MS Society's advertising agency made this argument in its guide for students, produced as a defence against criticisms of the campaign (Needham 1993).

The second step in the campaign introduced another figure into the imagery, so that the torn spines and ripped eyes disappeared and the now collapsed body of the person with MS was being held up by another beautiful body. Now the slogan read: 'MS Society, A Hope in Hell'. MS was presented as a hell in which the only hope was the society. To rescue the beautiful body from hell and damnation required of the public that they contribute to the Society. The Society thus prospered on the proposition that all people with MS were damned without it (even though the majority of people with MS are not acute sufferers with massive disabilities, however physically and psychologically debilitating their experience may be). Both campaigns won prizes from the advertising industry for marketing effectiveness.

The British MS campaign allows us to understand the relationship between the political economy of the disability industry in the contemporary era, the wider political and economic environment, the political environment for disability activism, and the representation of people with disabilities in the public culture. The Society understood that with the decline in government support and the rapidly rising demand for services by people with disabilities, the community and corporate donation pool was the only source for survival. Yet every other charity was in the same position, competing to locate itself in the public mind as the most deserving destination for charitable donations. An image which could touch the deepest fears of the population – to be beautiful and suddenly become ugly, to be healthy and become ill – was needed to break through the sea of competing cries of worthiness. And if the self-image and self-worth of people with MS had to suffer in the process, then so be it. The agency and the Society both seemed to take the position that most people with MS would understand the need to shock a complaisant public into awareness.

The market approach can also be seen in the Australian context with another large charitable agency. It was a state-based organization, though part of a national federation with its own autonomy, which had the typical dual function of fundraising and service provision. In 1994 the organization established a marketing and development business unit, with a brief to position the organization as a leading service delivery agency, not only in relation to its 'own' disability community, but in the marketplace as a service supplier to people with other disabilities who could afford to purchase its services.

Its development plan is a carefully structured example of contemporary marketing, and it is only with some difficulty that one realizes that the product being marketed is disability. The situational analysis covers competitors (that is, other charities seeking to survive in the New Right economic environment of the state); a history (of fundraising and the profits made from it); current market trends in fundraising; and a SWOT analysis (identifying strengths, weaknesses, opportunities and threats). The plan then goes on to identify the key theme and messages which are to be sold, and the audiences who are to be the targets for these messages. The crucial elements in the plan relate to events – defined points in the year when the message can be communicated to specific audiences. Priorities are given to particular events and the year structured to maintain a regular rhythm of material designed to elicit donations.

Corporate image is made a crucial part of the exercise. A new logo is designed, suggestive of efficiency and caring and a businesslike attitude. New signs are prepared, in corporate style, again reflective of modernity and efficiency. A style and content manual is prepared, ensuring consistency and maintaining the corporate image. Then a variety of materials designed for potential corporate or private sponsors – audio-visual aids, cassettes to be played in the car, a video. From these, there emerges a more detailed set of moves around sponsorship – a media kit, a strategy to raise the profile of the CEO, an identification of 'new business' – where the organization can offer new services or find new fundraisers. A government and health sector program is developed, with an information kit, special luncheons for sector managers, and tours over various facilities. Volunteers are identified as an important part of the process, with their recruitment and recognition (or reward) presented as significant components. Finally a critical path is drawn for the marketing and selling of the disability and the agency.

There are also a public relations strategy, a special events strategy, a specific community and children involvement project, raffles, shops, 'deferred giving' (being written into wills), major gifts and their solicitation, the development of a corporate donations program (including breakfasts and dinners with champions), the development of packages to make the organization attractive to charitable trusts and foundations, direct marketing associated with important public holidays (including an assessment of how to retain donors and why they lapse).

The public relations strategy provides further insights into the way in which media/organizational links are to be nurtured. The plan looks at the pay-off for advertorials (ads disguised as editorial or news copy) and direct advertising, the development of news releases, gaining electronic coverage, the development of a story-bank of 'good stories' already researched and ready for journalists to follow up, the publication of special advertising supplements in the press, a regular series of media luncheons (for key journalists) and briefings, the development of good photo opportunities, the publication of internal and external newsletters, and an annual calendar. Finally the work of the organization is framed in an annual 'day', 'week' or, for the truly ambitious, 'month' for the disability – as in National Mental Health Week, or Cancer Week or Red Nose Day (for SIDS – sudden infant death syndrome).

It is salutary to note that, despite government policies which try to improve the employment of people with disabilities, the organization employs very few people with a disability, and none with the condition it was established to ameliorate. This stands in stark contrast to the rapidly increasing number of jobs, many of them very well paid, in the new charitable service delivery bodies and their government partners.

The public images of disabilities, the presentation of the disabled body to the public gaze, the position that observers of disability are led to take, and the linking of the position to the cash donation – the gift – indicates that the process through which the gaze is both educated and satiated remains a central issue for analysis. For the industry works at creating consumers of disability as spectacle, and as they experience the emotions of pity, fear, horror, sympathy, gratitude (for their escape) they are urged to give to charity – their 'ticket' to the spectacle is their donation to the disability body. Thus the processes through which public images of disability are created in a number of media – as objects of entertainment, pity, fear, horror, humour and pathos – serve to extend and deepen the spectacle and the spectatorial gaze. We turn now to an examination of cinema and disability as one avenue for gaining a purchase on the complexity of the dynamics at work here.

Images of disability

The ideologies of capitalism and democracy, argues Denzin, simultaneously 'reproduce and inscribe the concept of the free, interacting, autonomous individual' (Denzin 1995: 6). The gaze turned upon this individual is gendered and racially signified – the bodies seen are always of a specific sex and race, and class. The aesthetics through which they are seen are formed through these dimensions of differentiation, giving birth in the process of being watched to the sense of the otherness of the disabled person. Yet the word 'person' masks these realities – for the disabled woman experiences the world differently from the disabled man, experiences different external expectations, different sets of assumptions, different social mores, and different self-perceptions. The disabled individual experiences at times other aspects of their identity which may prevail for that moment over the impairment and subsequent discrimination. For the gaze which frames the space inhabited by the 'free individual' is a male gaze, with male able-bodied points of view, drawn with middle-class and white inflections.

Thus public images of women framed by the male gaze are historically represented as the objects of men's desire, such that 'the determining male gaze projects its phantasy onto the female figure which is styled accordingly . . . women are simultaneously looked at and displayed' (Mulvey 1985: 808). Yet representations of the disabled female challenge the male gaze – challenge it in myriad cinematic and other portrayals, triggering a transformation of the gaze into one of voyeuristic exploitation – the central concern of which becomes whether she can be a 'real' woman, as lover, wife and mother. The image of male disability also tends to focus on sexuality, and masculinity. The constant concern seems to be the sexual prowess of the wounded male which is his defining characteristic of 'normality'. The dynamic becomes one of either eradicating the disability – the cure – or eradicating the person – death (Darke 1995: 4).

Norden (1994) has argued in his history of Hollywood movies and disability that the social mores of the time often determine the image of disability in the movies. Thus the earlier part of the century offered disability as a freakshow and the disabled as sources of entertainment and humour, from the first short movies with one-legged thieves and beggars through to the grand work of *Freaks* in the 1930s, with its cultural ambiguities and triumphant charge by the disabled circus performers against the cruel arrogance of the able bodied and aesthetically powerful (the strongman and his trapeze artiste lover). In the post-World War II period, the Hollywood media addressed disability primarily through the genre of the disabled war veteran and his survival in the new society. Films such as *The Men* (with Marlon Brando in his first role) and *Bright Victory* marked a high point for Hollywood, as politically progressive directors and writers, including some who were strongly anti-war such as Carl Foreman, worked with disabled veterans and screen actors to develop realistic representations of newly disabled men and their engagement with social hostility. Traditional themes or focal points remain – the veterans in *The Men* are paraplegics, with their genital sexual capacity destroyed but their emotional sexuality alive. Norden quotes a key line in the film in criticism of the position taken by the writer – 'It's not in the nature of the normal woman to be in love with one of us. Normal is normal and crippled is crippled and never the twain shall meet' (Norden 1994: 179). And yet the sense of the normal as being tied to a particular notion of heterosexual genital sexuality remains a continuing fascination of mainstream ideologies both of disability and the media.

In the wake of the House Un-American Activities Committee investigation into Hollywood, many progressive actors, writers and directors were blacklisted from movie production. In general the studios fled from what had been seen as progressive themes, and Foreman for one, was banned. Hollywood films tended then towards representations of disability that stressed the individual's struggle against adversity – though disabled women were often presented as apathetic victims. The denial of disability and a desire to escape the disabled state mark many of these films. The disabled person overcoming her disability offered great spiritual value, according to actress Jane Wyman (Norden 1994: 221). Conversely, the reality of disabilities where 'overcoming' was not on the agenda was rarely represented, and for audiences of people with disabilities the message was absolutely clear. Survival for the individual was a personal matter, one of moral strength, of heroic actions. Failure to 'overcome' was a sign of moral collapse and failure, where despite the reality of everyday mundane victories, only the grand gesture was of any significance (see also Zola 1984).

By the late 1970s and 80s the disability movement began to gain more significant purchase on the Hollywood agenda. The Vietnam war produced a similar round of films to those about veterans in the aftermath of World War II. *Coming Home* was initiated by Jane Fonda's IPC (Indochina Peace Campaign) company; Jon Voight played a disabled vet – again, paralysed from the waist down, with the central storyline focusing on whether Jane Fonda can bring his sexuality back to life.

The stars in these films and others of the 1980s and 90s were still able-bodied people masquerading as disabled: Dustin Hoffman in *The Rain Man*, Barbara Hershey in *Beaches*, or Daniel Day Lewis in *My Left Foot*. Norden argues that many of the Hollywood 1980s films were still toned down and softened for audiences by producers not ready to allow the harder edges of disability to intrude.

Indeed it is not until Neil Jiminez's *Waterdance*, based on his own life experience, that we see a director/writer with a disability presenting the world view of people with disabilities. For Jiminez the film is about masculinity and its reconstruction for paraplegic men from different backgrounds of race and class (Norden 1994). The older, 'trickster' view of the disabled person not only survives but has re-emerged in full flower. In the 1995 cinema noir hit *Usual Suspects*, the leading character 'Verbal Kent', whose fictitious narrative structures the film, is presented as a man affected by cerebral palsy, his 'cp' determining his possibilities in life. Yet he is the trickster, for his fantastic lies protect his 'real' identity, that of the master criminal 'Keyser Soze', as in the final scenes his shuffling gait is transformed into strong steps, his curved and lifeless hand stretches and clenches, and he escapes. Here bodily disability is made to represent a devious mind, and offers a suggestion that disability is to be suspected as a manipulative device for those of criminal intent.

The gender dynamics of cinema's treatment of disability expose deeper issues – the disabled man is usually brought back to full masculinity by the action of a woman which revitalizes his sexuality. However, the woman's body is offered under the gaze of the male professional – surgeon or psychiatrist or trainer. It is his normalizing gaze and structuring of the situation which is required before she can overcome her situation. His magic intervention is crucial to her survival. For in the movies it seems that masculine disability stands for men's fear of castration, the loss of limbs and functioning acting as a metaphor for some deeper psychic apprehension. Women lose their sexuality as a whole (becoming in Norden's analysis (p. 321) simply bodies upon which symptoms are inscribed) while they are disabled, and only in overcoming their disability do they gain back their femininity/objectivity to the male gaze. There is a dark parallel here with both the historic and current fate of many institutionalized men and women, whose sexuality and reproductive capacities have been forcibly curtailed through drastic surgery, these organs being considered 'useless', because disabled people should not be permitted to reproduce. New film-makers are confronting these traditions, challenged by media producers who have experienced the disability movement as part of their personal histories.

The late Irving Zola (1985) suggested in a key paper that disability in the media served as metaphor and message, and was affected by the medium through which the messages were delivered. He noted that the Independent Living Movement, while modelling itself on many other liberation movements, could not easily assert a disabled identity as a focus for pride – rather disability was presented as a real part of the lives of disabled people. But disability could be constructed by the movement as a metaphor for survival – rather than as it had been by the media so often, as a metaphor for exclusion and disaster. However it is only when the movement began to influence representation that such a change in metaphor could occur.

The disability movement and social justice

The rise of the disability movement reflects wider social mobilization around what has come to be known as identity politics (Meekosha and Pettman 1991). With its strongest base in North America and Scandinavia the movement has spread internationally, linking activists and non-government organizations in countries throughout the world. From the first struggles for the independent living centres in the US, through to the establishment of organizations such as Disabled Peoples' International and international conferences (World Assembly) such as that held in Sydney Australia in December 1994, the movement has grown into an organized lobby able to make demands more effectively for control over the disability agenda.

It is surprising therefore that so little work has been done by scholars in Australia and elsewhere to recognize the impact of the movement on public culture and social change. Recent studies such as those by Burgmann (1993) and Pakulski (1991) make no mention of the disability movement among their investigations of gender, sexuality and environmental movements, and literature reviews of the social movements area (a major research committee of the International Sociological Association) indicate this lack of interest is international.

Any assessment of the relation between social justice and disability rights has to come to terms with the role of the movement of disabled people in struggles around these issues. The movement stands for the right to communicate, participate and assert self-determined social identities. In a sense the denial of the humanity of people with disabilities marks the most central issue for a social justice agenda on disability. Representation in relation to disability has two dimensions: one meaning pursues representation in the sense of cultural studies, where images and ideas about disability are cultivated and communicated through various public media. The second meaning is political – the process through which people with disabilities assert their subjectivity and identities in the forums of power. The movement has been increasingly active in the latter of these processes.

In the UK, the Conservative government has resisted time and again attempts by the movement to bring about legal recognition of disability rights and the commitment of public resources to promote the take-up of rights. Frustration has been widespread, with local action by disabled people in many centres, on (for example) transport, accommodation and health services. In the USA as we have seen, the conservative Bush administration enacted the Americans with Disabilities legislation (1990) after two decades of direct action by the movement.

In the Australian context the Disability Discrimination Act (1992) has emerged as a governmental initiative designed to minimize the pressures from the disability lobby, though the particular situation in Australia allows for federal legislation to be used to press for rights from state governments and local bodies. Thus positive action by the disability movement has focused on areas such as government transport accessibility. Meanwhile some states have used new government investigative bodies to pursue issues associated with the denial of human rights to people with developmental disabilities. However, the disability movement in Australia has voiced serious concerns with the nature of its representation in policy processes. Two leading activists have argued that

> the fundamental changes that integration promised, structurally and in attitude, remain for the most part as far off as they ever did. Government has hijacked integration and in its place, while maintaining the rhetoric, substituted its own agenda. People with disabilities are now experiencing a new institutionalisation . . . [it] is not being adequately challenged by the Disability Rights Movement . . . it remains our view that to a large extent the 'fire has gone out of the belly' of the Disability Rights Movement . . . some organizations . . . [are at] the point where it is hard to work out whether they are the representatives of people with disabilities or the representatives of Government in the Disability Rights Movement . . . Fundamentally tough disabled people must re-appropriate integration and once again define it in our own terms.
>
> In our view the starting point is participation; participation in social activity that gives people a sense of worth and of meaning . . . The next stage is for people with disabilities to be in control.
>
> (Harding and Attrill 1992)

The struggle for participation in political processes of representation is advancing and will have major impact on the participation of people with disabilities in the future. The right to participate in decisions and representation raises particular issues for children with disabilities and people with severe intellectual disabilities, whose interests have traditionally been represented by carers, parents, guardians and institutional officials. Given the pressures toward control and regulation that Harding and Attrill (1992) identify, there are particular challanges associated with groups such as these gaining power over their own representation. It is clear that for them cultural participation and representation will be one major avenue through which such empowerment can be approached.

In general and specifically for particular groups, the cultural meaning of representation remains relatively unaddressed. The corporatization of disability service provision and the establishment of a sophisticated co-option system for advising government, combined with exclusionary practices in the realm of the media, have made it difficult for a disability movement agenda to colonize the spaces constructed by the mainstream to contain and normalize disabled people. Yet for people with disabilities, stereotypical representations or exclusion from the public culture of contemporary societies clearly affects their participation in wider public life – especially in the lack of role models for younger people, and the sustained exclusion of images which are accessible and valuable.

The medicalization or distinctive categorization of disability which characterizes much which passes as disability studies in tertiary education is also problematic. The move towards social justice is clearly tied to the empowerment of people with disabilities in the processes which determine their representation in both the senses used here. Their cultural empowerment is clearly a central constitutive component of this process.

References

Alexander, R. (1995) Understanding the Americans with Disabilities Act, http://www.seamless.com/talf/txt/disact.html.

Bernauer, J. and Mahon, M. (1994) The ethics of Michel Foucault, in G. Gutting (ed.) *The Cambridge Companion to Foucault*. Cambridge: Cambridge University Press, pp. 141–58.

BMP DDB Needham (1993) The Multiple Sclerosis Society: a short paper for students reviewing the role played by advertising in promoting its cause, London, February.

Burgmann, V. (1993) *Power and Protest: Movements for Change in Australian Society*. St Leonards: Allen and Unwin.

Darke, P. (1995) Screening lies, introductory essay in *Disability in the Cinema* film season catalogue, Watershed Media Centre, pp. 2–5.

Denzin, N. (1995) *The Cinematic Society: the Voyeur's Gaze*. London: Sage.

Gilman, S. (1995) *Health and Illness: Images of Difference*. London: Reaktion Books.

Harding, M. and Attrill, P. (1992) The Disability Rights Movement: is it in crisis? *DEAC News*, February.

Johnson, M. (1991) Media miss the disability rights issue: 'courageous cripples' instead of access activists, *Extra*, 5–6.

Meekosha, H. (1986) *Breaking in and Breaking out: Women, Disability and Rehabilitation*. Canberra: Department of Community Services and Health.

Meekosha, H. and Pettman, J. (1991) Beyond category politics, *Hecate*, 17(2): 75–92.

Mulvey, L. (1985) Visual pleasure and narrative cinema, in G. Mast and M. Cohen (eds) *Film Theory and Criticism*. New York: Oxford University Press.

Norden, M. (1994) *The Cinema of Isolation: a History of Physical Disability in the Movies*. New Brunswick, NJ: Rutgers University Press.

Pakulski, J. (1991) *Social Movements: the Politics of Moral Protest*. Melbourne: Longman Cheshire.

Rawls, J. (1972) *A Theory of Justice*. Cambridge, MA: Harvard University Press.

Rawls, J. (1993) *Political Liberalism*. New York: Columbia University Press.

Shapiro, J. (1994) The new civil rights, Modern Maturity, Nov/Dec, http://www.eskimo.com/~dempt/crights.htm.

Theophanous, A. (1994) *Understanding Social Justice: an Australian Perspective*. Melbourne: Eilkia Books.

Wolfensberger, W. (1970) The principle of normalization and its implications for psychiatric services, *American Journal of Psychiatry*, 127: 291–7.

Wolfensberger, W. (1995) Social role valorization is too conservative. No, it is too radical, *Disability and Society*, 10(3): 245–7.

Woodward, J. with M. Elliott (1992) Developing a language, Disability Rag May/June 1992 13:2 on line at: gopher://gopher.etext.org:70/00/Politics/Disability Rag/dr13.2.gz.

Zola, I. (1984) Communication barriers between 'the able-bodied' and 'the handicapped', in R. Marinelli and A. Dell Orto (eds) *The Psychological and Social Impact of Physical Disability*, 2nd edn. New York: Springer, pp. 139–47.

Zola, I. (1985) Depictions of disability – metaphor, message, and medium in the media: a research and political agenda, *The Social Science Journal*, 22(4): October, 5–17.

Disability, class and poverty: school structures and policing identities

Introduction

In a moment of autobiographical reflection upon his schooling and experience of disability, at a disability seminar in Hull, disabled researcher Colin Barnes declared that he thought he was oppressed because he was working class until someone told him that he was disabled! It is not a difficult task to draw on data to make clear and persuasive the oppressive intersections of disability, class and poverty (Abberley 1987; Katz 1989; Thompson *et al.* 1990; Barnes 1991; HREOC 1993). School stands at the centre of the production of these intersections as a structural gatekeeper determining and dispensing identities of disability. The focus for this chapter could thus proceed from this point by citing the correlation between class and disability (Oliver 1990; Abberley 1994) and indicating the dimensions of poverty among those categorized as disabled (Ronalds 1990; Thompson *et al.* 1990; HREOC 1993). Materialist conceptions of disability press us to rehearse educational reproduction theory. Our conclusion may then be to call in the architects of distributive justice to design accommodating schools.

At one level such an account of disablement, poverty and schooling would attend to the project of challenging the pervasive discourses of individual difference and medical models of dysfunctional student pathologies (Kirk 1972; Ward *et al.* 1987; Ashman and Elkins 1990; Butler 1990) that dominate education departments' and the academies' thinking about 'special educational needs', segregated provision, integration and inclusion. A major shortcoming of such an approach, however, may lie in its failure to look beyond distributive notions of justice, providing little more than compensatory educational responses. Iris Marion Young warns against such reductionism:

> Contemporary . . . theories of social justice tend to restrict the meaning of social justice to the morally proper distribution of benefits and

burdens among society's members ... while distributive issues are crucial to a satisfactory conception of justice, it is a mistake to reduce social justice to distribution.

(Young 1990: 15)

For Young, a major problem with the distributive paradigm is that it concentrates 'thinking about social justice on the allocation of material goods ... or on the distribution of social positions', ignoring 'the social structure and institutional context that often help determine distributive patterns' (p. 15). This chapter will argue that this is central to the management of difference by machine bureaucracies within what have become regulatory discourses of equity and social justice. Mainstreaming, integration and inclusion have all been framed within a narrow technicist reading of disability and its relationship to educational provision. What this means is that integration and inclusion, like segregated special education, have become a bureaucratic means to the minimization of difference in order to maintain the existing structural and cultural relations of schooling (Tomlinson 1982; Branson and Miller 1989; Fulcher 1989; Skrtic 1991; Slee 1993a).

The issue of disablement, like racism and sexism, speaks both to complex structural relations as well as to the politics of identity and representation (Fraser 1995). Sociologies of disability, consistent with social theory in general, are having to acknowledge and deal with the interruptions to deterministic single-theory narratives of social organization and relations issued by poststructuralist debates (Barton 1996). This is not to deny the structural realities of the political economy of disability, rather it calls for greater acknowledgement of conflicting theoretical representations (Yeatman 1994), of disabilities and consideration of their implications for educational organization and practices. In other words, we might be asking for too much when deferring to single theory for complex and 'messy' social phenomena (Ball 1990: 9). Such elaboration of theory provides the space for a more comprehensive analysis of disablement and its material and cultural consequences than class theory is able to yield. There is, however, a danger of collapsing into the despair and apathy of relativism.

Redistribution remains central to changing the material conditions of disabled people. However, it is limiting to set this as the primary or exclusive task for constructing inclusive schools. Indeed the task requires more complex interventions which will contribute to cultural and social reconstruction. Education remains a central institutional agent in such a process. Poverty and disability is not an economic problem, nor is it a problem of deficient individuals (Wright Mills 1959; Ryan 1971); it needs to be set as a political problematic.

This chapter will attempt to draw together this wide-ranging discussion; however, it cannot promise closure. Divided into three parts, the discussion will:

- consider the relationship between disability and poverty;
- insert ontological and epistemological questions about the relationship between disability, 'special educational needs' and schooling, and 'inclusive' education policy;
- tentatively suggest guidelines for a new agenda for the educational reconstruction of schooling with a view to the enablement of student bodies.

Pondering Colin Barnes's crisis in identities provides a useful, if not intentional, dilemma for initiating a reconsideration of the relationship between disabling education, class and poverty.

Disablement, poverty and class – a social theory of disability

Rejecting individualized 'personal tragedy' accounts of disability and impairment as disconnected, disabled researchers such as Hahn (1985), Finklestein (1980), Oliver (1986, 1990) and Abberley (1987) sought the development of a social theory of disability to demonstrate the structural and cultural antecedents to what Miller and Gwynne (1972) depict as the 'social death' attendant to disability. Earlier studies in deviance provided theoretical tools to demonstrate the social construction and maintenance of marginal identities and status (for example, Lemert 1951; Goffman 1961, 1963; Becker 1963, 1964; Cohen 1971; Schur 1971). Positivist claims of objectivity in the 'scientific' ascription of abnormality were refuted, deviants and social scientists alike refusing to 'concur in the verdict' (Davis 1964: 119). Defining and mapping difference according to categories of disability coincided with aspirations of governmentality; the regulation of 'the subnormal' and 'normal' alike (Foucault 1967; Rose 1979).

Labelling and deviance theories accepted as given that as a consequence of differences, those relegated to positions of inferior status would receive inferior entitlements to cultural and material well-being. In other words, the relationship between disability and poverty was not capricious, it was systematic. For Abberley (1987), the undertheorization of this relationship reflected an 'absence of good sociology'. Taking to task the popular characterization of 'impairment as personal tragedy and disability as social responses to impairment' (World Health Organization 1980; OPCS 1986), the medical notion of the disabled person as a *patient* whose impairment caused *their* disability was argued to be an ideological construct deployed to manage unproductive citizens. Marx, Comte, Weber, Gramsci and Althusser were summoned to explicate the social origin of material and biological phenomena which produce impairment (Abberley 1987: 12; Oliver 1990: 15–42). Put simply, the complex interaction of material (political economy) and non-material (biological) factors conspired to disable people in 'real social and historical contexts'.

The mode of production bore a direct relationship to disablement in that some people were impaired through accidents during their engagement in productive labour, others' physical or intellectual status excluded them from participation in the workforce. Whereas the deaf and the blind had previously been capable of productive labour in agrarian social organization, industrialization deskilled and impoverished these sections of the population (Topliss 1979). The capitalist disruption to feudal social organization called for state intervention in the form of the proliferation of large institutions for the displaced poor.

> In the institution, the state had found a successful method of dealing with the problem of order . . . But it still faced the age-old problem of separating out those who would not from those who could not conform to the new order. Hence throughout the eighteenth and nineteenth centuries institutions became ever more specific in their purposes and selective in their personnel . . . These developments then, facilitated the segregation of disabled people, initially in workhouses and asylums, but gradually in more specialist institutions . . .
>
> (Oliver 1990: 33)

Policy interventions for the excluded and disabled such as Poor Law legislation and disability welfare entitlements find logical coherence within this materialist reading of history. Moreover the continuity of impairment and disability as historically, socially and ideologically specific phenomena finds contemporary application. Changing reproductive technologies produce specific biological impairments; changing modes of transport contribute to accelerated rates of impairment; new forms of leisure contribute to divergent patterns of impairment and disablement; colonial wars alter the form and rate of disability within a nation or specific region.

The relationship between disability and poverty would seem axiomatic. British researchers Berthoud, Lakey and McKay (1993) conservatively estimate that half of all disabled people are living in poverty. There exists a growing mass of international statistical data which demonstrates the materially precarious position of disabled people (Dupont 1980; Lipton *et al.* 1983; Rees and Emerson 1983; Chetwynd 1985; Fuller Torrey 1988; Martin *et al.* 1989; Matthews and Truscott 1990; Barnes 1991; Disability Advisory Council of Australia 1991; Disability Task Force 1991; Wightman and Foreman 1991; New South Wales Council for Intellectual Disability 1992; ABS 1993a,b; Government Statistical Service 1993; HREOC 1993). These data are augmented by personal accounts of the pernicious impact of disablement (Morris 1991; Potts and Fido 1991; Abberley 1993).

A disabled feminist researcher and writer, Jenny Morris (1991: 77) reports on a House of Commons debate on abortion in 1985 when Peter Thurnham

MP declared the abortion of a 'handicapped foetus could well save the country £1 million over the course of a lifetime'. Thurnham's statement is significant for a number of reasons. First it demonstrates the politics of disablement. Clearly disability is erected as an individual characteristic belonging to the impaired person. It is not produced by complex social structure and relations. Moreover, according to this reductionist schema, disabled people, having nothing to offer, are a cost and burden to the able-bodied community. Elizabeth Hastings, the Australian Federal Disability Discrimination Commissioner reflects further on this in noting that the Australian Department for Immigration retains a notable exemption from Federal Disability Discrimination legislation. In her own case, she tells of how her parents who immigrated to Australia on the assisted passages scheme had to pay for their disabled daughter (Commissioner Hastings) who was perceived as a child who would be a long-term burden to the Australian state (Slee 1993b: 9–10).

Second, it reflects the economic reality that disability can have significant financial costs, 'costs that would be even higher if adequate resources were devoted to ensuring a good quality of life' (Morris 1991: 77). In crude terms, the impoverishment of disabled people revolves around segregation from the paid labour market, enforced dependency, the high costs of support and housing for independent and community living, and the pervasive impact of economic rationalism on the public policy and welfare provision. Abberley depicts the situation in the context of scorched earth Thatcher/Major social policy:

> Under the new Social Fund, the higher long-term benefit rate was abolished and the Additional Requirement Payments (ARPs) replaced by flat-rate premiums, which are not geared to specific needs but based on two categories of basic and severe disability . . . The Social Fund, limited in expenditure to £203 million in its first year [down from £350 million] made discretionary loans, with no right to appeal decisions. The system involves an obligation to provide evidence of having sought help from charities, friends and relations, and even if this can be provided and the request deemed a reasonable one, no payment will be forthcoming if it involves the breach of cash limits.
>
> Hardship is clearly caused to disabled people (40,000 on government estimates, up to half a million according to the Disablement Income Group) who are able to live in the community . . . For individuals wishing to make the move from institutional care to living in the community the situation is far more problematic than it was before . . . *disabled people experience these 'reforms' as an attack on their human right not to be incarcerated without trial and conviction* . . .
>
> (Abberley 1993: 112, my emphasis)

Attention has recently been paid in Australia to the disproportionate homelessness of people with mental illness. Both Burdekin's original inquiry into youth homelessness (HREOC 1989), and the more recent *Report of the National Inquiry into the Human Rights of People with Mental Illness* (HREOC 1993) drew media attention to the lack of adequate support, housing and medical treatment for people with mental illness throughout Australia. The extreme impoverishment of those with mental illness is not idiosyncratic. It is particularly useful to consider studies of homelessness and poverty in America (Katz 1989; Blau 1992; Gans 1995). Such analysis debunks the linear logic which suggests that since the mentally ill figure prominently in homelessness data, mental illness is a cause of poverty and homelessness. Homelessness is symptomatic of a political economy which places 'non-productive' people at risk.

Mental illness increases risk since typically people may be unable to maintain unsupported work regimens. A particularly potent argument has been that emptying out large institutions has caused homelessness and that deinstitutionalization is therefore the culprit to be targeted. Contrary to popular belief, Blau argues, from the vantage of comprehensive data on psychiatric hospitalization and institutional census data from 1904 to the present, that

> It has long been customary to assert that since the policy of deinsti-tutionalization failed the mentally ill, it must be the primary cause of homelessness. First heard when homelessness proliferated in the early 1980's, this argument got weaker with the passage of time. Sixty-five percent of the decline in the hospital census had already occurred before 1975. Deinstitutionalization therefore cannot explain very much about the spread of homelessness one decade later.
>
> (Blau 1992: 85)

Blau asserts that the emptying out of large institutions commenced in earnest in the 1950s in response to the growing cost of institutional care being shouldered by state legislatures.

> Economics and medical science were soon wed. Apart from local aid, mental illness was the single largest expense in the New York State budget, and bonds were issued regularly for the construction of new hospitals. The discovery of psychotropic drugs presented Harriman with an opportunity to do something about this cost ... Drugs tranquilized not only the patients to whom they were administered but also the growth rate of the state's mental health budget.
>
> (p. 81)

For Blau the 'issue, then, is the quality, rather than the locus, of care' (p. 88). The homeless mentally disabled share much in common with other homeless people: insufficient income underwritten by ineligibility and the lack of a support system, but this is exacerbated by emotional frailty (p. 90).

Institutionalization, a metaphor for social severance, conceals impoverishment from the public gaze. This finds parallel expression in the proliferation of what have been euphemistically called sheltered workshops. Considerable heated debate has been provoked by challenges to these discriminatory work practices (Branson and Miller 1992; Kendrick 1992; Stern 1992, 1993, 1994). Within a discourse of benevolence, segregated workshops are defended on the grounds that they provide 'meaning' and the occupation of time for people who would otherwise not be engaged by a discriminating labour market. This remains a poor defence and a calculated deflection from the injustice of appalling working conditions and slave-like remunerations. Special schools, operating on minimal academic expectations and repetitive manual curriculum programmes provide the recruiting ground for participation in sheltered workshops and, as Bodna's (1987) research so disturbingly indicates, disproportionately high rates of incarceration.

The structural arrangements of production, labour and consumption establish the sites for the disablement of groups of people. This process of disablement through the interplay of material and non-material factors is historically and culturally specific. Structural theories provide analytical tools to demonstrate linkages between impairment, disablement, class and poverty. Such an analysis does however simplify some of the complexities of agency and apparent contradictions in the deployment of discourses of disability to argue entitlement on behalf of the middle class. The burgeoning categories of specific learning disabilities are indicative. Our consideration of schooling and disablement directs our attention to such issues and assists in confronting the shortcomings of working exclusively within a distributive paradigm of justice.

Schooling and the production of disabling identities

Eleven years after the publication of *Integration in Victorian Education: Report of the Ministerial Review of Educational Services for the Disabled* (Ministry of Education – Victoria 1984) and three years following the enactment of the *Commonwealth Disability Discrimination Act 1992* there exists little evidence for one to feel sanguine about Australian schooling as a site for inclusive education. Following a review of the 'first five years of integration policy in Victoria' (Lewis, Cook and Sword 1989), John Lewis (1993: 22) was suspicious of claims by the Victorian Ministry of Education that the

> outstanding achievement of the integration program has been to increase the participation of students with disabilities in the social and

educational life of Victorian schools from 500 in 1985 to 5000 in 1991. Attainment of such far-reaching change is a progressive process.

(Victorian Ministry of Education, 1992 cited in Lewis 1993: 22)

For Lewis, integration in Victorian schools did not represent a benchmark of progressive social reconstruction. The new category of 'integration student' rapidly became a pejorative special educational classification:

In this way 'integration children' have formed a new category of disability, and are used as a vehicle to legitimise a new period of expansion of special education interests – albeit within a rhetoric of integration. The current 5000 'integration students' represent a new and large set of potential clients for special education at a time when many of its practices are being questioned.

(Lewis 1993: 22)

The attendant professional intrusion into this new category of special educational provision is entirely consistent with Tomlinson's observations in the United Kingdom (see Chapter 11). The report *Integration in Victorian Education* (Ministry of Education – Victoria 1984) had suggested that integration policy would be funded by the transfer of resources from segregated settings correspondent to the transfer of students from one system to another:

The integration process, which was considered to be largely self-funding from resources deployed from a gradually devitalized special education system, is currently costing the state $43 million a year, while in the period 1984–1991 the cost of the special school system grew from about $50 million to $100 million.

(Lewis 1993: 23)

Fulcher (1985) observed the entrapment of integration within struggles over resources. Schools now required integration teachers and aides, and the support of psychologists and special educators in order to integrate students with disabilities. Paradoxically integration in Victoria was not simply a question of relocating students from segregated settings in the educational mainstream, it also prompted the identification of students with impairments, disabilities and 'problems with schooling' already attending regular classrooms. Integration became the mechanism for the management of students with behavioural problems, ('socially and emotionally disturbed students'), as well as for minimizing the impact of disability on school programs and structures. Advanced within a discourse of social justice and equity, integration was a regulatory framework for the surveillance and management of students who presented challenges to schooling: ' "Integration" is another version of the same [segregation policy], another sibling of the triad – disability, handicap, policy – a policy spawning programmes designed in terms of the demands of effective administration' (Branson and Miller 1989: 144).

The ministerial review, and subsequent policy statements, declared that all children had a right to be enrolled in their neighbourhood school. While the policy seemed unequivocal, a bureaucratic sleight of hand was effected so that schools would enrol students, but delay their admission until the resources to enable their instruction to proceed were in place. This translated into frequently bitter disputes over the determination of what level of resourcing would be required for each child (Marks 1993; Slee 1993a). These determinations were characteristically made by those who had traditionally presided over the segregated system of special education, psychologists and special education experts. Psychologists, special educators, academics, teachers, school administrators and bureaucrats discarded old segregative lexicons and used the discourse of inclusion, equity and social justice to ply old practices in new sites (Slee 1993a). In this way the special education fraternity were able to rearticulate their authority over those they considered disabled.

Declining enrolments in Victorian state schools exacerbated the exclusion of disabled students. Shortly after the publication of *Integration in Victorian Education* (Ministry of Education – Victoria 1984) schools with shrinking student numbers faced closure and amalgamation with neighbouring schools. The urgency of attracting students was evident in the efforts of schools to project the right image to their constituencies. Having a reputation for successfully including students with disabilities is seldom seen as a good marketing vehicle. Integration may be construed as a diminution of academic standards. It was reported that schools were using the delayed admissions procedures to discourage enrolments (Slee 1993a).

This finds its sequel in the current marketing of education in British schools (Gold *et al.* 1993; Ball 1994). Ball (1994: 124) cites Whitty's (1991: 20) early proposition that 'current reforms [in the UK] would seem to relate to a version of post-modernity that emphasises "distinction" and "hierarchy" within a fragmented social order, rather than one that positively celebrates "difference" and heterogeneity'.

In examining the ways in which framing education within a discourse of markets and choice exacerbates the divisions of class, Ball demonstrates the relative privilege of the middle class in entering into the rituals of choice and the self-exclusion of certain other class groups. Though not specifically speaking to issues of disability he does point out the 'fractioning' of 'the class differentials of the market . . . along ethnic, religious and gender lines' (Ball 1994: 123). The vulnerability of disabled students is intensified by the press for inflexible national testing and a 'return to standards' in a narrowing 'back to basics' curriculum (Barton 1987; Wiltshire *et al.* 1994; Clark *et al.* 1995).

Victoria is not an isolated example of policy contests over education and disability. Other states and territories in Australia have been subsumed by similar resourcing debates which impede the rights of passage of disabled students into regular schools and classrooms (Lewis and Cook 1993). The Queensland Teachers Union and the Australian Parent Advocacy (a conservative backlash against inclusion) have lobbied the Queensland state government for the retention of segregated special schools. This is part of an acrimonious struggle prompted by an Anti-Discrimination Commission inquiry into the exclusion of a disabled student from a Brisbane primary school (Butler 1995: 1).

Much of what is issued from education authorities as integration or inclusive education policy is an attempt to combine incompatible discourses of social justice and equity with antithetical languages of special education based on a medical model of disability and corporate managerialism (e.g. Andrews *et al*. 1993). It is hardly surprising that policy represents attempts to manage contests and orchestrate compromises. It is worth exploring this conceptual terrain in order to interrogate further the nature of the relationship between schooling and disablement.

For many inclusion for disabled students is an actuarial quest. Equity, according to this crude arithmetic, equals disabled student plus additional resources, or $E = DS + AR$.

> The success of integration programs depends to a large extent on the degree to which teachers, regular class students and parents are prepared to assist in the socialisation of students with handicaps . . . Real levels of success have occurred . . . only where some kind of mandated service model has been put in place or where there has been a substantial allocation of government funds to special education programs.
>
> (Cole 1991: 20)

Cole's remarks are unremarkable in the discourse of special education. They show the reductionist view that equity is a question of distributive calculus rather than a challenge to the structure and culture of schooling. There is also a carelessness in the interchanging of concepts such as handicap and disability. Students have disabilities and handicaps which may be ameliorated through the deployment of special services with students to the 'least restrictive environment'. Disability is intrinsic to the child. Schools and teachers are not included in the diagnostic gaze. No consideration is given to the role of schools in disabling or enabling students. Integration and special education programs are seen to hold a symbiotic relationship. The greater the range of differences presented by the child to challenge the organizational tranquillity of the school, the greater the level of resourcing that will be required to support the child's tenure in the regular classroom. Intense surveillance of the disabled student will be maintained through Integration Support Group meetings (Marks 1993) and Individual Education Programmes (Gilbert and Low 1994).

Nowhere is the calculus of 'special needs' given greater bureaucratic refinement than in the six-tiered schedule employed by the Queensland Department of Education to ascertain the educational needs of disabled students. In a meeting of parents with the Canadian disability rights advocate, Bruce Uditsky, in Brisbane earlier this year stories were recounted of the intrusive, irrelevant and insulting nature of some of the questions asked in the ascertainment rituals. Disparities between regions in the determination of criteria for student levels reveals the bureaucratic imperative of drawing lines across expenditure columns. Moreover, given anecdotal reportage of disabled children doing better in some schools than in others, it would seem apposite that any instrument of ascertainment be applied also to the diagnosis of defective school pathologies. However, inclusion continues to be advanced as a technical issue focusing almost exclusively upon the redistribution of material and human resources.

When the resourcing formulae fail a more legalistic approach is adopted to reconcile institutional needs. Carefully scripted clauses of conditionality are invoked to release schools from the appearance of discriminatory practice (Slee 1996). Professional judgement is called in to interpret 'least restrictive environment', 'undue institutional hardship', or 'most appropriate setting'. In this way the considerable latitude of professional discretion and power is reflected in the variety of definitions of inclusion that are offered (Lewis and Cook 1993; Slee 1995). Inclusion can mean the unconditional entry of a child into the regular educational and social programme of the school. It may be interpreted as attendance for two days a week augmented by a special placement elsewhere, or it may even describe the placement of a group of students in a separate unit in the school precinct. All may be defended as the integration program.

Where in all of this are disabled children, their parents and advocates? Finding answers reveals further complexity and challenges class-based explanations. Rather than rehearse anecdotal evidence of the powerlessness of parents and disabled students (Ireland 1993; Lyons 1993; Rice 1993; Walsh 1993) or the analysis of power relations in integration fora (Marks 1993), I will point to some recent anomalies which demonstrate the confusing twists in the political economy of schooling.

As a member of a New South Wales Special Education Advisory Panel I travelled to a number of regional centres where parents, teachers, school administrators, education department personnel and community members were invited to make representations to the panel to discuss what they saw as problems in the provision of special needs services for students. Predictably many parents spoke of the deleterious impact of disabling labels, lowered expectations and discriminatory practices upon the academic and social progress of their children. Their stories were frequently horrific and their arguments thoroughly informed by research literature. They urged the panel to consider:

- the removal of labels from their children;
- the raising of expectations for their success; and
- more flexible approaches to schooling to enable the participation of all children.

Paradoxically a growing group of articulate predominantly middle-class parents and professionals made representations to extend the application of categories of disability to attract additional resources and special educational treatment for their children. Labels and the accompanying extra provision would assist, they proposed, in offsetting the failure of schools to teach across a range of student differences. Specific learning disabilities and Attention Deficit Disorder Syndrome (ADD/ADHD) were most commonly cited. Both groups of parents, notwithstanding the apparent privilege and leverage of the latter, were reduced to the status of beggars pleading for crumbs from the bureaucratic table. The politics of disablement in the management of special (i.e. inclusive) education policy, in its various sites (Fulcher 1989) is palpable.

Attention deficit disorder: the troubling epidemic

The recent Australian and American (Kingston 1995) epidemics of ADD/ ADHD provide a useful means for examining the machinations of disablement and the dispensing of 'scholastic identities' (Ball 1990: 4) in schools. Serfontein (1990) introduces this 'hidden handicap' as the experience of difficulty in paying attention for a reasonable period of time.

> In other words these children have difficulty in focusing and sustaining their attention long enough to initiate and complete any set task. They tend to be easily distracted from the task at hand by other stimuli, such as noise or movement. Significant disturbances in concentration may lead to daydreaming and 'switching off'.
>
> (Serfontein 1990: 19)

According to Bowley and Walter (1992: 39) ADD/ADHD is a biological disorder consistent with an imbalance or deficiency of one or more neurotransmitter in the brain. Diagnosis is made by a physician or psychologist matching a child's reported behaviour against a checklist from the American Psychiatric Association (1994). The correlation, devoid of contextualization, is both random and normative; 'Attention Deficit Disorder is not a disease, it's just part of the spectrum of children's behaviour. The issue is to find the line where abnormality stops and normality begins . . . and the line moves according to who's drawing it' (*Speed for Breakfast* 1995).

Geographical disproportionality in diagnosis seems to indicate the prevalence of diagnostic predisposition as a causal factor. Swann's research reveals that in an average school of 1000 students in Victoria, not even one child would be receiving treatment for ADD/ADHD. In Western Australia and

New South Wales approximately ten students are being treated. In the United States, Swann estimates, on the basis of Barkley's data (1990), there would be up to 80 ADD/ADHD students in a school of 1000. Kingston (1995: 2), writing for the *Guardian*, reports that 5 per cent of American children are being placed in the ADD/ADHD category. It is worth noting Kingston continues, that although the condition is 'commonly recognised in the US and Australia' it has not gained wide recognition in the UK.

Diagnosis and treatments for this syndrome generate controversy. We have noted the random subjectivity of matching decontextualized behaviours listed in the American Psychiatric Association (1994) inventory. The Serfontein Clinic in Sydney employs an apparently more sophisticated diagnostic tool called neurometrics. Neurometrics involves the scrutinizing of brain waves from different parts of the brain to ascertain 'abnormalities' on coloured graphs. Neurologists remain sceptical about whether ADD/ADHD has a patterned abnormality, or even whether computers have the capacity for depicting the complex patterning of the brain's electrical impulses (Swann 1995).

Treatments include behavioural therapy and or chemical interventions. The most popular treatment is the prescribing of amphetamines, the most popular of which is Ritalin. Ritalin acts on the central nervous system to sedate the child. Govoni and Hayes (1988: 778–9) warn of the contraindications of the drug, which include the repression of growth, impeded cardiovascular function, the development of ticks, and nausea. This list is indicative rather than exhaustive. No controlled studies using placebos of the drug have been undertaken so that there is no basis for proving or disproving its effects.

ADD/ADHD is a beguiling syndrome. For both teachers and parents it provides a palatable explanation for the errant behaviour of an increasing number of children who are difficult to manage. For parents it grasps at respectability. Better for their child to be seen as pathologically impaired than as bad. For teachers it resists applying diagnostic probes to difficult questions about pedagogy, curriculum and school organization. Moreover it offers relief through chemical treatment and the promise of a cure. Increasing numbers of 'naughty' children are being pathologized and are now framed as ADD/ADHD children who require special needs intervention. The pervasiveness of such a category as a disciplinary technology of surveillance and control is evident in the growing incidence of self-diagnosis where parents voluntarily submit their children to diagnosis and treatment following suggestion or complaint from the school.

Another reading of this text is possible and plausible. We might commence with the proposition that ADD/ADHD deflects for a school system struggling against the ravages of history. Schools have always produced failure. In the past schools have had little difficulty in managing failure. The problem of failure in schools was depoliticized through individualization. Deficient children failed school. These children could be accommodated and managed. The unskilled labour market and a segregated system of special education colluded in the concealment of the failure of schools to provide a comprehensive education for all comers. Structural changes in the unskilled youth labour market (Polk and Tait 1990; Freeland 1992) and in the patterns of school retention (Freeland 1992; Marginson 1993; Slee 1995b) make failure both apparent and problematic. Increasing numbers of young people look to the end of their academic careers and know that school is unable to deliver its promise of successful transition to independent working life. Resistance in this context seems not an indication of impaired human pathologies, it resonates with a deeply troubled social pathology.

The distributive calculus fails to compute with equity. Special educational diagnosis and the proliferation of compensatory programs is an impoverished reading of dysfunctional schooling. Changing students so that they become compliant with a system of schooling that ignores changing social and economic realities makes schooling a particularly risky business for increasing numbers of students who will be awarded disabling identities and excluded from regular educational provision. The intersection of such conditions of disablement and class, race and ethnicity is not coincidental. Exclusion is selective, it is not benign. This is revealed by data from Pupil Referral Units in the UK, where race and class are reliable predictors for referral (Ofsted 1993; Pyke 1993).

New agendas for enabling schools

In a recent seminar considering sociologies of disability, Shakespeare and Watson (1995:2) acknowledged the theoretical and political importance of the development of a social model of disability in refuting the 'political nature of biological essentialism and biological determinism'. Drawing parallels between Oliver's (1990) and the theoretical and political project of second-wave feminists such as Mitchell (1971) and Millett (1977), they argue that just as the second-wave feminists identified masculinity and femininity as socially constructed roles as distinct from notions of male and female bodies, the positing of a social model of disability overcame the biological distraction of impairment (Shakespeare and Watson 1995:2). Embracing the range of theoretical tools provided by poststructural contributions to more recent feminist and lesbian and gay studies, Shakespeare and Watson contend that disability studies is prone to reductionism in its theorization. While having played an important rhetorical and political role, the task now centres upon a multilevelled consideration of the interplay between identities and social structure.

Contiguous with feminist recognition of the theoretical and political importance of the personal, subjectivities have to become a part of theorizing disability. Jenny Morris takes this up in pointing to the absence of disabled and older women from western feminist theory:

> Disabled people – men and women – have little opportunity to portray our experiences within the general culture, or within radical political movements. Our experience is isolated, individualised; the definitions which society places on us centre on judgements of individual capacities and personalities. This lack of voice, of the representation of our subjective reality means that it is difficult for non-disabled feminists to incorporate our reality into their research and their theories, unless it is in terms of the way the non-disabled world sees us.
>
> (Morris 1991: 8)

Morris invites social constructionist theories of disability to write agency into their text:

> there is a tendency within the social model of disability to deny the experience of our own bodies, insisting that our physical differences and restrictions are entirely *socially created*. While environmental barriers and social attitudes are a crucial part of our experience of disability – and do indeed disable us – to suggest that this is all there is to it is to deny the personal experience of physical or intellectual restrictions, of illness, of fear of dying.
>
> (Morris 1991: 10, original emphasis)

Issues of material support, identity, the politics of recognition and representation, and voice become central to the project of enabling schooling. Fraser's analysis of the redistribution – recognition dilemma is theoretically and strategically useful:

> The redistribution–recognition dilemma is real. There is no neat theoretical move by which it can be wholly dissolved or resolved. The best we can do is try to soften the dilemma by finding approaches that minimise conflicts between redistribution and recognition in cases where both must be pursued simultaneously.
>
> (Fraser 1995: 92)

Clearly redistribution is central to the task of ensuring that schools provide physical facilities and learning environments which enable young people to participate successfully in programs which increase rather than restrict opportunities. Hitherto, integration has proceeded from a series of unacknowledged assumptions. At the centre stands the assumption that the regular school provides an education worth being included in. Regular schooling, it is inferred, is worthwhile for students currently attending it. This position lays a functionalist path to educational reform. The objective is to include disabled students through redistributing resources and personnel to minimize those differences which demand alteration to the educational program. The quest, rearticulated as 'inclusion', 'integration' and the delivery of 'social justice', is the relocation of special educational services to sustain school bureaucracies (Skrtic 1991).

There is much that would indicate, not least our discussion of the framing of disruptive students as disabled (ADD/ADHD), that the regular school is in need of reconstruction so that it recognizes a range of identities and resists the current deployment of the discourse of the market to reassert old class hierarchies (Ball 1994). Inclusion, a euphemism for containment and assimilation, ignores the need for deconstruction and recognition across a range of boundaries. In practical terms, where does this leave us? Albeit briefly, I will suggest a number of points for the enabling schools discussion agenda:

- debating inclusive schooling – voices and representation
- disability and research in education
- teaching teachers
- pathologizing schools.

From that point we can take leave to debate our own conclusions, if indeed conclusions exist.

Debating inclusive schooling

Australian education departments have turned the management of integration and inclusion, and the epistemological authority, over to the experts in the field of 'special educational needs'. The tacit acceptance of this expert knowledge obstructs divergent representations of the experience of disability in education and reasserts the unequal power relations of disability. The failure to broaden the debate to critiques of regular educational as well as special educational practices restricts the possibilities for a reconstruction of schooling which values a range of different identities.

Confronting questions of gender discrimination and disadvantage was not expedited by allowing the men who 'knew' about women's issues to set the agenda. Aboriginal and Torres Strait Islander students and educators insisted not only on the presence of their people in the policy fora, they also established the authority of their voice as legitimate and enriching in the redefinition of Australian history and culture. Slippage occurs when it comes to representation in the formation of disability policy. Consequently inclusion remains a compensatory program. The assumption that the only beneficiaries of inclusion are disabled students is a compounding factor.

Impatience for solutions, usually political expediencies, can present barriers to the progress of knowledge and improvement of educational practice. Consideration of representations from a range of constituencies is seen as an indulgence that confuses where closure is sought. Typical is resorting to prescriptive formulae for 'effective schools' (Reynolds 1995).

Disability and research in education

The production of Australian education theory, dominated by psychological discourses, has not devoted sufficient intellectual effort to disablement. Central to this problematic is the structure of research funding. Major research grants in the area of inclusion and disability studies continue to be awarded to those who are recognized as 'expert' in the area. The special education research centres at Macquarie University, University of Queensland and Burwood Campus of Deakin predominate. Peer review supports the concentration and control of the production of research knowledge. Disabled voices which call the expert to account and insert new critiques of the old canons will have difficulty in crossing the institutional barriers.

Teaching teachers

Training in inclusive education has largely been interpreted as the insertion of a core unit on 'special educational needs'. Such units are characterized by descriptions of categories of defective students, hints for recognition of these students, and sequential programmes for their remediation. Few have taken up the challenge that inclusion ought to presuppose a critical examination of current educational programs and bureaucratic procedures, or challenge the epistemological binary of special and regular educational knowledge. Moreover, student teachers will tend to receive their knowledge from those who traditionally presided over segregation. Few will receive instruction from disabled people.

Pathologizing schools?

As we have noted, inclusion is obsessed with categorial division and provision. The 'dysfunctional child' is placed at the centre of the inclusionary focus. While not removing children from focus, we need to consider the refractions of the lens employed. If we are fixated on determining scales of deficiencies for compensatory intervention, we condemn ourselves to the marginalization of students whose longer-term options will be limited. Alternatively, through the representation and registration of a range of experiences, we might consider the characteristics of a school which responds to children's needs across the range of human variation in ways that value their participation and increase their options.

Summary

Disablement in schools restricts students' options and reinforces existing class hierarchies. Handing education over to market discourses that proclaim choice, efficiency and quality re-establishes the vulnerability of students along class lines. Where the state attempted levels of redistribution of opportunity through comprehensive educational provision, 'choice' actually eschews diversity and reverts to narrow preconceptions of worthwhile curriculum and standards. Those 'unfit' to compete are dislodged (Ball 1994). The management of the growing body of the 'unfit' is facilitated through the rearticulation of special education in the guise of inclusive education. Special educators relocate their practice and preside over this expanding clientele with special needs. The discourse of meeting needs is misleading. Evidence of the expansion of opportunity for these young people has not yet been furnished. Inclusion cannot simply be an exercise in the redistribution or resiting of support to accommodate disabled students with their able-bodied peers. It demands the interrogation of the conditions that serve to construct hierarchies of identities, some of which are recognized and others that are not. Retheorizing the form and practice of regular education is central to this project. As Ramsay (1993: 44) observes in relation to feminist theory and politics, inserting an authentic language which describe specific forms of oppression from the vantage of the oppressed is the first step.

References

Abberley, P. (1987) The concept of oppression and the development of a social theory of disability, *Disability, Handicap and Society*, 2(1): 5–19.
Abberley, P. (1994) Disabled people and normality, in J. Swain, V. Finkelstein, S. French and M. Oliver (eds) *Disabling Barriers – Enabling Environments*. London: Sage.
American Psychiatric Association (1994) *Diagnostic and Statistical Manual of Mental Disorders*. Washington, DC: APA.
Andrews, R. J., Elkins, J. and Christie, R. (1993) *Report and Operational Plan for the Provision of Special Educational Needs 1993–1996*. Brisbane: Metropolitan East Region, Queensland Department of Education.
Ashman, A. and Elkins, J. (eds) (1990) *Educating Children with Special Needs*. Sydney: Prentice-Hall.
Australian Bureau of Statistics [ABS] (1993a) *Disability Ageing and Carers: a Summary of Findings*. Canberra: Australian Government Printer.

Australian Bureau of Statistics [ABS] (1993b) *1991 Census of Population and Housing: Basic Community Profile*. Canberra: Australian Government Printer.

Ball, S. J. (ed.) (1990) *Foucault and Education: Discipline and Knowledge*. London: Routledge.

Ball, S. J. (1994) *Education Reform: a Critical and Post-structural Approach*. Buckingham: Open University Press.

Barkley, R. A. (1990) *Attention Deficit Hyperactivity Disorder: a Handbook for Diagnosis and Treatment*. New York: Guildford Press.

Barnes, C. (1991) *Disabled People in Britain and Discrimination: a Case for Anti-discrimination Legislation*. London: Hurst.

Barton, L. (ed.) (1987) *The Politics of Special Educational Needs*. Lewes: Falmer Press.

Barton, L. (1996) Sociology and disability: some emerging issues, in L. Barton (ed.) *Disability and Society: Emerging Issues and Insights*. London: Longman.

Becker, H. S. (1963) *Outsiders: Studies in the Sociology of Deviance*. New York: The Free Press.

Becker, H. S. (ed.) (1964) *The Other Side: Perspectives on Deviance*. New York: The Free Press.

Berthoud, R., Lakey, J. and McKay, S. (1993) *The Economic Problems of Disabled People*. London: Policy Studies Institute.

Blau, J. (1992) *The Visible Poor: Homelessness in the United States*. New York: Oxford University Press.

Bodna, B. (1987) People with intellectual disability and the criminal justice system, in D. Challinger (ed.) *Intellectually Disabled Offenders*. Canberra: Australian Institute of Criminology.

Bowley, C. and Walter, E. (1992) Attention deficit disorders and the role of the school counsellor, *Elementary School Guidance and Counselling*, 27: 39–46.

Branson, J. and Miller, D. (1989) Beyond policy: the deconstruction of disability, in L. Barton (ed.) *Integration: Myth or Reality?* Lewes: Falmer Press.

Branson, J. and Miller, D. (1992) Normalisation, community care and the politics of difference, *Australian Disability Review*, 4: 17–28.

Butler, G. (1995) Disabled kids row widens, *Courier Mail*, 11 August: 1.

Butler, S. R. (ed.) (1990) *The Exceptional Child: an Introduction to Special Education*. Sydney, Australia: Harcourt Brace Jovanovich.

Chetwynd, J. (1985) Some costs of caring at home for an intellectually handicapped child, *Australia and New Zealand Journal of Developmental Disabilities*, 11(1): 35–40.

Clark, C., Dyson, A. and Millward, A. (eds) (1995) *Towards Inclusive Schools?* London: David Fulton.

Cohen, S. (ed.) (1971) *Images of Deviance*. Harmondsworth: Penguin.

Cole, P. (1991) Two models of integration. A review of some of the recent literature on the effects of integration in schools, in A. Ashman (ed.) *Current Themes in Integration – the Exceptional Child Monograph Number 2*, St Lucia: Fred and Eleanor Schonell Special Education Research Centre.

Davis, F. (1964) Deviance disavowal: the management of strained interaction by the visibly handicapped, in H. S. Becker (ed.) *The Other Side: Perspectives on Deviance*. New York: The Free Press.

Disability Advisory Council of Australia (1991) *Consultation with People with Disabilities and their Families*. Canberra: DACA.

Disability Task Force (1991) *Discussion Paper on the Additional Costs Faced by People with Disabilities*. Canberra: Department of Social Security.

Dupont, A. (1980) A study concerning the time related and other burdens when severely handicapped children are reared at home, *Acta Psychiatrica Scandinavia*, Supplement 285, 62: 249–57.

Finkelstein, V. (1980) *Attitudes and Disabled People: Issues for Discussion*. New York: World Rehabilitation Fund.

Foucault, M. (1967) *Madness and Civilization: a History of Insanity in the Age of Reason*. London: Tavistock.

Fraser, N. (1995) From redistribution to recognition? Dilemmas of justice in a 'post-socialist' age, *New Left Review*, July/August: 68–93.

Freeland, J. (1992) Education and training for the school to work transition, in T. Seddon and C. Deer (eds) *A Curriculum for the Senior Secondary Years*. Hawthorn: ACER.

Fulcher, G. (1985) Integration locks into fight over resources, *The Age*, 8 October.

Fulcher, G. (1989) *Disabling Policies?* Lewes: Falmer Press.

Fuller Torrey, E. (1988) *Nowhere to Go: the Tragic Odyssey of the Homeless Mentally Ill*. New York: Harper and Row.

Gans, H. J. (1995) *The War Against the Poor: the Underclass and Antipoverty Policy*. New York: Basic Books.

Gilbert, R. and Low, P. (1994) Discourse and power in education: analysing institutional processes in schools, *The Australian Educational Researcher*, 21(3): 1–24.

Goffman, E. (1961) *Asylums*. New York: Doubleday.

Goffman, E. (1963) *Stigma: Some Notes on the Management of Spoiled Identity*. Harmondsworth: Penguin.

Gold, A., Bowe, R. and Ball, S. J. (1993) Special educational needs in a new context: micropolitics, money and education for all, in R. Slee (ed.) *Is There a Desk with my Name on it? The Politics of Integration*. London: Falmer Press.

Government Statistical Service (1993) *Disability Working Allowance Statistics*. London: HMSO.

Govoni, L. E. and Hayes, J. E. (1988) *Drugs and Nursing Implications*. Englewood Cliffs, NJ: Prentice-Hall.

Hahn, H. (1985) Disability policy and the problem of discrimination, *American Behavioural Scientist*, 28(3): 293–318.

Human Rights and Equal Opportunities Commission [HREOC] (1989) *Our Homeless Children: Report of the National Committee of Inquiry into Homeless Children*. Canberra: Australian Government Publishing Service.

Human Rights and Equal Opportunities Commission [HREOC] (1993) *Report of the National Inquiry into the Human Rights of People with Mental Illness*. Canberra: Australian Government Printing Service.

Ireland, M. (1993) Taking the challenge of disability within the tertiary education system, *Australian Disability Review*, 2: 54–5.

Katz, M. B. (1989) *The Undeserving Poor: From the War on Poverty to the War on Welfare*. New York: Pantheon Books.

Kendrick, M. (1992) Additional thoughts on 'rationality' and the service system, *Australian Disability Review*, 4: 11–16.

Kingston, P. (1995) Give peace a chance, *Guardian Education*, Tuesday, October 31: 2.

Kirk, S. A. (1972) *Educating Exceptional Children*, 2nd edn. Boston, MA: Houghton Mifflin.

Lemert, E. (1951) *Social Pathology*. New York: McGraw Hill.

Lewis, J. (1993) Integration in Victorian schools: radical social policy or old wine? in R. Slee (ed.) *Is There a Desk with my Name on it? The Politics of Integration*. London: Falmer Press.

Lewis, J. and Cook, S. (1993) Possible directions in school integration, *Australian Disability Review*, 1: 28–37.

Lewis, J., Cook, S. and Sword, B. (1989) 'The first five years of integration policy in Victoria', unpublished report. Melbourne: Victorian Ministry of Education.

Lipton, F., Sabatini, A. and Katz, S. E. (1983) Down and out in the city: the homeless mentally ill, *Hospital and Community Psychiatry*, 34(9): 817–21.

Lyons, A. (1993) A parent's perspective, in R. Slee (ed.) *Is There a Desk with my Name on it? The Politics of Integration*. London: Falmer Press.

Marks, G. (1993) Contests in decision-making at the school level, in R. Slee (ed.) *Is There a Desk with my Name on it? The Politics of Integration*. London: Falmer Press.

Marginson, S. (1993) *Education and Public Policy in Australia*. Cambridge: Cambridge University Press.

Martin, J., White, A. and Meltzer, H. (1989) *Disabled Adults: Services, Transport and Employment, Office of Population Censuses and Surveys Survey of Disability in Great Britain*, Report No. 4. London: HMSO.

Matthews, A. and Truscott, P. (1990) *Disability, Household Income and Expenditure, Department of Social Security Research Report No. 2*. London: HMSO.

Miller, E. and Gwynne, G. (1972) *A Life Apart*. London: Tavistock.

Millett, K. (1977) *Sexual Politics*. London: Virago.

Ministry of Education – Victoria (1984) *Integration in Victorian Education: Report of the Ministerial Review of Educational Services for the Disabled*. Melbourne: Victorian Government Printer.

Mitchell, J. (1971) *Women's Estate*. Harmondsworth: Penguin.

Morris, J. (1991) *Pride Against Prejudice: Transforming Attitudes to Disability*. London: The Women's Press.

New South Wales Council for Intellectual Disability (1992) Missing services, *Newsletter No. 1*, November.

Ofsted (1993) *Education for Disaffected Pupils*. London: Department for Education, Office for Standards in Education.

OPCS [Office of Population Censuses and Surveys] (1986) *Surveys of Disability in Great Britain*. London: HMSO.

Oliver, M. (1986) Social policy and disability: some theoretical issues, *Disability, Handicap and Society*, 1(1): 5–18.

Oliver, M. (1990) *The Politics of Disablement*. Basingstoke: Macmillan.

Polk, K. and Tait, D. (1990) Changing youth labour markets and youth lifestyles, *Youth Studies*, 9(1): 17–23.

Potts, M. and Fido, R. (1991) *'A Fit Person to be Removed': Personal Accounts of Life in a Mental Deficiency Institution*. Plymouth: Northcote House.

Pyke, N. (1993) Banished to the exclusion zone, *Times Educational Supplement*, 2 April: 6.

Ramsay, E. (1993) Linguistic omissions marginalising women managers, in D. Baker and M. Fogarty (eds) *A Gendered Culture: Educational Management in the Nineties*. Melbourne: Victoria University of Technology.

Rees, S. and Emerson, A. (1983) The costs of caring for disabled children at home, *Australian Rehabilitation Review*, 7(3): 26–31.

Reynolds, D. (1995) Using school effectiveness knowledge for children with special needs – the problems and possibilities, in C. Clark, A. Dyson and A. Millward (eds) *Towards Inclusive Schools?* London: David Fulton.

Rice, M. (1993) Integration: another form of specialism, in R. Slee (ed.) *Is There a Desk with my Name on it? The Politics of Integration*. London: Falmer Press.

Ronalds, C. (1990) *National Employment Initiatives for People with Disabilities: a Discussion Paper*. Canberra: Australian Government Publishing Service.

Rose, N. (1979) The psychological complex: mental measurement and social administration, *Ideology and Consciousness*, 5: 5–68.

Ryan, W. (1971) *Blaming the Victim*. New York: Vintage Books.

Schur, E. M. (1971) *Labelling Deviant Behaviour*. New York: Harper and Row.

Serfontein, G. (1990) *The Hidden Handicap*. Sydney: Simon and Schuster Australia.

Shakespeare, T. and Watson, N. (1995) The body line controversy: a new direction for disability studies? Hull, Sociologies of Disability seminar.

Skrtic, T. (1991) *Behind Special Education: a Critical Analysis of Professional Culture and School Organisation*. Denver, CO: Love.

Slee, R. (1993a) The politics of integration – new sites for old practices? *Disability, Handicap and Society*, 8(4): 351–60.

Slee, R. (1993b) Interview with Disability Discrimination Commissioner Elizabeth Hastings, *Australian Disability Review*, 1: 4–13.

Slee, R. (1995) *Changing Theories and Practices of Discipline*. London: Falmer Press.

Slee, R. (1996) Clauses of conditionality: the 'reasonable' accommodation of language, in L. Barton (ed.) *Disability and Society: Emerging Issues and Insights*. London: Longman.

Speed for Breakfast (1995) ABC television documentary, 12 February.

Stern, W. (1992) A plea for rationality, *Australian Disability Review*, 4: 3–10.

Stern, W. (1993) A further plea for rationality, *Australian Disability Review*, 1: 14–21.

Stern, W. (1994) Good intentions are not enough – are we on the right track? *Australian Disability Review*, 3: 73–91.

Thompson, P., Buckle, J. and Lavery, M. (1990) *Short Changed by Disability*. London: Disablement Income Group.

Tomlinson, S. (1982) *A Sociology of Special Education*. London: Routledge and Kegan Paul.

Topliss, E. (1979) *Provision for the Disabled*, 2nd edn. Oxford: Basil Blackwell.

Walsh, B. (1993) How disabling any handicap is depends on the attitudes and actions of others: a student's perspective, in R. Slee (ed.) *Is There a Desk with my Name on it? The Politics of Integration*. London: Falmer Press.

Ward, J., Bochner, S., Center, Y., Outhred, L. and Pieterse, M. (eds) (1987) *Educating Children with Special Needs in Regular Classrooms: an Australian Perspective*. North Ryde: Special Education Centre, Macquaries University.

Whitty, G. (1991) Making sense of urban education after Thatcher, seminar paper, University of Liverpool, Department of Education, 1 May.

Wightman, P. and Foreman, H. (1991) *Costs of Disability, Social Policy Research Paper No. 59*. Canberra: Australian Government Printing Service.

Wiltshire, K., McMeniman, M. and Tolhurst, T. (1994) *Shaping the Future: Report of the Review of the Queensland School Curriculum*. Brisbane: The State of Queensland.

World Health Organization (1980) *Classification of Impairment, Disability and Handicap*. Geneva: WHO.

Wright Mills, C. (1959) *The Sociological Imagination*. New York: Oxford University Press.

Yeatman, A. (1994) *Postmodern Revisionings of the Political*. New York: Routledge.

Young, I. M. (1990) *Justice and the Politics of Difference*. Princeton, NJ: Princeton University Press.

Coming out as gendered adults: gender, sexuality and disability

Introduction

Beyond doubt, disability and gender are political issues. It is not so much the disabling effects of different impairments on people of different genders that are of concern here, as the issues of power, control, and the various ways difference is perceived and constructed, by outsiders, as well as by people with disabilities themselves. Disability itself is socially constructed in relation to gender and sexuality. But disability and gender, both individually and combined, must be addressed as issues of oppression.

Care must be taken, however, to avoid the reductionism that is so common when considering disability. To 'reduce political subjects to a unity and to value commonness and sameness over specificity and difference' (Young, 1990: 3) is to valorize the oppression of those who are different. This not only applies to the difference that disabilities corporeally inscribe. There is a tendency to assume that all people with disabilities will be equally ungendered, or in some cases, equally oversexed, but seldom entitled to diversity of gender and sexuality. Brown notes, for example: 'Fears and myths about sexuality have been projected onto people with learning disabilities, they are framed as asexual, or oversexed, innocents or perverts. Historically service models have been predicated on the need to maintain sexual boundaries between people with learning disabilities and the general public' (Brown 1994: 125).

For a person with a disability, it is seldom easy to avoid the 'normative gaze' (Young 1990: 11) that so readily demands sameness. Whether the disability be one that requires the use of a wheelchair or a white cane, or one that marks a body as Other, such as size or disfigurement, or one that involves behaviour regarded as aberrant, there is condemnation, and often revulsion. Such a normative view 'locates bodies on a single aesthetic scale that constructs some kinds of bodies as ugly, disgusting or degenerate' (Young

1990: 11). The articulation of such oppression with gender, however, is a more complicated matter still.

So who may speak for whom?

This chapter does not pretend to be a definitive exploration of the articulations between disability and gender. By drawing on several examples of the way things are, it focuses on the way things could possibly be in the future. But as will become clear in this exploration of the ways political relationships between gender and disability are manifested, we primarily need to be concerned with the issue of who is entitled to 'speak' in this debate. To identify as disabled, and as gendered, is less complicated than to consider who, within such diversity, may speak for whom. It is certainly true that groups are constituted by individuals. 'A person's particular sense of history, affinity, and separateness, even the person's mode of reasoning, evaluating, and expressing feeling, are constituted mainly by his or her group affinities' (Young 1990: 45).

But individuals *do* transcend group identities. Further, individuals seldom belong to one group. A homosexual man with a hearing impairment will not necessarily view the world through the same lens as another homosexual man with a hearing impairment. Less likely still is that he would take the same position on gender and disability as a single mother with an intellectual disability. It must be stressed that the politics of difference does not 'work according to a strict binary, oppositional logic' (Gunew 1993: xxii). Nor indeed, are disability and gender simply a matter of binaries. While it may be possible individually to 'ontologize' either disability or gender, it is both devaluing and disempowering to do so.

Since disability always exists in articulation with gender and sexuality, it is essential to value the differences that exist within particular categories if we are to move forward in debates on social justice and disability. Because there is no universal subject and no universal definition of oppression, the emancipatory needs of all people with disabilities cannot be generalized. Cross-gender and sexuality positionings, as well as cross-disability positionings, will influence the nature of social alliances and political activities that are both possible and desirable. 'A politics of difference within an emancipatory movement makes explicit the contradictory nature of emancipation itself, its orientation of both interest and ethics' (Yeatman 1993: 229).

Coming out, or coming in?

Gender and sexuality are articulated with disability in many ways, but seldom are their expressions unproblematic. In order to explore the ways 'sexual and gendered identities' (Hall 1992: 290) are articulated with disability, in this chapter I will consider three different social positionings. The first of these concerns marriage and parenting, which is often considered to be a right of all adults, and indeed, is viewed as a marker of adulthood. Despite such beliefs, marriage and parenting are frequently denied to people with disabilities on various grounds. To varying degrees, and in differing ways, both men and women with disabilities are frequently denied this basic human right to their sexual identity.

The second positioning relates to women with disabilities performing unwaged work, not only within marriage, where 'women's oppression consists partly in a systematic and unreciprocated transfer of power from women to men' (Young, 1990: 50), but also in their role as carers outside marriage for aged or ill parents or siblings. In discussions of women as carers, it is often assumed that the women are able-bodied, but are caring for the frail or disabled. This is frequently far from the truth, but has been essentially overlooked by feminists in their arguments about women as unpaid workers.

Being gay and having a disability is the third positioning around which I will discuss the issues of articulation between gender and disability. It is an area that is only now beginning to capture the imagination of researchers. The denial, or invisibility, of homosexuality generally is greatly exacerbated within the disabled community. School sex education programs seldom address homosexuality, so for people with disability, who have limited access to information and resources, the articulation of their sexuality with their disability may be especially problematic. The compulsion to pass as 'ordinary' or 'normal' is a key theme, whether it be in regard to parenting, to Gay Pride or to the workforce. For people with disabilities, coming out of schools is hard enough, but coming out as gendered adults is even more difficult.

The discussion will seek to show how exploitation on the basis of gender is as much an issue for people with disabilities as it is for those without. Furthermore, it will be clear that when people with disabilities 'assert their rights to sexual lives they heighten their visibility rather than increase their chances of integration and acceptance' (Brown 1994: 124). This will be confirmed in an examination of the issue of gender and disability, and how it is perceived by social movements such as feminism and Gay Pride. Evidence suggests that these social movements, however progressive, have failed to consider the needs, or indeed the existence, of people with disabilities. By the same token, however, disability movements fail many people by overlooking the needs of women, or by ignoring the articulation of homosexuality with disability.

Marriage and parenting

Women with disability frequently have a different starting point from that of men with disability when challenging oppression. Lloyd (1992: 212) contends:

'The women are as concerned as the men to affirm that it is society which disables and oppresses, but the discussion is not confined to the modes of economic and social discrimination identified by disabled men.' For women with disabilities, it is also important to explore issues of sexuality and sexual identity, often in relation to motherhood. Whether beset by the 'helpless child' role (in which it is assumed that marriage and/or parenting is unacceptable), the challenge to 'be sexy from a wheelchair' (Lloyd 1992), or the demand to nurture men within marriage, women with disabilities face issues that are gender-specific.

This is not to suggest that oppression in relation to marriage and parenting does not also apply to men with disabilities. It is true that men with disabilities may not enjoy the 'freedom, status, and self-realization' afforded to able-bodied men. However, as Young (1990: 50) observes, 'Gender exploitation has two aspects, transfer of the fruits of material labour to men and transfer of the nurturing of sexual energies to men.' In other words, the nature of oppression in relation to marriage is different for women with disabilities. Hanna and Rogovsky (1991: 56) assert: 'There is a big difference between a disabled husband and a disabled wife. A disabled husband needs a wife to nurture him, but a disabled wife is not seen by society as capable of nurturing a husband who is not disabled.'

The right of women (and therefore, men) with disabilities to procreate, and then raise their own children, is not taken for granted. Too often, it is a rarely granted privilege rather than a right. This denial applies not only to women considered to have intellectual disabilities, but also to those who use wheelchairs, for example. Hanna and Rogovsky (1991) report that in a recent case, a court in California ruled that a woman who used a wheelchair be forced to give up her two sons for adoption. They also found that mothers with disabilities also experienced opposition to their motherhood from a range of sources. For example, one woman observed: 'My mothering worries everybody else. Even my mother thinks I should never have children. But it sure doesn't worry me. It'll take me longer to do things, but I'll do it' (p. 56).

In Australia, there is considerable opposition from community service providers to women with intellectual disabilities raising their own children. Child protection workers argue that each case is evaluated on its individual merits, but the records in the courts do little to convince advocacy organizations that this is genuinely the case. It seems that once a family comes to the notice of the government-run community services organization, there is little chance of the mother who has a disability keeping her children at home. This does not seem to be confined to Australia, but rather reflects a prevailing attitude about the appropriateness of certain child-rearing practices, and the skills needed for successful parenting.

In a recent case, a family moved into a large regional town from an interstate capital city. Both parents have an intellectual disability, and the father was raised in an institution. Prior to the couple leaving the previous city, state welfare workers removed the couple's oldest child from their care, and placed the child in an institution. Understandably distressed, and denied regular access (although there is no record of physical abuse), the couple moved interstate and started a new family. At the time of coming to the attention of child protection workers in their new district, the eldest child in the new family was nearly school age, and the youngest was a toddler.

The child protection agency argued that the children were neglected, and that the mother had no parenting skills. After some months, they suggested that she had no interest in acquiring those skills, and moved that the court remove the children and place them in custodial care. Not surprisingly, the mother immediately became pregnant again, in anticipation of losing her other children. Eventually, and perhaps predictably, the court ruled that the children be taken from their mother, and that the unborn child be removed at birth.

This case highlights some interesting predicaments and contradictions. It is true that the children were ill-kempt. They rarely wore shoes, despite the often cold weather. Frequently, they were unwashed, and the court reported that on occasions, the youngest slept on a bed without sheets. Dishes were often left unwashed, and dirty washing accumulated around the house. The situation was described as neglect and abuse. It must be stressed that the children were not beaten, or even threatened. All witnesses agreed that the children were much loved, and were happy.

Had the parents been exceedingly poor, but without disability, the situation would likely have been read as poverty. If the family had been indigenous, what was termed neglect would have been considered cultural difference. Had the mother been white and middle class, the situation would probably have been overlooked entirely, or it would have been suggested that the mother was under stress, and needed either home help or emotional support. But because the parents, and in particular the mother, were labelled as having an intellectual disability, child-rearing practices that did not conform with middle-class white expectations were described as neglect and abuse.

Such denial of a woman's rights as a gendered adult, to parent, and of children's rights to be in a loving and safe family, is not isolated to one area of Australia. It typifies the way parents with disabilities are viewed across the western world. Booth and Booth (1993) have recently reported a similar case in Britain. The young mother described had already lost one child to the welfare system. The mother was fortunate, however, in that she had been allowed to keep her second and third children, although she was clearly being closely monitored by the welfare workers. The mother observed: 'Community Nurse doesn't interfere. She says how're you getting on, that's all. It's just for file, just to make sure we're all right and kids all right. That's the reason why they come, to make sure they're all right' (p. 382). Surveillance is subtle, but nonetheless real.

Women with disabilities and unwaged work

While much has been written about the exploitation of women performing unwaged work, these discussions seldom examine the issue in relation to women with disabilities. Certainly, such discussions underestimate their relevance to women with disabilities (WinVisible 1994). Yet for women with disabilities, the problem is sometimes even more significant. Brown (1994), for example, raises concerns about women with learning disabilities who are placed in group homes, with no choice of coresidents, and are expected to perform unwaged work for the male residents of those homes.

The British organization, Women with Visible and Invisible Disabilities (WinVisible), has expressed particular concern about the nature of unpaid work for women with disabilities. They note that unpaid work performed by women with disabilities does not just fall into the realm of working as carers. Women, as with all people with disabilities,

> do the unwaged work of disability and health, sometimes caring for others, always caring for ourselves: getting about, communicating, arranging transport, following and preparing special diets, dealing with agencies and authorities about money and services, becoming our own health experts, directing others about when we do or don't need help, trying to get the helper to do the job more nearly the way we want, and so on. Those of us who are physically dependent on others have to do more of the taxing emotional work of handling these relationships and of grappling with being dependent.
>
> (WinVisible 1994: 55–6)

Yet at the same time, people with disabilities are frequently living on the poverty line, which creates additional dependency on family and friends. This, WinVisible rightly contends, is the unpaid work universally experienced by people with disabilities, irrespective of gender. 'It is reproductive work which is a huge contribution to society, entitling us to resources of all kinds, not as charity, but as rights and reparations we are owed. We are unpaid workers who save the Treasury billions of pounds every year' (p. 56).

Recent moves towards economic rationalism have also created new problems for people for disabilities in their determination to get wage justice. The rationalist call for increased levels of productivity, and the view that 'only those who do "productive" work deserve to live' (p. 59), has significant implications for people with disabilities. Furthermore, the demand on unwaged carers to support people with disabilities has decreased the potential of the carers to be economically productive (p. 59). This ideological push may be witnessed in the kind of courses that are now provided in the Technical and Further Education (TAFE) sector in Australia. Until recently, people with disabilities had a choice. If they wished to attend TAFE to study skills relating to their interests or to their unwaged work of caring for themselves or others, the option was there. Now such courses are considered to be the domain of community providers, and the TAFE system focuses purely on vocational education and training in line with the narrowly framed requirements of economic rationalism.

It is important though, not to overlook that there are significant gender implications in the applicability of the idea of unpaid work to women with disabilities. There is a perpetual conflict between the need for care, and the perception of woman as carers. It is taken as read in our society that women are nurturers by nature, and so women with disabilities are placed in what may only be described as a very peculiar position. As Rae (1993: 431) writes: 'This is very strange, because in all other aspects of our womanhood, womanliness in us is denied.' It is, perhaps, for this reason, that men with disabilities are more likely to receive the support of relatives, neighbours and community service providers than are women with disability. This, Rae argues, is also 'received wisdom' among women with disability.

Interestingly, even though it is generally assumed that women with disabilities will not, or should not, have children, they are taught how to housekeep, presumably in the expectation that they will care for others. 'It is extraordinary that society, at least the part of society who are service providers, who perceive disabled people as passive and helpless, absorb the belief that on the whole disabled women can "manage"' (p. 432). To request additional support frequently requires lengthy justification of why women need support now, when they appear to have managed in the past. Furthermore, if the woman happens to be married, or living with a male partner who is also disabled, then there are questions asked about the capacity of the woman to be in the 'caring wife role' (p. 432).

For women with disabilities then, there is a 'contested fragility' of adulthood and womanhood (Jenkins 1989, quoted in Walmsley 1993: 129). The roles that we traditionally associate with adulthood, such as wife, sexual partner, parent, paid worker and householder are held out as incentives; and are yet denied. At the same time, however, women with disabilities, like so many other women, are called on to perform the unpaid work of carers. Not only are they denied their basic human rights as adults, but they are exploited in the unpaid work they do, and marginalized in both the regular workforce and as women. That women with disabilities should be seen as requiring care, yet admonished for needing assistance is contradictory enough. That they should also frequently be called on to take the role of carer (Walmsley 1993), while being considered incompetent to care for their own children, is astonishing.

Disability and gayness

The significance of the issue of sexual orientation for people with disabilities is too readily overlooked when considering the articulation between disability and gender. Yet models of normalization, such as PASSING, encourage only 'heterosexual socialisation activities' (Wolfensberger and Glenn 1975, reported in Brown 1994: 128). Brown suggests that 'Sex education for people with learning disabilities tends to have focused on biological rather than social issues and to have assumed a heterosexist preference and a familial context for all relationships even where neither seems applicable to the person's current life or foreseeable future' (p. 131).

Furthermore, people with disabilities who show a preference for same-sex relationships face opposition on the grounds of normalization. There is, in fact, a cultural imperialism that demands that people with disabilities be 'more normal than normal'. The possibility of homosexuality is rendered invisible, possibly because to be homosexual further stereotypes people with disability as Other. 'Resisting heterosexist norms is problematical if you are visible in other ways' (Brown 1994: 136). It adds an additional edge to the idea of 'coming out', an edge that for many people with disabilities, is too difficult to bear. As Young so succinctly observes: 'The culturally dominated undergo a paradoxical oppression, in that they are both marked out by stereotypes and at the same time rendered invisible' (Young 1990: 59).

Yet both homosexuality and disability are socially constructed, and may be subject to reconsideration and restructuring. According to Young: 'Those living under cultural imperialism find themselves defined from the outside, positioned, placed, by a network of dominant meanings they experience as arising from elsewhere, from those with whom they do not identify and who do not identify with them' (p. 59).

Perhaps one of the most publicized cases of the unacceptability of the articulation of disability and lesbianism is that of a young American lesbian, Sharon Kowalski. Sharon was injured in a car accident, and both her communication and motor skills were seriously affected. Following the accident, there was a protracted and bitter legal guardianship battle between Sharon's father, and her lover. The issue was taken on board by both the disability movement, and the lesbian and feminist movements. Eventually, the decision that Sharon's father should have guardianship was reversed, and Sharon's lover was granted guardianship. In retrospect, it appears 'that her [Sharon's] parents would rather have contained and controlled her as an asexual person rather than accept her as a disabled lesbian' (Appleby 1994: 21).

For Corbett, this denial of the reality of people who are gay or lesbian, and disabled 'is a suffocation of what makes us exist as unique individuals. It disempowers and weakens us. To gain a proud label, we need to fight this denial and use the language of our 'actual identity . . . Language needs expression, not silence; substance, not shadows. Pride has to be audible and visible' (Corbett 1994: 347). Yet, she suggests, for people with disability, the 'impetus to pass' and assimilate at all costs 'carries a high price in terms of human suffering and frustration' (p. 348). It seems that for people with disability, the fear of exposure of their homosexuality may be even greater than it is for people without disability. 'Hiding our identities and presenting social masks is presented as an element of social decorum and an essential ingredient of social assimilation' (p. 348). To be homosexual, as well as a person with a disability, is to be doubly Other, and doubly oppressed.

Disability and social movements

Bearing in mind all that has already been said in this chapter, one would expect to find considerable support from the feminist and gay movements for the potential members who have disabilities. Yet, with limited exceptions, such as the Sharon Kowalski case, this has been far from the case. In fact, at times, it seems these social movements have actually gone out of their way to make life difficult for people with disabilities in their midst. When Appleby observes that 'Being disabled is a reflection of the power relationship that segregates some members of society by organising the environment only around the needs of its able bodied members' (Appleby 1994: 19), she might well have been reflecting specifically on the responses of the feminist organizations to women with disabilities, or the responses of the gay movement and organizations to gay men and lesbians with disability.

Not only are people with disabilities stereotyped as Other within mainstream society and organizations, but they also appear to be similarly stereotyped within social movements of groups who are otherwise themselves viewed as Other. When Gay Pride and other homosexual organizations, in response to oppression by dominant heterosexist viewpoints, create a safe social, intellectual and philosophical environment for homosexuals, it does less well in providing for its members who have disability. A brief glance through the gay press immediately confirms such a perspective.

In the Australian lesbian monthly, *Lesbians on the Loose* (August 1995), for example, Aboriginality, Grey Power, sex workers, women with HIV and IV drug users all get a mention. But despite a large number of feature articles on lesbians doing various unusual and interesting things, there is not one who has a visible disability. In the same issue, among the over 50 advertisements for lesbian-friendly entertainment, holiday accommodation, businesses and services, not one had information about physical accessibility. This was minimally compensated for by a side bar on the inside back cover that featured accessibility information for the various entertainment venues; but of the 26 Sydney venues named, only six were wheelchair accessible. Not only are lesbians with disability discriminated against through a silence about their existence in the feature and news articles, and by a failure of advertisers to acknowledge their existence, but it appears little thought has been put into ensuring lesbian social events are held in locations that are accessible.

Similarly, in a current edition of *Capital Q Weekly*, a Sydney gay and lesbian newspaper with wide circulation, there were no advertisements that specified physical accessibility. This is particularly surprising considering the amount of news coverage the paper contains around the issue of HIV/AIDS, which must be considered to be a variety of disability, as it is covered by the Australian Disability Discrimination Act. Many people in the later stages of AIDS-related illnesses are exceedingly frail, and access to services, venues and so on is an issue. But perhaps, once again, it is assumed that these people will not want to access such services.

This form of oppression and exclusion is not distinctively Australian, of course. It is an international issue. Lucy, a lesbian with a disability, has perhaps thrown some light on the issue. She claimed that members of the lesbian movement assumed her to be asexual firstly, and that discos were held in venues that were not physically accessible. According to Lucy: 'Disability means weakness, and the whole focus of building a lesbian community is about women uniting in strength. It's a strength thing and uniting in power, and presenting as powerful. Basically disability issues aren't about strength' (quoted in Appleby 1994: 23). For Lucy, as for myriad lesbians with disability, there was support in rhetoric, but not in reality.

However, if the gay movement has failed to meet the needs of people with disabilities, the women's movement has done no better. 'Lest it be assumed at this point that the true home for disabled women is located within the women's movement, it is necessary to restate the reality: non-disabled feminists have consistently failed to recognize disability issues' (Lloyd 1992: 213). The academic disability journals are full of articles written by women with disabilities bemoaning the failure of the feminist movements to adopt the cause of women with disabilities (Keith 1992; Lloyd 1992; Morris 1992). Lloyd (1992) goes so far as to say: 'The charge can justifiably be levied at non-disabled feminists that their "blindness" in relation to disability issues has contributed to disabled women finding the disability movement more hospitable than the women's movement' (p. 213). She does, however, admit that the disability movement also fails to embrace adequately the needs of women. For women with disability, this is an invidious double bind. Within the women's movement, they are invisible as disabled; within the disability movement, they are invisible as women.

Inevitably, what this means is that women with disabilities essentially remain invisible and silent, condemned to the status of Other. And in a very real sense, this is a self-perpetuating situation. If women with disabilities remain silent, or indeed silenced, then neither the feminists, nor the disability movement will see the need to seek out their opinions and voices. 'This lack of a voice, of the representation of our subjective reality, means that it is difficult for non-disabled feminists to incorporate our reality into their research, their theories, unless it is in terms of the way the non-disabled world sees us' (Morris 1992: 161).

This is not, however, to deny the value of the work done by both the disability movement and the women's movement. As Keith (1992: 173) writes: 'Feminist theory has given us some useful concepts to help us understand the ways in which women are oppressed and marginalised and have their world defined by others. They have shown how this oppression isn't inevitable, that it has consequences for *everyone* in society and must be changed.' However, these understandings of women's oppression have certainly not been based on the experiences of women with disabilities, any more than they have been based on the experiences of black women. They grow, instead, out of a white, middle-class, and able-bodied view of the world.

What does the future hold?

It is Yeatman's contention that 'Multiple interests in emancipation have tabled difference as a central axiom in the contemporary politics of justice. Not only do the various emancipatory movements have to accept each other's presence, but they have to work with this presence as part of their *internal* politics' (Yeatman 1993: 228). Yet in relation to the articulation of disability with gender, it would seem that difference and diversity have at best been undervalued, and at worst, deliberately repressed. Despite the emergence of 'new cultural boundaries and spaces . . . crisscrossed with a diversity of Otherness' (Giroux 1993: 100), and despite the contestation of oppressive notions of representation, cultural imperialism prevails.

People with disabilities, when making decisions about sexuality and gender, continue to experience the uneasy paradox of invisibility combined with overt Otherness. Groups otherwise marginal themselves, such as the women's movement, the gay movement and the disability movement, take the dominant position, and thus render invisible women with disabilities, and homosexual men with disabilities. Emancipatory intent, in the case of these social movements, cannot be assumed to be generally applied. 'This, then, is the injustice of cultural imperialism: that the oppressed group's own experience and interpretation of social life finds little expression that touches the dominant culture, while the same culture imposes on the oppressed group its experience and interpretation of social life' (Young 1990: 60).

It is no longer acceptable for social movements with transformational intent to continue to oppress marginalized groups within their potential membership. The politics of difference demands that emancipatory movements contest the oppression of people with disabilities, and move towards 'an inclusive politics of voice and representation' (Yeatman 1993: 231). A recognition of the need to value diversity and difference in matters of disability, gender and sexuality must not be viewed as secondary to the emancipatory intent of social movements. The dislocating fragmentation of the cultural landscape, constitutes, as Hall argues, a '"crisis of identity" for the individual' (Hall 1992: 275). For people with disabilities, coming out of school into society at large is difficult enough, but coming out as gendered adults is even more difficult. More difficult still, however, is the coming out of fear and oppression. This, however, should be seen as the way forward.

References

Appleby, Y. (1994) Out in the margins, *Disability and Society*, 9(1): 19–32.

Booth, W. and Booth, T. (1993) Accentuate the positive: a personal profile of a parent with learning difficulties, *Disability, Handicap and Society*, 8(4): 377–92.

Brown, H. (1994) 'An ordinary sexual life?': a review of the normalisation principle as it applies to the sexual options of people with learning disabilities, *Disability and Society*, 9(2): 123–44.

Capital Q Weekly, Issue 151, 18 August 1995.

Corbett, J. (1994) A proud label: exploring the relationship between disability politics and gay pride, *Disability and Society*, 9(3): 343–57.

Giroux, H. (1993) *Living Dangerously. Multiculturalism and the Politics of Difference*. New York: Peter Lang.

Gunew, S. (1993) Feminism and the politics of irreducible differences: multi-culturalism/ethnicity/race, in S. Gunew and A. Yeatman (eds) *Feminism and the Politics of Difference*. Sydney: Allen and Unwin.

Hall, S. (1992) The question of cultural identity, in S. Hall, D. Held and T. McGew *Modernity and Its Futures*. Cambridge: Polity, in association with Basil Blackwell and the Open University.

Hanna, W. and Rogovsky, B. (1991) Women with disabilities: two handicaps plus, *Disability, Handicap and Society*, 6(1): 49–64.

Keith, L. (1992) Who cares wins? Women, caring and disability, *Disability, Handicap and Society*, 7(2): 167–75.

Lesbians on the Loose, August 1995, 6(8).

Lloyd, M. (1992) 'Does she boil eggs?' Towards a feminist model of disability, *Disability, Handicap and Society*, 7(3): 207–21.

Morris, J. (1992) Personal and political: a feminist perspective on researching physical disability, *Disability, Handicap and Society*, 7(2): 157–66.

Rae, A. (1993) Independent living, personal assistance and disabled women – the double bind? *Disability, Handicap and Society*, 8(4): 431–3.

Walmsley, J. (1993) Contradictions in caring: reciprocity and interdependence, *Disability, Handicap and Society*, 8(2): 129–39.

WinVisible (1994) Women with disabilities count our unwaged work, *Australian Disability Review*, 3(94): 55–62.

Yeatman, A. (1993) Voice and representation in the politics of difference, in S. Gunew and A. Yeatman (eds) *Feminism and the Politics of Difference*. Sydney: Allen and Unwin.

Young, I. M. (1990) *Justice and the Politics of Difference*. Princeton, NJ: Princeton University Press.

'The ideology of expertism': the framing of special education and racial equality policies in the local state

Introduction

In this chapter we want to look at the way 'social justice' informs the educational discourse of 'special education'. Our particular interest is in the way this discourse is framed within local state policies. We intend to show that the understanding of social justice which figures in this discourse has deleterious consequences for the development, organization and provision of special education. In this context, local state policies for special education are especially apposite because they exemplify the continuing prevalence of 'the ideology of expertism' (Young 1990: 80). This is a distinctly liberal approach which emphasizes 'needs', 'vulnerabilities' and 'deficiencies'. Our concern is that local state policies in this area legitimate a deficit, perhaps pathological, and certainly individualized, conception of 'special education'.

This emphasis on 'private troubles' rather than 'public issues' (Wright Mills 1959) in special education contrasts sharply with certain other educational discourses which are also operationalized within the local state. Consider, for instance, racial equality. There, individualism and the 'ideology of expertism' have far less of a grip on understandings of, and the mobilization against racism within local settings. Rather, the discourse here articulates, ostensibly at least, with a concern for the rights and entitlements of minority *groups* perceived as racially or ethnically different (Troyna and Williams 1986; Ball and Solomos 1990).

Our analysis crystallizes around the conviction that social justice is differentially packaged by the local state in its policies for special education and racial equality. In the former, there is a firm, unequivocal commitment to social justice as a means of redistributing scarce resources to 'needy' individuals. In the latter, the alleged commitment is to compensate members of perceived racial minority groups, *qua* group members, who have suffered racist discrimination in education, historically and currently. However, it is our contention in this chapter that these differences in the conception and articulation of social justice are not as profound as they first appear. Indeed, they exist largely at the level of political rhetoric.

We will illustrate our arguments both empirically and theoretically. Empirically, by referring to our respective studies of special education and racial equality in England and Wales; theoretically, by drawing on the work of Iris Marion Young who, in her book, *Justice and the Politics of Difference* (1990), questions prevailing ideologies of social justice, especially as they operate in, and are legitimated by, the workings of the state.

Special education and social justice

In this section, we want to concentrate on the way in which special education is understood in a specific context: that of the local state. The local state is, of course, a 'site of struggle' between competing ideologies and political perspectives (Ben Tovim *et al.* 1986; Troyna and Williams 1986; Dale 1989). Nonetheless, laying aside for a moment differences between localities, it is possible to say that, within the local state, special education is organized and administered by welfare professionals who claim a right to define problems and formulate solutions. This right is justified on the basis of their professional knowledge and training, or what Patrick McAuslan calls 'the ideology of public interest' (1980: 2; see also Yeatman 1990; Cole and Furbey 1994). Paul Wilding's view is that the pre-eminence of professional knowledge and training leads to

a depoliticising of social problems, treating them rather as personal problems susceptible to individual solutions by experts. The growth of a host of helping professions has implicitly propagated the notion that the problems with which they deal could be solved within the existing pattern of economic and social relations, that such problems were marginal, technical and susceptible to solution by appropriate prescriptions of modern medicine or the latest planning, educational or social work orthodoxies.

(Wilding 1982: 63)

In the specific area of special education, this process of depoliticization and concomitant reliance on 'individual solutions' is writ large. Here, after all, the professional imperative is to compensate for the perceived 'inadequacies' of children with 'special needs'. Several critics of this perspective (Abberley

1987; Sigmon 1987; Barton and Oliver 1992) argue that it articulates with a model of disability as

> a medical problem, belonging to the individual concerned, which needs treating, curing or at least ameliorating. It is fundamental to the philosophy of segregation which separates young children from each other on the basis of their medical diagnoses, and then designs a curriculum which is aimed at 'normalizing' the child as far as possible.
>
> (Mason 1992: 223)

Mike Oliver (1986) develops this argument by suggesting that 'disability', in terms of its effect upon the individual, is seen as a personal tragedy. As a result, the disabled person is positioned as one who is in need of charity which is provided and administered within the welfare capitalist system. In this scenario, the state projects itself as a benign influence, committed to the amelioration of 'private troubles'. Sally Tomlinson characterizes this relationship between the state and the individual as 'benevolent humanitarianism'. She sees this as an ideology sustaining the creation and maintenance of a separate system of provision, either for children with disabilities, or for those who are experiencing difficulties in learning. Such a system, according to Tomlinson, constitutes an 'instance of the obligation placed upon civilised society to care for its *weaker* members' (Tomlinson 1982: 5, emphasis added).

Thomas Skrtic (1991) extends the insights provided by Tomlinson's analysis. In *Behind Special Education*, he identifies functionalism and liberalism as the dominant values that characterize special education. He defines a 'functionalist world view' as stressing a conservative, technicist approach to the management of change. He concludes:

> True to both the functionalist and liberal ideologies, justice for the special education community historically has been based on accepting the inevitability of the status quo in public education, whilst at the same time seeking rational-technical progress in the form of quantitative and bureaucratic solutions to educational inequities. Thus for the special education community, progress toward a just educational system is calculated in terms of identifying more students as disabled and securing for them more rights, resources and participation within the general education system.
>
> (Skrtic 1991: 107)

These ideologies contribute to a view of social justice that emphasizes the achievement of equality through 'enabling' individuals; that is, through the allocation of additional provision and resources to support 'vulnerable' individuals in the quest for equality of opportunity.

The veracity of Tomlinson's and Skrtic's analyses can be seen in the nature of professional support for the integration of a select group of 'special needs' children into the mainstream. The position which these professionals adopt is rationalized, as we have already suggested, in terms of equality of opportunity; that is, some of those children – especially those with physical or sensory disabilities or mild learning difficulties – should be educated in mainstream schools, not segregated into special schools. It is contended that segregation from the educational and social experiences of mainstream school life is seen as stigmatizing for children and liable to result in inequality of outcomes.

On the face of it, this proposal for integration seems commendable. However, as Barton and Tomlinson (1984) argue, a process which integrates a few relatively easily accommodated individuals into the mainstream is limited, for three reasons in particular. First, because 'integration' is a reformist strategy which fails to address the ways in which the curriculum is presented and learning is organized. Second, it is an *exclusive* conception of integration, selecting only those pupils who are least likely to cause disruption to the *status quo*. Third, it fails to mitigate, let alone acknowledge, other structural inequalities based on class, gender and ethnicity. In this analysis, 'integration' is a statist approach which flatters to deceive. It can only scratch the surface of inequalities and injustice based, in this instance, on notions of 'ability' and 'disability'.

However, critics such as Barton and Tomlinson have made relatively little impact on the prevailing discourses of special education which inform the work of professionals in the local state. Instead, as Skrtic (1991) noted earlier, energy has gone into improving the systems and bureaucracies responsible for the administration of special education predicated on these dubious, some might say, offensive grounds (see also Johnstone 1993).

'Special ed.' in practice

We now want to provide some empirical examples of the ways in which the hegemonic status of the 'ideology of expertism' is expressed in special education.

A good place to start is with the 1994 *Code of Practice* which forms the government's guidance on special education in England and Wales. This had been promised by the 1993 Education Act which is itself intended to support and extend the restructuring of the education system which the Conservative Party started with the 1988 Education Reform Act (Riddell and Brown 1994). The Code of Practice lays down a framework for all schools and local education authorities (LEAs) to follow in identifying, assessing and providing for 'children with special educational needs'. It represents what Skrtic (1991) describes as a 'rational-technical' initiative designed to make the bureaucracy function more efficiently and distribute resources more effectively. It does

not, however, question the definitions and assumptions of 'special educational need', 'learning difficulty', or 'statementing'. Consequently, the
intrinsic values and principles which structure the prevailing discourse of
'special education', and which guide its associated practices, remain sacro-
sanct. It follows from what we have already said that the Code defers to the
'ideology of expertism' in its reproduction of dominant professional
concerns. As a corollary, it overlooks the way in which structural inequalities
mould and distort relationships between individuals and groups (CCCS
1981; Walkerdine 1983).

John Wright's (1994) anxieties about the resourcing of special education
draw attention to another way in which the 'ideology of expertism' assumes
centre-stage. He insists that as local government continues to struggle with
budgetary constraints, the primary concern for professional officers is with
the 'fair' distribution of resources and their equal allocation, irrespective of
the results. His fear is that this will result in some children, who have
statements of special educational need, failing to receive the resources
detailed on that statement, and that any shortcomings in provision will be
justified in terms of what he calls the professionals' ' "in time of famine,
spread it thin" model' (Wright 1994: 9).

Wright's concern about the conception of equality of opportunity which
guides professional 'experts' criteria for funding special education is well
founded. In the context of the resourcing of special education, equality of
opportunity is defined by what Dixon (1991) calls 'horizontal equity'. This
involves the establishment of allegedly 'objective' rules and regulations which
are procedurally just and equitable, and therefore, ostensibly, fair to all.

A recent study (Vincent *et al.* 1994, 1995) of the effects of school-based
management and delegation of funding on special education explored further
professionals' understanding of equality of opportunity and how this defines
the organization of special education in the local state. The research
comprised interviews with local education authority officers, elected politicians, teachers and governors. We want to highlight two of the issues arising
from this study.

To begin with, the majority of personnel in the local education authorities
did not appear to make explicit links between special education and their
local equal opportunities policies. Even where such links were made, special
education was still treated as separate and different. However, this false
dichotomy was not entirely lost on some of the respondents. In 'Jaston', one
of the LEAs in the study, the head of the learning support services told the
researchers that local teachers had begun to realize that the authority's equal
opportunities policy had been artificially compartmentalized:

> Teachers in [Jaston] have got very used to equal opportunities as far as
> race goes when one talks about pupils, and have also gone a long way
> towards equal opportunities as far as gender goes . . . They're accepting

that disability special needs hasn't really been part of that policy up to now, but that it should be.

A second issue arising from the study was that, in reflecting on their roles, professionals believed that equality of opportunity for children with perceived 'special needs' would be best achieved by their 'benign' intervention. In 'Morton', for instance, the Chair of the Education Committee described the LEA's special education services as follows:

> In [this policy document] it says people who are vulnerable and in need, we should take care of them. That's going to be useful because I'm going to have to go back to the [city council] for more money on the special needs situation . . . [The policy document] sounds alright. It's about fairness and all these sort of things . . . At the end of the day, the most vulnerable are the special needs [children].

A special education officer in 'Hillshire', another LEA in the study, described his councillors' attitude towards special education in similar terms:

> Within the majority group [of elected politicians] the view is, you know, that we delegate as much [funding] as possible, if not absolutely everything . . . [but] with the Chairs that I've worked with, it seems to me there's always been almost a protectiveness [about special education], that's probably the wrong word, that's perhaps too paternalistic, but a feeling that [LEA control] is the best way to deliver services, and we need to protect that in some way, and therefore we'll resist delegating [the special education budget] for as long as possible.

Not only do these views offer an insight into how equality of opportunity is understood within the professional discourse of special education, they also strengthen one of our earlier points: that special education is seen by local professional officers and elected politicians in paternalistic terms, with the children regarded as vulnerable and in need of care and protection. To repeat: this is the language not of 'rights' and 'equality', but of 'benevolent humanitarianism', largesse and protection for those individuals who seemingly cannot fight for themselves.

Paradigms of social justice

The 'ideology of expertism' as operationalized by special education professionals draws on a definition of equality which resonates closely with what Iris Marion Young terms the *distributive* paradigm of social justice. Accordingly, its primary concerns are issues of resourcing and access. As Young notes:

> The paradigm assumes a single model for all analyses of justice: all situations in which justice is at issue are analogous to the situation of

persons dividing a stock of goods and comparing the size of the portions individuals have. Such a model implicitly assumes that individuals or other agents lie as nodes, points in the social field, among whom larger or smaller bundles of social goods are assigned.

(Young 1990: 18)

In this setting the emphasis is very much on the potential capacity of individual rights to deliver social justice. Young claims that this obsession obscures a consideration of broader questions about 'the social structure and institutional context that often help determine distributive patterns' (Young 1990: 15; also Corson 1993).

Bob Connell's (1993) analysis of the term 'social justice' complements Young's critique and extends it to the field of education. He shares the view that the distributive paradigm draws undue attention to the allocation of the 'social good' (i.e. education). By this he means that the efficacy of various reformist measures, such as compensatory education and the statementing process, are designed to ensure a more equitable distribution of the 'social good'. It is this that tends to dominate discussions about social justice and education while debates about the nature of the 'social good' itself take place in an entirely separate context, that of curriculum theory, teaching method and the psychology of learning. In an argument which elaborates upon Barton and Tomlinson's (1984) more specific concerns about integration, Connell suggests that the problem with the distributive model of 'social justice' in education is 'its indifference to the nature of education itself'. He continues: 'education is a social process in which the "how much" cannot be separated from the "what". *There is an inescapable link between distribution and content*' (Connell 1993: 18, emphasis added).

We have seen that the distributive paradigm of social justice is accorded hegemonic status in special education. We have also implied that it constitutes a restricted and restrictive framework. Restricted because it privileges a concern with 'who gets what'; restrictive because it brackets out questions about the nature of the 'what' and the influences which are brought to bear upon it.

In contrast to the distributive paradigm, Young argues in favour of conceptions of justice (and citizenship) in relation to heterogeneous and differentiated communities. She suggests that differentiation on the various axes of oppression (such as class, gender, age, disability, ethnicity, sexuality and perceived racial group), generate distinct versions of what 'justice' looks like. Young concludes that concepts of domination and oppression, not the concept of distribution, should be the starting point for a politics of social justice. This means giving priority to the analysis of social structures and institutional contexts which influence the nature of distribution. This is Young's reasoning:

While distributive issues are important concerns of social justice, an approach that focuses solely on distribution tends to obscure questions of the justice of social institutions (that are) at least as important as distributions. . . . Insofar as this paradigm of justice limits evaluation to distribution, ignoring and obscuring questions of the justice of institutional organisation, it serves an ideological function; it implicitly supports the institutional relations it assumes as given.

(Young 1990: 198)

We now want to spend some time looking at local state policies on racial equality in education. This affords us the opportunity to see how far Young's alternative paradigm of social justice has impacted upon policymakers' understandings of *racial* justice.

Racial justice in education

Britain in the 1990s is experiencing a backlash against the promotion and affirmation of anti-discriminatory policies and legislation (see Troyna and Carrington 1990; Troyna 1993). In Kate Myers's view, the 1990s constitute a period of 'equiphobia', where there is a prevailing and 'irrational hatred and fear of anything to do with equal opportunities' (1990: 295). This contrasts with the previous decade when Britain witnessed a proliferation of local state policies geared towards questions of racial inequality. What distinguished a number of these policies from their predecessors of the 1970s was their support for anti-racist rather than multicultural education (Troyna 1993). Ostensibly, they sought to deal not only with issues of access and curricular reform, but also to expose and challenge those structures and assumptions which perpetuate racist discrimination in education and beyond. One of the distinctive features of the anti-racist discourse has been its emphasis on collective rights. In contrast to special education, therefore, locally developed anti-racist education policies tend to show less concern with individual rights. The centrality accorded to 'institutional racism' and cognate radical terms in these policies is testimony to the exceptional nature of the anti-racist discourse.

In their analysis of LEA policies on anti-racist education in the 1980s, Troyna and Williams (1986) found clear evidence of the local state's enthusiasm for the language of radicalism. The research also revealed the extent to which local professional officers and politicians believed that their policies constituted an accurate reflection of the views of local black activists, parents and their children as expressed through local consultative processes (see also Gibson 1987). These were policies which were said to pay close attention to the 'real', rather than perceived injustices experienced by members of local black communities. There was no place here, it seemed, for the 'ideology of expertism' or the 'depoliticization' of the 'social problem' of racism (Wilding 1982). The commitment appeared to be to viewing 'race' and racism as 'public issues' not 'private troubles', to return once again to the terms coined by Wright Mills (1959).

It is undoubtedly the case that these policies gave some authority, support and legitimacy to those working in schools and colleges who were committed to initiating changes along anti-racist lines. Furthermore, the policies generated unprecedented debate around the subject of 'race' and education within the local state. Robin Richardson, one of the pioneering influences in local state initiatives on anti-racist education, assessed the value of these policies in the following terms:

> First, they may facilitate the provision of new, or a redistribution of existing resources for the development of multicultural/antiracist initiatives in the local context. Second, policies may lead to desired structural, procedural and cognitive changes in the local education department and committee. Third, they may constitute a valuable resource for teachers already engaged in integrating multicultural/ antiracist perspectives into their routine practices and who wish to mobilise the concern and involvement of others in the process. Finally, pressure groups may use the policy statement as a campaigning instrument.
>
> (cited in Troyna and Ball 1985: 166)

However, while acknowledging the value of policies couched in the language of anti-racism, it is difficult to avoid the conclusion that many suffered from delusions of grandeur. Indeed, micropolitical analyses of settings in which these policies emerged revealed several weaknesses in the status and efficacy of the policies and the practice they encouraged. We want to draw attention to three of these weaknesses.

First, and despite protestations to the contrary, the consultative process was often superficial and perfunctory. Consequently, the policies operated in a political vacuum, abstracted from the political struggles taking place 'outside' local town halls. Careful analysis of the consultations which took place showed that local state bureaucrats tended to operate with different criteria of success from others within the local 'race policy environment' (Saggar 1991; see also Gibson 1987; Ball and Solomos 1990). On the basis of his research in two local authorities, Shamit Saggar concluded that 'success from the point of view of the local authority administration often leads to failure in the eyes of other policy actors, including ethnic minority activists' (1991: 153). More recently, Hatcher, Troyna and Gewirtz (1996) identified a similar disparity in expectations within the local race policy environment (RPE) in 'Woodshire' LEA, as local state bureaucrats attempted to adjust their policy on 'race' in the light of the 1988 Education Reform Act. The LEA initiatives were strongly condemned by other members of the RPE, especially black activists and representatives from the local Racial Equality Council. It seems, therefore, that the 'ideology of expertism' *has* been endorsed and reproduced by local racial equality policies, although in less pronounced forms than those revealed in special education policies.

Another weakness of local anti-racist education policies of the 1980s centred on the conception of 'municipal anti-racism' within which such education policies figured prominently. Paul Gilroy, one of the more vociferous leftist critics of this reformist initiative, questionned what he regarded as the vacuous concept of racism on which these policies were predicated. He argued against the approach, common to these initiatives and policies, which saw racism as a superficial feature of British society, an

> unfortunate excresence on a democratic polity which is essentially sound, and . . . with the right ideological tools and political elbow grease, racism can be dealt with once and for all, leaving the basic structures and relations of the British economy and society essentially unchanged.
>
> (Gilroy 1990: 195)

One final and crucial observation about the nature and thrust of these so-called radical policies on 'race' is that they showed a disinclination to challenge the liberal conception of social justice. Behind the rhetoric (or 'symbolic political language' to use Murray Edelman's (1964) term) of anti-racism lay a policy which operated with a model of social justice firmly based on the distributive paradigm. In this sense, the anti-racist statements shared with special education policies an obsession with 'who gets what'. Troyna and Williams (1986) showed that for local state bureaucrats, 'racial justice' could only exist in an educational context which was either 'colour blind' or self-consciously non-discriminatory. Whichever course of action the local state bureaucrats chose to underwrite in their policies, the message was clear: there is a need for ameliorative action by the school, the local state, perhaps even the national state. And this action often demanded a redistribution of scarce resources.

We have highlighted some of the limitations of 'municipal racism' and the education policies which it spawned. But we do not want to be nihilistic in our appraisal of these policies. Although those involved in the framing and diffusion of racial equality policies in the 1980s were constrained by political expedience and professional defensiveness they did, nonetheless, assign lay members of the local community some role in the nexus of decision-making. We recognize that their actions in this regard were driven more by the pressure applied by groups of ethnic minority activists and parents (see Carter 1986; Troyna and Williams 1986 for discussion) than by a determination to diffuse power. However, the net result of these political developments constituted a significant challenge to the sanctity of the 'ideology of expertism' in the way race-related matters were handled in these settings. Therefore, while these local state initiatives in participation and consultation were circumscribed by micro- and macropolitical considerations, they went some way towards questionning professionals' understandings of social justice, by introducing new perspectives into the debate. In short, political pragmatism and occupational self-interest combined to ensure that local state policy-makers involved in racial equality policies and practices realized only some of the ambitions associated with a participatory ethos. However, the process was a step in the right direction.

Conclusion

So to what extent do the lessons learnt from municipal anti-racism provide the basis for an alternative strategy within special education? Put another way, how can special education be freed from the 'ideology of expertism' without falling into the trap of an overreliance on symbolic political language and perfunctory consultation processes?

In the same way that we highlighted the key role of the 'outside' activists and parents in altering the 'ideology of expertism' in relation to racial equality, we see a similar potential for challenging professional approaches towards special education lying with voluntary groups campaigning in this area. There are signs that parent groups active in special education are no longer obsessed simply with issues of distribution and resourcing and are increasingly assertive and confrontational as they begin to challenge the ways in which their children have been defined and categorized. For example, local voluntary groups, such as the London-based Parents in Partnership, have tackled entrenched professional notions of 'ability' and 'disability' by lobbying local councils and by making a determined effort to ensure that their voice is heard in the policy-making process (Mason 1992). These efforts are replicated in the activities of other local parent groups, operating alone or as part of loosely federated national organizations (e.g. the British Dyslexia Association and the Down's Syndrome Association) who have won themselves a place in local decision-making processes. In 'Midshire' LEA, for instance, an alliance between schools, voluntary groups and activists campaigning on educational provision for autistic and deaf children proved a powerful combination. Consequently, the LEA has established a regular liaison group which consults with the voluntary groups on all aspects of LEA special education policy (personal communication). At present, however, the activities of these voluntary groups tend to be fragmented and uncoordinated, and their political influence both transitory and diffuse. Nevertheless, they remain the primary mechanism through which parents can collectively influence the organization and provision of special education in local settings.

These *collective*, grassroots endeavours to challenge the 'ideology of expertism' contrast with central government's recent attempts to enhance parental influence and participation. Initiatives such as the Parents Charter (DES 1991) concentrate on 'enabling' *individual* parents to contest the status of professional discretion. More specific examples of central government's strategy with regard to special education can be found in the 1993 Education Act and the accompanying Code of Practice. These recommend that local authorities institute 'named persons' to act as independent sources of advice and support to parents whose children are undergoing statutory assessment. The Special Education Tribunal, also established by the 1993 Act, is an independent forum where individual parents can challenge local authority decisions. Functioning within the distributive paradigm, the Tribunal concerns itself primarily with issues of resourcing and provision for children designated as being in need of 'special education'.

All in all, then, and despite their incursions in some localities, collective campaigns which parents have organized in this sphere of education remain structurally peripheral to and marginalized by the direction and nature of decision and policy-making process in special education. Parent groups which operate in a collective fashion currently lack the political clout either to undermine or reorientate recent conceptions of (and provision for) special education.

Within this somewhat bleak scenario we remain convinced that collective action organized by parent groups foreshadows the emergence of more effective and coordinated attempts to subvert the 'ideology of expertism'. This would not be entirely without precedent as our discussion of racial equality initiatives in the local state testifies. Furthermore, as we noted earlier, the local state is a 'site of struggle' and in these circumstances there remains the potential for closer alliances between professionals, parents and their children in attempts to challenge the hegemonic status of the 'ideology of expertism'. This scenario presumes a 'dynamic as opposed to deterministic relationship between different social interests' (Armstrong 1995: 126) which, in this context, refers to professional and lay interpretations of how alternative forms of social justice might be advanced through special education. For some this might seem a forlorn expectation, but we suggest that to think otherwise is to submit to political quiescence and the language of defeatism.

References

Abberley, P. (1987) The concept of oppression and the development of a social theory of disability, *Disability, Handicap and Society*, 2(1): 5–19.
Armstrong, D. (1995) *Power and Partnership in Education*. London: Routledge.
Ball, W. and Solomos, J. (eds) (1990) *Race and Local Politics*. London: Macmillan.
Barton, L. and Oliver, M. (1992) Special needs: personal trouble or public issue? in M. Arnot and L. Barton (eds) *Voicing Concerns*. Oxford: Triangle Books.
Barton, L. and Tomlinson, S. (eds) (1984) *Special Education and Social Interests*. London: Croom Helm.

Ben-Tovim, G., Gabriel, J., Law, I. and Stredder, K. (1986) *The Local Politics of Race*. London: Methuen.

Carter, T. (1986) *Shattering Illusions*. London: Lawrence and Wishart.

CCCS [Centre for Contemporary Cultural Studies] (1981) *Unpopular Education*. London: Hutchinson.

Cole, I. and Furbey, R. (1994) *The Eclipse of Council Housing*. London: Routledge.

Connell, R. (1993) *Schools and Social Justice*. Philadelphia, PA: Temple University Press.

Corson, D. (1993) *Language, Minority Education, and Gender*. Clevedon: Multi-lingual Matters.

Dale, R. (1989) *The State and Education Policy*. Milton Keynes: Open University Press.

Department for Education and Science [DES] (1991) *The Parents Charter*. London: HMSO.

Dixon, R. (1991) Repercussions of LMS, *Educational Management and Administration*, 19(1): 52–61.

Edelman, M. (1964) *The Symbolic Uses of Politics*. Urbana, IL: University of Illinois Press.

Gibson, D. (1987) Hearing and listening: a case study of the consultation process undertaken by a local education department and black groups, in B. Troyna (ed.) *Racial Inequality in Education*. London: Tavistock Press.

Gilroy, P. (1990) The end of anti-racism, in W. Ball and J. Solomos (eds) *Race and Local Politics*. London: Macmillan.

Hatcher, R., Troyna, B. and Gewirtz, D. (1996) *The Local Management of Schools and Racial Equality*. Stoke-on-Trent: Trentham Books.

Johnstone, P. (1993) Critical view 1, in P. Johnstone and J. Perry, The social justice of mainstreaming students with disabilities: two critical views, in A. Reid and B. Johnson (eds) *Critical Issues in Australian Education in the 1990s*. Adelaide: University of South Australia Education Department.

Mason, M. (1992) The Integration Alliance: background and manifesto, in T. Booth, W.Swann, M. Masterton and P. Potts (eds) *Policies for Diversity in Education*. London: Open University/Routledge.

McAuslan, P. (1980) *The Ideologies of Planning Law*. Oxford: Pergamon Press.

Myers, K. (1990) Review of 'Equal Opportunities in the New ERA', *Education*, 5 October: 295.

Oliver, M. (1986) Social policy and disability: some theoretical issues, *Disability, Handicap and Society*, 1(1): 5–18.

Riddell, S. and Brown, S. (eds) (1994) *Special Needs Policies into the '90s: Warnock in the Market Place*. London: Routledge.

Saggar, S. (1991) *Race and Public Policy*. Aldershot: Avebury Press.

Sigmon, S. (1987) *Radical Analysis of Special Education*. London: Falmer.

Skrtic, T. (1991) *Behind Special Education*. Denver, CO: Love.

Tomlinson, S. (1982) *A Sociology of Special Education*. London: Routledge and Kegan Paul.

Troyna, B. (1993) *Racism and Education: Research Perspectives*. Buckingham: Open University Press.

Troyna, B. and Ball, W. (1985) Styles of LEA policy intervention in multicultural/antiracist education, *Educational Review*, 17(2): 165–75.

Troyna, B. and Carrington, C. (1990) *Education, Racism and Reform*. London: Routledge.

Troyna, B. and Williams, J. (1986) *Racism, Education and the State*. Beckenham: Croom Helm.

Vincent, C., Evans, J., Lunt, I. and Young, P. (1994) The market forces? the effect of Local Management of Schools on special educational needs provision, *British Educational Research Journal*, 20(3): 261–77.

Vincent, C., Evans, J., Lunt, I. and Young, P. (1995) Policy and practice: the changing nature of special educational provision in schools, *British Journal of Special Education*, 22(1): 4–11.

Walkerdine, V. (1983) It's only natural: rethinking child-centred pedagogy, in A. M. Wolpe and J. Donald (eds) *Is There Anyone Here From Education?* London: Pluto Press.

Wilding, P. (1982) *Professional Power and Social Welfare*. London: Routledge and Kegan Paul.

Wright, J. (1994) Crumbs! Is that all? *Special Children*, 73: 9–10.

Wright Mills, C. (1959) *The Sociological Imagination*. Oxford: Oxford University Press.

Yeatman, A. (1990) *Bureaucrats, Technocrats, Femocrats*. Sydney: Allen and Unwin.

Young, I. M. (1990) *Justice and the Politics of Difference*. Princeton, NJ: Princeton University Press.

Equity requires inclusion: the future for all students with disabilities

Equity in education is a term used in relation to racial and language minorities, women and the poor. Generally, it has not been applied to students with disabilities. In part, this reflects the general societal attitude toward issues of disability. Also, it is a general belief that students with disabilities have special needs as a function of their handicaps, therefore special treatment is appropriate. A part of that special treatment is the special education system.

Funk (1987), a founder of the Disability Rights Education and Defense Fund (DREDF), links these points:

> organized society, its decision makers, and program and policy implementors do not understand the concepts of integration and equal opportunity as it relates to the inclusion and participation of disabled adults and children in the social, political, and economic mainstream. This unwillingness or inability to understand and utilize these concepts as they apply to disabled adults and children is rooted in the overriding influence of the persisting images of disabled people as deviant, incompetent, unhealthy objects of fear who are perpetually dependent upon the welfare and charity of others; and the resulting inability of society to view the confirmed exclusion, segregation, and denial of equal opportunity as unlawful and harmful discrimination.
>
> The myriad of disability-specific programs and policies, the segregation of disabled people, the inability to gain access to organized society, *to experience an integrated and adequate education*, to obtain meaningful employment, and to socially interact and participate has resulted in a politically powerless and diffuse class of people who are unable to coalesce with other groups of disabled people on common issues, to vote, to be seen or heard. This class has accepted the stigma and cause of second-class citizenship and the incorrect judgment of social inferiority.

The concepts of equal opportunity and integration must be based on the reality of the differing needs and potential of people who are disabled. Thus equal opportunity must be defined as providing each individual with the chance to achieve, to develop their abilities and potential to the fullest.

(Funk 1987: 23, emphasis added)

The continuation of the current special education system – separate and unequal – violates these standards. Put affirmatively, honouring the fundamental rights of children with disabilities *requires* that they be provided effective educational opportunities in the mainstream of the educational system. This is the meaning of the current status of the law, the necessary condition for the full participation as contributing members of persons with disabilities in the life of the society, and the obligations of decency and morality. And, it is in keeping with the current capacity of school systems.

Background

The history of public education in the United States can be seen as the progressive inclusion of groups of students. In the colonial period, publicly provided education, in one or another colony, excluded youth based upon their gender, religion, colour, class (that is whether their parents were property owners), as well as disability. Over the course of the history of the republic, each of these exclusions was removed. The last of these was disability.

Increasingly in the years following *Brown*, parents of children with disabilities fought to have their children provided publicly funded education. This struggle culminated with the passage in 1975 of PL 94–142, The Education of All Handicapped Children Act. The most important word in the Act's title is the smallest, 'all'. The debate at the time was whether some children were, in the term of the special education field, 'educable'. The Congress, after hearing the differing views of the professionals, declared that *all* children with disabilities were entitled to a 'free appropriate public education'. Implicit here was that all children could benefit from education, i.e. were 'educable'. This was more a matter of belief and philosophy, rather than based upon evidence from research.

While the law has been successful in providing access for all children with disabilities, it has been less so in terms of the quality of the education provided and in the inclusion of students with disabilities with their non-disabled peers. These failures are inextricably linked and are both cause and consequence of the failure to provide equity to students with disabilities.

One of the authors of PL 94–142 (Walker 1987), described Congressional intent in establishing the principle (encompassed in the phrase 'least restrictive environment') that disabled children need not be removed from regular classes: 'Congress was interested in the normalization of services for disabled children, in the belief that the presence of a disability did not necessarily require separation and removal from regular classrooms, or the neighborhood school environment, or from regular academic classes' (Walker 1987: 99).

The concerns of parents, other advocates, practitioners and researchers were presented by Gartner and Lipsky (1987). They drew together four strands of concern:

1 the longstanding concern of many special educators and parents regarding the lack of inclusion for students with severe handicaps;
2 the 'Regular Education Initiative', promulgated by the then US Department of Education Assistant Secretary Madeline Will, concerning the need to include students with mild and moderate handicapping conditions in regular education;
3 attention to the emerging data concerning the negative academic and long-term outcomes of separate special education services;
4 the growing role of the disability rights movement in education.

Commenting on the failure to remove barriers between special and general education, Walker (1987) said about PL 94–142:

It did not anticipate that the artifice of delivery systems in schools might drive the maintenance of separate services and keep students from the mainstream, that the resource base for special education and other remedial services would be constrained by economic forces, or that special education might continue to be dead-end programs in many school systems. Nor could it anticipate how deeply ingrained were our assumptions about the differences between students with learning problems and those without and the substantial power of high (or, unfortunately, low) expectations for learning.

(Walker 1987: 109)

In effect, Walker has identified three factors:

1 'the artifice of delivery systems', i.e. school factors (e.g. district, school and classroom organization; instructional and curricular issues; personnel preparation);
2 'the resource base', both the strain on separate resources and the encouragement of separation of current funding formulae;[1]
3 'deeply ingrained . . . assumptions', i.e. attitudinal issues.

A 1993 report prepared for the Massachusetts Department of Education by Ed Moscovich, Cape Ann Economics, reaches similar conclusions:

Special education programs at the local school level are a logical result of the laws which bring them into being and the regulations by which they are run. The problems of the special education program, and *the failure to move more rapidly toward integrated programming*, are not the result of a failure properly to administer the program, but are rather *the inevitable result of a set of programmatic regulations no longer appropriate to current school or fiscal realities.*

(Moscovich 1993, emphasis added)

The current situation

The special education system serves close to 10 per cent of school age children, more than five million youngsters, at an annual cost of approximately $30 billion. There can be little doubt that the current system is not working. We see this in an increasing flow of reports describing outcomes for students with disabilities:

- high drop-out rates, often double that of other students;
- low graduation rates – only 45 per cent of the students with disabilities leave school with a diploma, a figure which must be understood in the context that more than half of the special education student population is classified as learning disabled, the least severely impaired students;
- limited success in post-secondary education. Special education graduates go on to post-secondary education at less than half the rate of general education graduates;
- high rates of unemployment; persons with disabilities have the highest unemployment rate of any population subgroup; and
- lack of success in community living, with too many parents reporting their children continuing to live at home.

These failures are not ones of the school system alone. We live in a society where there continue to be barriers for persons with disabilities, both physical and attitudinal. While the Americans with Disabilities Act is a major step forward, there is much yet to do to assure that the United States is a country of openness and opportunity for persons with disabilities.

In a very real sense, school systems and special education professionals have done what was expected of them, and they did it very well. They created two separate systems, and neither the general education system nor the special education system is working very well.

Since the passage of PL 94–142, nearly two decades ago, there have been two major developments: first, an increase in the number of students served – nearly 1.2 million more students are served now than were in the 1976–7 school year. The percentage increase last year was greater than in any year since the passage of the law. This is an extraordinary achievement in terms of *access*. Second, despite this substantial change in numbers, and the great increase there has been among those labelled as 'learning disabled', the least impaired, the placement pattern has remained nearly identical for the past decade and a half – about a third of the students served in regular classes, a third in resource rooms, and a third in special classes and more segregated settings.

In the face of this pattern of substantial separation, a combination of court decisions, pronouncements from the US Department of Education, parent groups and policy statements from national education organizations have championed a new design, one of inclusive education for all students with disabilities.

Court decisions

Federal district courts in four circuits have in the past two years issued similar decisions, each supporting inclusion. The cases involve an 11-year-old with Down's syndrome, a 9-year-old labelled as mentally retarded, a kindergarten student with severe behaviour problems, and a student with severe mental retardation and physical disabilities. (See Lipton 1994 for a summary of these cases.)

While differing in details, these court decisions each support inclusion. In *Oberti v. Board of Education of the Borough of Clementon School District*, in 1992 the court held that 'Inclusion is a right, not a privilege for a select few.' Affirming this decision, the court of appeals stated: 'We construe IDEA's mainstreaming requirement to prohibit a school from placing a child with disabilities outside of a regular classroom if educating the child in the regular classroom, with supplementary aids and support services, can be achieved satisfactorily.'

The Department of Education

The Office of Special Education and rehabilitative services is now directed by a strong supporter of inclusion, Judith Heumann. The Department has distributed the *Oberti* decision to chief state school officers, superintendents of schools and to special education directors. And it has filed an *amicus* brief in another of the cases, *Holland v. Sacramento Unified School District*, stating that IDEA 'prohibits a school district from placing a child with disabilities outside the regular classroom if educating the child in the regular classroom, with supplementary aids and support services, can be achieved satisfactorily'. Here, the court of appeals has upheld the decision of the court below, and the US Supreme Court has denied review.

Parental support

There is a widening network of support among parents and their organiz-ations. The Association for Persons with Severe Handicaps (TASH), the nation's largest organization of professionals and parents concerned with children with severe handicaps, continues its longstanding championing of full inclusion. Many of the recent books supporting inclusion have been written by parents. The PEAK Parent centre, in Colorado, has been funded by the Department of Education to focus on issues of inclusion. Across the country chapters of SAFE (Schools Are For Everyone) advocate full inclusion.

Support from educators

Support for full inclusion has long been the case among some general and some special educators. A positive new development is the support from general education organizations, including the Association for Supervision and Curriculum Development (ASCD); the National Association of State Boards of Education (NASBE), which urges states 'to create a new belief system' of inclusion, and calls for retraining teachers and revision of funding formulas; and the National Education Association (NEA), the nation's largest teacher organization. NEA has declared, 'The current state of knowledge about successful practice makes this an opportune time to reflect on how schools can achieve high quality outcomes in integrated settings for all students.'

The national scope of inclusion

Many terms have been used concerning issues of placement of students with disabilities: 'least restrictive environment' (LRE) is the law's term; 'main-streaming', although not found in the law, is the term commonly used, generally referring to special education students participating with general education students for a part of the school day, mostly in non-academic settings. Both LRE and 'mainstreaming' assume the existence of two separate systems, special education and general education, in which students labelled as 'handicapped' spend a portion of time in one and a portion of time in the other.

'Inclusive education' (or inclusion) combines placement (LRE) with the appropriateness of the services provided, i.e. the law's requirement for the provision of a 'free appropriate public education'. At a minimum, we believe inclusion means: *providing to all students, including those with severe handicaps, equitable opportunities to receive effective educational services, with the needed supplementary aids and support services, in age-appropriate classes in their neighbourhood schools, in order to prepare students for contributing lives as full members of society.*

The National Center on Educational Restructuring and Inclusion (NCERI), at The Graduate School and University Center, The City University of New York, has conducted a national survey of inclusion programs

(NCERI 1994). Chief state school officers and state directors of special education were contacted to identify inclusion programs within their state. Preliminary analysis of the survey indicates:

- inclusion programs are taking place across the country;
- inclusion programs are taking place in a wide range of locations – in urban, suburban, and rural school districts;
- inclusion programs are being initiated by administrators, teachers, parents, university faculty, state education departments, and as a result of court orders;
- while programs are occurring at all school levels, there is a concentration in the early grades;
- some districts 'include' all students with disabilities, while others focus either on those with mild or moderate handicapping conditions and others on those with more severe impairments;
- the evaluation of programs is taking place, addressing issues of implementation, outcomes and financing;
- there is an emerging network of individuals and organizations involved in inclusive education practices;
- there is a wide array of materials on inclusive education practices, for teachers, administrators and parents, including videos, printed material, and training opportunities.

These developments do not mean, of course, that inclusive education is the common practice in the United States. It is not. Most students with disabilities continue to be educated in separate settings.

Nor are the indicators of support for inclusion (noted earlier) representative of universal support. That is not the case. Some parents and organizations remain committed to separationist designs. Others are concerned that the needs of particular groups of students will not be met. There are differences of opinion within some disability groups concerning the inclusion of students, particularly those with deafness or blindness. Others fear that inclusion is a way for a society, tired of committing resources to social programs, to save money, here at the expense of students with disabilities. Yet others fear that teachers who may already feel burdened may not be given the adequate resources, training or support necessary to meet the needs of students with disabilities in general education settings. Many of the critics (e.g. Kauffman 1993; Fuchs and Fuchs 1994; Shanker 1994) fail to acknowledge that proponents of inclusive education emphasize the necessity of providing supplementary aids and support services in order to make the general education setting appropriate for students with disabilities. This point is summarized by Judith Heumann, Assistant Secretary for Special Education and Rehabilitative Services, US Department of Education:

Historically, we have had two educational systems, one for students with disabilities and one for everyone else. We are working to create one educational system that values all students. The regular classroom in the neighborhood school should be the first option for students with disabilities. Administrators and teacher must receive the training and the help [i.e. supplementary aids and support services] they need to make that the best option as well.[2]

Equity and autonomy[3]

Carol Christensen and Fazal Rizvi capture the issue here:

> the compassion view of social justice sits uneasily with the access, equity and empowerment views. The former view often characterizes practices where professionals are motivated by care, concern and compassion for those in society who are seen as 'less' fortunate. The critics suggest that this leads to client helplessness and contrasts with a view of social justice linked to the idea of autonomy and empowerment.
>
> (Christensen and Rizvi 1995: 3)

Autonomy is something granted to persons who are valued. For individuals to be autonomous reflects acceptance of three interrelated beliefs. They are:

1 a statement as to the *right* to control one's own life;
2 an expression of belief in the individual's *capacity* to do so; and
3 a recognition of the *benefits* to the individual of doing so.

For persons with disabilities, autonomy is limited by at least three factors. These are:

1 the limitation inherent upon the *impairment*;
2 broad societal *attitudes* toward persons with disabilities; and
3 the nature of current *human services practices*.

While the impairment may in certain circumstances warrant some limitations on autonomy, such limits should come only *after* the limits caused by factors 2 and 3, in the second list, are fully removed. Even then, great care must be exercised in coming to a priori assumptions as to the extent of such limitations. Until an accommodating society is established, the full range of an individual's capacity and the extent to which apparent limitations are inherent or a function of externally imposed barriers will not be known.

In the majority decision in *School Board of Nassau County* v. *Arline*, US Supreme Court Justice William Brennan wrote: 'Congress acknowledged that society's accumulated myths and fears about disability and disease are as handicapping as are the physical limitations that flow from actual impairment.'

In general, human services practices, including education, operate from a deficit model. That is, the consumer (e.g. student, patient or client) is seen as having some inadequacy, shortcoming, failure or disease. The provider (e.g. teacher, doctor or therapist) is seen as knowing something, doing something or having something that will overcome the deficit, fix the problem or cure the disease. Central to this formulation is the assumption that in exchange for accepting and not challenging the expertise of the provider, the consumer is excused from normal obligations. That is, the consumer is allowed to be dependent, and, thus, not autonomous. Such a deficit-based model is at odds with the beliefs that undergird autonomy.

In special education, while progressive when they were developed, the concepts of a 'continuum' of placements (Reynolds 1962), a 'cascade' of services (Deno 1970) and 'least restrictive environment' (LRE) today do not promote the full inclusion of persons with disabilities in all aspects of societal life, nor do they serve as appropriate guiding principles for the education that is the necessary means toward the goals' achievement. Taylor (1988) presents a trenchant critique of LRE. He writes that LRE:

- legitimates restrictive environments;
- confuses segregation and integration on the one hand with intensity of services on the other;
- is based on a 'readiness' model;
- supports the primacy of professional decision-making;
- sanctions infringements on people's rights;
- implies that people must move as they develop and change;
- directs attention to physical settings rather than to the services and supports people need to be integrated into the community.

Conclusion

Equity in education for *all* students with disabilities, including those with severe disabilities, requires:

- unfettered access to publicly and adequately funded education;
- educational services provided in an inclusive setting, that is in the same school available to their non-disabled peers in age-appropriate classes;
- educational programs that offer effective opportunities for success, in schooling and life; and
- holding those who govern and manage schools accountable for the achievement of that success.

In no country today are these requirements of equity met for students with disabilities. In many countries, including Australia, Canada, Italy, New Zealand and Sweden, among others, efforts are underway to address aspects of the first two or three of these factors. We have written about the developments in the United States, not because it has been successful in all four of these areas; it has not. Rather, it is because its intellectual hegemony has consequences for others.

Only in settings of full inclusion can individuals with disabilities exercise the autonomy which is an essential component of their full participation in society. The establishment of such settings, with supplementary aids and support services, is the *necessary* requirement for equity for students with disabilities.

Notes

1 Parrish (1993) reports convincingly on the separationist consequences of many state funding formulae.
2 This was in a 1993 press release of the US Justice Department, announcing that an *amicus curiae* petition had been filed with the US Supreme Court, on behalf of the US Department of Education, in the case, *Holland v. Sacramento Public Schools*, a case concerning parents seeking a fully inclusive placement for their daughter, Rachel. The court refused to review the case, thus leaving standing the Court of Appeals decision upholding the ruling of the federal district court supporting the parent's request.
3 For a fuller discussion of these issues, see Hahn (1989) and Lipsky and Gartner (1989).

References

Christensen, C. and Rizvi, F. (1995) 'Disability, education and social justice', unpublished paper. The University of Queensland, Australia.

Deno, E. (1970) Special education as developmental capital, *Exceptional Children*, 37(1): 229–37.

Fuchs, D. and Fuchs, L. S. (1994) Inclusive schools movement and the radicalization of special education reform. *Exceptional Children*, 60(4): 294–309.

Funk, R. (1987) Disability rights: from caste to class in the context of civil rights, in A. Gartner and T. Joe (eds) *Images of the Disabled, Disabling Images*. New York: Praeger, pp. 7–30.

Gartner, A. and Lipsky, D. K. (1987) Beyond separate education: toward a quality system for all students, *Harvard Educational Review*, 57(4): 367–95.

Hahn, H. (1989) The politics of special education, in D. K. Lipsky and A. Gartner (eds) *Beyond Separate Education: Quality Education for All*. Baltimore, MD: Paul H. Brookes, pp. 225–41.

Kauffman, J. M. (1993) How we might achieve the radical reform of special education, *Exceptional Children*, 60(1): 6–16.

Lipsky, D. K. and Gartner, A. (1989) Building the future, in D. K. Lipsky and A. Gartner (eds) *Beyond Separate Education: Quality Education for All*. Baltimore, MD: Paul H. Brookes, pp. 255–90.

Lipton, D. (1994) The 'full inclusion' court cases: 1989–1994, *NCERI Bulletin*, 1(2).

Moscovich, E. (1993) *Special Education: Good Intentions Gone Awry*. Boston: Pioneer Institute for Public Policy Research.

National Center on Educational Restructuring and Inclusion [NCERI] (1994) *National Study of Inclusive Education*. New York: NCERI, The Graduate School and University Center, The City University of New York.

Parrish, T. B. (1993) State funding procedures and least restrictive environment: implications for federal policy, *CSEF Brief*, no. 2.

Reynolds, M. C. (1962) A framework for considering some issues in special education, *Exceptional Children*, 28(3): 367–70.

Shanker, A. (1994) Inclusion and ideology, *New York Times*, 6 February.

Taylor, S. J. (1988) Caught in the continuum: a critical analysis of the principle of least restrictive environment, *Journal of the Association of Persons with Severe Handicaps*, 13(1): 41–53.

Walker, L. J. (1987) Procedural rights in the wrong system: special education is not enough, in A. Gartner and T. Joe (eds) *Images of the Disabled, Disabling Images*. New York: Praeger, pp. 97–116.

Reforming special education: beyond 'inclusion'

Often outside the awareness of its practitioners, special education contains elements that make it subversive to universal public education systems. Special education's focus and priorities challenge schools to produce a radical form of social justice: equality of educational opportunity for students who are sometimes characterized by extreme individual differences. Attempting to accommodate these differences raises questions as well about the meaning of equality, the meaning of opportunity, and indeed the relationship between schooling and education. Much of the American understanding of equality of educational opportunity begins with assumptions of normal – i.e. typical or modal – ability and learning potential. School policies and structures have evolved following more or less implicit expectations that children develop and learn 'normally' (i.e. in a tolerably similar manner).

However, it is a simple fact that some children, for a variety of reasons, are handicapped as learners by a complex interaction of individual characteristics and circumstances, on the one hand, and constraints imposed by social structures or material scarcities, on the other. Their observed trajectory of development and learning is atypical, sometimes profoundly so. Mass public schooling was not designed and has not evolved with these children in mind. Therefore, the very concept of a 'special' education can be and has been subversive to the extent that accommodation of extreme individual differences tends to undermine those structures within schools that have evolved to satisfy both expectations of tolerable similarity among children as well as the several social and political purposes of schools.

As I will attempt to show in this chapter, the current reform movement in special education – 'inclusion' – is merely a variation on a theme. I will argue that the stridency of reformers bent on inclusion inadvertently nurtures and legitimizes attempts by school administrators and policy-makers to regain control over an enterprise that for a hundred years has threatened the traditional structure, economy and culture of American public schooling.

Contradiction and conflict

It is not well understood that the conflict between mass public education and 'special' education is fundamental. It has always existed and, during eras of school reform, it frequently has made special education a source of deep discontent, a focus of controversy and a target of criticism. The public tends to view special education as a loose collection of unusual practices used by specially prepared teachers to instruct and manage an exotic, homogeneous population. In fact, special education in the twentieth century is better understood as a school enterprise, as an organizational strategy schools have adopted to accommodate sometimes extreme differences in children. That is, schools create, organize and allocate resources to satisfy instructional demands presented by the challenging behaviours of students with disabilities. Historically, special educational programming emerges as the unavoidable consequence of the immutable fact of human differences in conflict with the ambition to build systems of universal mass education. As a result, special education has proved to be a troubling and troublesome offspring to public school officials, chronically demanding extraordinary effort, contingent resources, and most of all, constant institutional transformation to achieve a radical form of social justice.

In many ways, special education's explicit concern for individual differences has been the source of its moral strength, but also its fatal political weakness. Even in societies professing democratic ideals, individuals are valued more at the high rather than low end of ability, achievement and performance distributions. The history of civil liberties flows from contemplation of social justice for competent more than for incompetent individuals. Historically, the latter individuals have been extended protection more often than opportunity following a common-sense expectation that equal social privileges and opportunities will fail to yield equal successes. Even when, in the first years of this century, special day classes seemed progressive and innovative, the subtle, unrelenting pressure exerted by special education advocacy for individual children was in contradiction to the mass educational system that school managers were attempting to build.

The heart of this contradiction lies in the distinction between access and opportunity. Mere access to the physical environment of schools or classrooms within schools confers no specific or necessarily appropriate opportunity to learn. Children who are very difficult to teach may provoke contingent and individual responses from teachers, but these responses do not necessarily constitute an 'opportunity'. Allowing such children into the schools in the early part of this century was an early form of inclusion that was popularly conceived as new educational opportunity for children with disabilities. But it wasn't until very difficult students received a planful response that was reasonably calculated to promote satisfactory progress in the curriculum that a real educational opportunity existed. It is, therefore,

unfortunate that contemporary reformers who urge 'inclusion' have emphasized place over instructional substance and confused 'participation' with
real opportunity (Kauffman 1993; Gerber 1995).

Criticism and reform

Despite its origins as a form of inclusion, special education is described today
by reformers as a segregating, insulated, self-protecting, racially biased
philosophy and array of practices, a product of an outdated modernism and
misguided scientific positivism, or merely as an ineffective, overblown
solution to easily solvable school problems (Dunn 1968; Heller *et al.* 1982;
Tomlinson 1982; Madden and Slavin 1983; Will 1986; Cole 1990; Skrtic
1991). Hardly ten years after the passage of a national special education
mandate, its most uncompromising critics had weighed its worth and found it
absolutely wanting, absolutely beyond redemption in its current forms
(Stainback and Stainback 1984; Gartner and Lipsky 1987; Wang *et al.*
1988). The remarkable policies of inclusion that led in this century from
special day classes to mandated public school education for *all* disabled
children in the 'least restrictive environment', policies that once were lauded
as dramatic signs of a profound social 'revolution', now seem to have lost
both the public's confidence and support amid a sea of change in political
attitudes about abnormal development, achievement and behaviour.

The current reform movement is complex, containing strands of various
interests that converge only on the perceived need to change special
education. Administrators and policy-makers, for example, using the
rhetoric of inclusion have advocated for integration of funding, more than for
integration of students, and deregulation more than improvement of
programs (National Association of State Boards of Education 1992;
'Governors seek authority to merge IDEA, other money' 1995). Policy
rhetoric and philosophical debate aside, administrators and other public
officials recognize a 'bottom line' – attempting to organize instructional
resources to suit the learning differences among children is very costly
(Chaikind *et al.* 1993; Bacdayan 1994). These critics are focused on
managing schools more efficiently and effectively, so their expressed concern
for improving special education must be evaluated in that light.

A quite different set of critics who strongly identify themselves with needs
and rights of disabled people, advocate a new more radical policy of
'inclusion' in place of existing forms of special education (Catlett and Osher
1994; Fuchs and Fuchs 1994). They aggressively demand and define
educational opportunity for all disabled students in terms of its location in
regular, age-appropriate classrooms. These critics believe and intend that,
under great moral and political pressure, schools, curriculum and instruction
will remould themselves to accommodate individual learning needs of

students with disabilities and, therefore, produce a fuller and more genuine equality of educational opportunity.

Advocates for special education resist these radical proposals as misguided zealotry and believe that the philosophical and legal framework created by legislation ultimately is a more powerful and reliable vehicle of change (Gerber 1989). Advocates for gradual, research-based improvement in implementing present policies believe that the political stress created by more radical reformers will be expropriated easily by school administrators and policy-makers who seek mainly to gain greater local control and discretion over educational programs for students with disabilities. These 'gradualists' believe that school administrators are supportive of changes in special education only because, as currently constituted, it evades local control and limits degrees of managerial freedom to such an extent that traditional forms of schooling are threatened (Kauffman *et al.* 1988; Gerber 1989, 1994; Kauffman and Hallahan 1995).

If the 'gradualists' are correct, it will be ironic if it is those who have most thwarted current policy by their bureaucratic resistance who ultimately benefit from the intense criticisms and political agitation of radical inclusionists. In fact, radical inclusionists and policy gradualists *both* seek improvement for students with disabilities although they have engaged in fractious, often harsh debate over who best speaks for the interests of children with disabilities (Fuchs and Fuchs 1994; Kauffman and Hallahan 1995). An objective analysis reveals that *both* positions and the courses of action they might recommend have an important underlying commonality. Followed to their logical conclusion, both represent the continuation of the same implicit threat to public schooling that was posed by the establishment of special day classes almost a hundred years ago.

Special education became a formal part of public schooling in the United States during the closing years of the nineteenth century while a system of mass public education was still emerging. The story of its origins reveals why over the ensuing years and especially today it so seriously threatens the *status quo* of public schooling. Beneath the progressivist – some might say, modernist – language of the story, however, is the hard material fact that extant knowledge and technology of instruction, organized for 'schooling' as it has been over most of this century, is incapable of providing either meaningfully equal or equally meaningful educational opportunity for all students. It is in reaction to this fact and its long-term implications that special education is singled out and vilified by current reformers.

Past is prologue

In response to rapid industrialization, urban growth and massive immigration, the institution of public schooling at the beginning of the twentieth century served several different public purposes. One set of purposes wished to secure and improve a democratic society by improving its citizenry and controlling those disintegrative and anarchistic forces thought to be latent in unsocialized – uneducated – people. Another set of purposes sought a general grading and upgrading of the labour force as one component in the production equation to support better expanding capitalist industry and interests.

At an accelerating rate, a subtle political consensus developed following the American Civil War. Different purposes and interests coalesced in support of universal, publically financed compulsory schooling. By 1900, fewer than half of the states had compulsory attendance laws, and those that did varied in the vigour of their enforcement. But public education was far more easily legislated than accomplished. Organizing and operating schools for so many children at the scale contemplated faced substantial practical barriers especially in fast-growing urban centres. Children appeared in classrooms who, for reasons of ability, background or motivation, caused teachers significant difficulties. Any first-order approximation to the kind of school system intended required management and control, not only of numerous but also highly diverse children. As early as 1894, for example, a researcher, Will S. Monroe, revealed that teachers perceived 2 per cent of their students as 'imbeciles' or 'idiots', and almost 9 per cent as 'mentally dull'. Monroe and others knew that children who were extremely low functioning would eventually find their way into state institutions. But he crystallized the core problem of universal compulsory education by pondering if schools were or could be the proper place for so many 'mentally dull' students who were so 'below the general average' (cited in Trent 1994: 147).

At the turn of the century, teaching consisted of oral presentation and recitation of subject-matter and an array of drill and practice for acquiring basic academic skills. Teachers expected and sought to command student behaviours conducive to large-group instruction in classrooms. Professional teaching, still in its infancy, was wholly unprepared for students who differed in so many obstructive ways. Teachers were not trained or encouraged to develop repertoires of adaptive methods or techniques suitable, let alone optimal, for addressing significant individual differences in learners.

In conventional wisdom, learning was a product of crudely understood interaction of opportunity, provided by schooling, and ability and character, sufficient amounts of which were assumed to exist in a 'typical' student. There was as yet no psychology of child development or useful educational psychology. Neither the intelligence-testing nor 'child study' movements had begun. In practice, school personnel made little formal distinction between students who were unwilling or unable to learn the curriculum teachers presented to them. Rather, they and the public at large believed that merely being at school provided students with an opportunity to learn. If they succeeded, then they had obviously used this opportunity to good advantage.

If they did not succeed, then just as obviously they had squandered their opportunity and must accept responsibility for doing so.

The first reform

In the first years of the century, however, a new progressivist philosophy gained a foothold in urban affairs and spread easily to urban schools particularly. According to Ravitch (1974), new ideas contributed to a vision of a 'new education' that undermined traditional thinking 'that school was a place to learn reading, writing, and arithmetic, and that students who failed had only themselves to blame' (p. 167). Progressivists urged schools as agents of the community to assume and accept more responsibility for the success of students' learning. Ultimately, the public's perception of the source of educational success or failure shifted away from students to what schools were thought to provide – how instruction was organized, the curriculum offered, the quality of teachers, and the nature of teaching itself. In this view, schools did not merely manufacture education by a set of technical production processes. Rather, schools, through the kind of educational opportunities offered, were vanguards of societal redemption and renewal.

It was natural, therefore, that someone would view educating children with learning and behavioural problems as similar to public health nursing or social work. One of the most prominent leaders of a new movement to establish special day classes for these children in schools was Elizabeth Farrell, a teacher in New York City. Farrell gained the active support of social activists associated with Lillian Wald's nearby settlement house and from other progressive figures, including New York City's Superintendent of Schools, William Maxwell (Sarason and Doris 1979; Hendrick and Mac-Millan 1989). As Farrell herself describes it, the idea for special day classes

> was not the result of any theory. It grew out of conditions in a neighborhood which furnished many and serious problems in truancy and discipline. The first class was made up of the odds and ends of a large school. There were over-age children, so-called naughty children, and the dull and stupid children . . . They had varied interests but the school, as they found it, had little or nothing for them.
> (cited in Sarason and Doris 1979: 297)

Thus, while the still-emerging concept of 'public school' emphasized universal exposure to a common curriculum in age-graded classes, early special education advocacy by teachers like Farrell promoted *differentiated* treatment and curriculum in *ungraded* classes for students considered wayward, mentally deficient or simply difficult to teach (Hoffman 1975). Despite what appear to be obvious contradictions in trying to incorporate special classes, teachers and curriculum within the otherwise rigid framework of public schooling, the idea caught fire. By 1913, there were special day classes and special schools.in 108 cities. Ten years later, this number had increased by 55 per cent with over 33,000 students in special education programs (Trent 1994: 147). Clearly, not every teacher or administrator shared Farrell's and Maxwell's enthusiasm for special class programs for retarded students within the context of graded public schools. Indeed, it isn't clear that Farrell and Maxwell had precisely the same motives or vision. It seems, rather, that the concept of special day classes was embraced widely because it satisfied different needs for different constituencies.

When Farrell, encouraged by local support, finally presented her ideas to members of the Board of Education, she was praised as a 'genius whose vision was essentially practical' (Lillian Wald, cited in Sarason and Doris 1979: 299). That phrase – a vision that is essentially practical – is a succinct expression of the unusual consensus achieved by the new 'special' education. To administrators, special day classes appeared to meet two important goals, attendance *and* containment, while also providing an orderly professional context for addressing significant management difficulties. However, although administrators won control and containment of a segment of the school population who were difficult to teach and manage, they failed to see how porous and troubling the boundaries between general practices and the new special education actually would prove to be. On the other hand, advocates for special day classes won a kind of autonomy within the school from which they hoped to organize more appropriate, more meaningful curriculum and instruction for students with disabilities, but failed to see how potentially threatening they would become to the deepest interests of those who built and supported public schooling.

Almost immediately, these different purposes began to conflict, surfacing as debate over how special day classes were to be administered, to what extent their curriculum would vary from normal curriculum, methods of identification and classification, and the nature of professional preparation and certification. Most school districts established separate supervisorial authorities and administrative channels to manage those specially designated teachers assigned to special day classes. It was separation, to be sure, but separation by mutual consent (Sarason and Doris 1979: 360). If special educators pushed the boundaries of their autonomy, general educators worked as aggressively to circumscribe, contain and limit the overall impact of special education on the general structure and operation of schools. Thus, the bifurcation of the public school system into two mutually contradicting, asymmetrically empowered strands – one for 'special' and one for 'normal' students – arose not from the insistent advocacy of any particular group, so much as from a tacit agreement about the practical conditions and possibilities of public schools. It was – it is – an unworkable arrangement as long as schools maintain their traditional structure, economy and culture.

In remembering Farrell's vision as it was shared with members of the Henry

Street Settlement House, Lillian Wald in 1935 understood more accurately than most the implications of what was being proposed by the young teacher. It was *not* simply about optimal development of every individual's potential. Rather,

> Miss Farrell's originality lay in applying the idea to the education of the atypical in the public schools. She was optimistic enough to believe that the largest and most complex school system in the country – perhaps in the world – with its hundreds of thousands of children, its rigid curriculum, its mass methods, could be modified to meet the needs of the atypical – often the least lovely and potentially the most troublesome of its pupils.
>
> (Wald, cited in Sarason and Doris 1979: 298)

Education, income and social justice

Without some reference to material well-being, the concept of social justice is ultimately a philosophical abstraction. Differences and variations in status or power or specific rights are important because they ultimately contribute to greater equality or inequality of material well-being. After 1900, greater social equality and material well-being, as indexed by distribution of income, was presumptively related to access to and equality of educational opportunity. In these terms, social justice does not require strict equality of income, but it does demand that some basic level of material and psychological well-being (i.e. income) should not be withheld from individuals by society for arbitrary or capricious reasons. There is historical confusion and room for debate, however, over what constitutes 'arbitrary' or 'capricious' justifications for social inequality.

In capitalist societies, apologists explain observed inequalities of income distribution as a product of supply and demand for qualities of labour as they are differentiated and allocated blindly by competitive market mechanisms. Beneath this explanation is a broad-based and tenacious conventional wisdom that lifespan social achievements of individuals reflect unfettered expressions of innate differences in ability in competition with one another. For some, this belief provides a satisfying explanation for income and social class disparities because natural abilities do not seem arbitrary or capricious. The concept that education obtained in schools frees natural ability for fair competition also establishes an explicit strategy for social advancement and, therefore, the value of an *equal* educational opportunity.

Much of the social value of publicly supported education in this century begins with an abiding faith in the transformative or modifying effects of learning as a process leading to expression of natural abilities. In American society, at least, there was no expectation that schools would produce absolute equality. Despite educational opportunity, income disparities certainly would still exist because individuals differ in natural ability. Following from this logic, public schools were embraced as an instrument of social justice for individuals in the marketplace and in society at large. For example, in a recent call for educational opportunity for African-Americans, John Hope Franklin has written: 'Economic and social progress in the United States has long been rooted in access to quality education. What worked so well for millions of immigrants must at last be made to work for black Americans' (Committee on Policy for Racial Justice 1989: ix). His statement succinctly captures how strong still is the popular expectation that American public education has the ability as well as the purpose to transform American social and economic life and promote social justice.

In the 1960s, when this belief was applied to the problem of substantial domestic poverty through a series of unprecedented education policies, it seemed logical that public schools could be recruited to redress income disparities simply by offering compensatory educational opportunities for those who were unfairly disadvantaged. The expected result was not the elimination of poverty so much as a correction of *disproportional* poverty among some social groups. Thus, the equality of opportunity sought was equality of opportunity to *compete* without restrictions other than those imposed by differences in ability. The core belief was unchanged that ability differences, once freed from unacceptable social suppression and enhanced by educational opportunity, were still the legitimate determinants of income disparities.

Limitations and disability

Individuals with disabilities occupy an ambiguous and sometimes paradoxical space in this scheme of things. In particular, there is only a tenuous relationship between access to schooling and economic well-being. As a group of learners, individuals with disabilities are heterogeneous. Despite confusion in individual identification, as a group they are neither like immigrants nor racial minorities. Also unlike these latter groups, we make no assumption that their social identification distorts or disguises an underlying average ability. Instead, we presume that they will face serious and chronic barriers to achievement over their lifespan and generally will not compete successfully with non-disabled individuals for employment.

To be sure, there is considerable debate over whether these perceived limitations are a product of innate characteristics or the result of arbitrary social assignment or some interaction of both. Teachers recognize children with disabilities less by diagnostic signs and more because they are relatively difficult to teach and less likely to benefit from typical instructional arrangements. On the other hand, inclusionists stridently argue that teachers either underestimate their achievement potential if professional training is improved, instructional environments modified and adequate support pro-vided. Whichever view one holds, it is difficult to dispute the fact of 'disabled' students' lower achievement compared to that of non-disabled peers. There is also little dispute that available remedies will cost more on a *per capita* basis than the public typically expends for students not considered disabled. And therein lies the source of the durable concern special education of any kind raises for school managers.

When the public perceives disabilities as unalterable barriers to achieve-ment and, thus, future employment, it is unwilling to invest scarce resources in what seems to be futile educational opportunities. On the other hand, especially during times of economic prosperity, the public also rejects the social devaluation and economic disadvantage that follows from little or no educational opportunity for individuals with disabilities. These two views ultimately are not reconcilable within the current economic and organiz-ational framework of public schooling. The special day class curriculum was designed with alternative, not simply lower, achievement and employment expectations. Contemporary special education is more complex, allowing for remedial and compensatory academic programs for some, alternative curricula for others. Nevertheless, whatever special education the public has supported inevitably reveals a critical paradox in nominally 'universal' schooling. It really cannot accommodate the full range of human differences without substantial cost and structural change.

Paradox revealed

To achieve its ambitious scale of universality, public schooling largely ignores individual differences that contribute to variable instructional outcomes. Special education throughout its almost one-hundred-year history has been concerned *mostly* with individual differences and how they might be accommodated by institutional transformations. The intrinsic nature of this paradox is revealed best by asking whether the claim that public schools work for *all* children, without exception, is supported by any extant evidence? More specifically, is equality of educational opportunity really offered to each and every American child, again without exception? What, indeed, does it mean to provide equality of educational opportunity for children with disabilities if these children will always be at a competitive disadvantage compared to their more normally achieving peers?

Under most existing instructional arrangements, exposure to precisely the same instruction designed for more normally achieving peers condemns children with disabilities to achievement below their potential and at great disadvantage for developing socially valued levels of independence and productivity. This, in essence, defines disability and is axiomatic in any construction of a 'special' education. Equal physical access to school and strict equality of instructional resources therein are precisely the conditions that created special education in the first place. The subversive quality of special education arises from the organizational disruption and fiscal burden imposed on schools when they legitimize attempts to provide individually variable levels of access and instructional resources.

Early special day class programs revealed this paradox because, in an attempt to gain control over the consequences of enrolling diverse, often difficult students, school officials legitimized the internal organization of special effort that was fundamentally antagonistic to the organization of the school as a whole. Special class teachers required *additional* resources but also used these resources *differently* to create instructional arrangements meant to obtain *different*, not just lower, achievement outcomes from those expected for students in the general program. Although now criticized by inclusionists and others, is it instructive to consider how special education seeks to establish equality of opportunity? That is, in what sense can a *different* instructional program aimed at *different* goals with *different* resources be considered equal? Clearly, any such description of equality must accept not only that children may consume different resources to reach similar goals, but also that they may consume different resources to reach *different*, equally valid goals.

In past decades, policy-makers have overemphasized the amount of school resources, or inputs, for calculating equality while ignoring whether similar resources provide an equally substantive educational opportunity for students who differ. For students with disabilities, substantive opportunity is not necessarily provided either by access or by social participation in universally accessible programs, but is provided when and if an individually tailored educational program exists that is reasonably calculated to promote at least satisfactory levels of development and achievement. If such opportunity is provided to each child, then educational opportunity is equally meaningful. The public school establishment, focused on equal access to equal resources, constrained by fiscal limitations and conflicting political demands, has recognized from the beginning both the resource and organizational implications of special education's more radical formulation of equality and, therefore, has resisted it at every turn.

Public schools may have *attempted*, at varying times and to varying degrees, to give access to *all* children, but truly universal public education remains really more of an ideal than a reality. Despite early advocacy for special day class programs, public schools in the United States have always acted to deny or restrict access – sometimes absolutely, sometimes contingently – for some students. As a matter of law, *all* American children were not guaranteed equal access to public education until 1975 and the passage of the Education of All Handicapped Children's Act (popularly known as Public Law 94–142, or simply PL 94–142 and revised and reauthorized in 1990 as

Individuals with Disabilities Education Act, or IDEA). Even so, schools still require students to demonstrate desirable general standards of conduct to *remain* in normal public school programs. Students with severe behaviour problems, particularly those whose behaviour is considered dangerous or otherwise criminal, tend to be segregated and eventually expelled from public schools.

The hot dispute currently raging over suspension and expulsion policies in the United States illustrates how special education disturbs school administrators and their sense of control over schools. Court decisions like *Honig v. Doe* underscore how strongly anti-exclusionist contemporary special education policy is in its philosophy and current regulatory scheme (Bartlett 1989; 'House IDEA draft would lift discipline barrier' 1995). Once identified, students are explicitly entitled to appropriate educational interventions that cannot be limited or interrupted by unilateral decisions by school administrators. School authorities perceive this policy as serious interference with their ability to suspend or expel unilaterally any student who is disruptive, aggressive or violent regardless of whether such behaviour is related to disability. Special education policy, on the other hand, permits no exclusion and, in any case, intends an active search for educational rather than administrative solutions to undesirable behaviour.

More important than loss of discretion over misbehaviour, schools balk at the open-ended and contingent commitment of resources that special education demands. In other recent litigation, *Timothy W. v. Rochester*, school officials sought relief from what they perceived to be a burdensome and inappropriate expenditure of scarce resources for a completely unresponsive profoundly retarded child. An appeals court, overturning a lower court's ruling in favour of the schools, indicated that federal law mandating special education required no test of educability as a precondition for the provision of special education and related services (Whitted 1991). Simply stated, children do not have to prove they can learn before schools must commit themselves to an exploratory effort to teach them.

This principle, central in special education history and policy, contradicts the traditional assumption around which traditional school organization has evolved, namely, that learning opportunities are provided and children may or may not take advantage of these opportunities. Either way, whether students are successful or not, the school's obligation ends with provision of whatever instructional arrangements it chooses to designate as an opportunity. Special education policy, on the other hand, imposes on schools an obligation to seek actively and continually means to instruct all students without exclusion. Society cannot presuppose or legislate individual outcomes, so what is required by such a mandate is effort itself. That is, special education law in the United States commits schools to invest effort in educating children who may not, when all is said and done, promise much return for that effort. Although from the perspective of educational resource managers, such a policy may seem folly, the *Timothy W.* case emphasizes how radically American special education policy endorses true universality and redefines equality of opportunity.

American special education policy also includes at least two other principles that have proved a chronic irritant to school officials. One is the requirement that parents formally participate in formulating and consent to an individualized educational plan (IEP) for their children. While not a legal contract, the IEP shares important characteristics with contracts. Most fundamentally, IEPs represent a negotiated agreement between parents who wish to lay claim to school resources for their child, and school administrators who manage and who are accountable to the public for the use of these resources. The IEP requirement, therefore, confers on parents an unusual degree of power over how schools respond to children. No tradition of schooling or other law so explicitly and so effectively extends to parents the right to modulate the school experiences of their children. Even though it is doubtful that all parents of disabled children take equal advantage of their legal rights, including judicial relief if necessary, enough do so that public school administrators feel challenged and burdened. Beneath their apparent support for the values espoused by inclusionists, administrators also clearly seek greater discretion and control when IEPs are contested by parents.

Another principle enshrined in contemporary American special education policy that can be antagonistic to traditional schooling is the requirement that special education, when provided, should occur in the 'least restrictive environment' (LRE). As a matter of law, the LRE requirement intends to separate questions of educational program and physical setting. That is, once parents and schools agree on an appropriate program, it is incumbent upon the school to provide that program in an environment that is different from regular classrooms and schedules only to the degree necessary. Gradualists have argued that the LRE provision provides and protects precisely what inclusionists propose – opportunity to learn in the same education environments as non-disabled children.

There is no disagreement that schools often circumvent the intent of this requirement by failing to acknowledge the possibility of providing some special education in regular classrooms, particularly for students with severe disabilities. But the failure in this regard has been a failure of schools not special education policy, a failure consistent with schools' historical reaction to the intrusiveness of special education. Acknowledgement of possibility requires an attempt; and the attempt to provide special education in regular classrooms, as inclusionists are beginning to learn, immediately creates demand for supplementation and contingent reconfiguration of resources available to any given class, including the kind of training and consultative support required by teachers. Schools attempting to exchange special education's current regulatory strictures for a vague inclusion policy will find themselves recreating the very thing they are trying to escape. Ironically, by adopting inclusionist philosophy to counter the perceived burden of special education policy without fundamental restructuring, administrators risk conflicts with general classroom teachers who, without adequate support, will resist the increased instructional burden of 'included' students. One hundred years after the first special day classes were instituted, then, schools will have come full circle.

Can schools change?

It really was not until the *Equality of Educational Opportunity (EEO)* report that the belief that public schooling promoted social mobility and was a force for social equality was ever seriously questioned (Coleman *et al.* 1966; *Harvard Educational Review* 1969; Mosteller and Moynihan 1972; Jencks and Brown 1975; Levine and Bane 1975). The massive study commissioned by the Office of Civil Rights and produced by Coleman and his colleagues sought only to demonstrate the magnitude of the injustice that almost everyone agreed must exist. Much to everyone's surprise, Coleman's data showed rather small differences in the resource infrastructure that characterized segregated white and black schools.

It is difficult to recapture in 1995 what profound implications seemed to attach to these findings in 1966. Coleman's findings were surprising because they could not demonstrate the expected inequality of resources that hypothetically accounted for achievement inequality. But they were shocking because they offered little evidence that schools, even with massive federal investment, could correct achievement differences in any case. This seemed to contradict precisely the policy course the federal government had already chosen by the time Coleman's data became known. And more darkly, it appeared to support the view that the real cause of unequal achievement was familial and not social (Jencks *et al.* 1972; Jencks and Brown 1975; Levine and Bane 1975).

Coleman's study instigated two decades of vigorous research to refute the politically unacceptable inference that schools sorted but did not really educate children (*Harvard Educational Review* 1969; Mosteller and Moynihan 1972; Hodgson 1975; Rutter 1983). Ever more sophisticated analytical methods were brought to bear on the general search for an educational production function – that combination of resource inputs that reliably and strongly would predict achievement outputs (Averch *et al.* 1972; Bridge *et al.* 1979). But after two decades, the evidence is still ambiguous and forcefully debated (Hanushek 1989, 1994; Wainer 1993; Hedges *et al.* 1994a,b).

Despite differences in analytical strategy, though, most research habitually focuses on average achievement in the school as the proper indicator of school effectiveness or success. Although policy-makers acknowledge that schools might produce more than one outcome, there has been an unwavering conviction that these multiple 'products' of schooling are simply different domains of achievement or growth, estimated as the *average* performance or status within a school.

Such blind faith in the arithmetic average has led us far astray and helped schools avoid recognizing that they 'produce' a distribution of human beings, not average levels of performance. Ignoring the fact that different outcomes are distributed by schools' instructional arrangements for different students causes periodic paroxysms of reform without ever changing traditional approaches to curriculum and instruction. Enshrining average rather than distributed outcomes permits schools to continue their historical treatment of diverse students as tolerably alike in learning characteristics and, therefore, tolerably alike in their responsiveness to a given curriculum or particular instructional method. Student diversity is reduced to a slogan and the organizational and resource implications of disability continue to be avoided or ignored (Gerber 1989; Gamoran 1992; Biemiller 1993a,b; Slavin 1993).

Questioning the importance of average performance in terms of its underlying distribution also threatens traditional notions of school effectiveness. Do we expect that as a manifestation of some natural law that high achieving students will always make the greatest gains? If so, we are actually expressing a preference for a particular achievement outcome, a distribution that is skewed towards already high achieving students. Because low achieving students, including most considered disabled, achieve at a lower rate, more instructional effort is required to obtain more similar (equal) levels of achievement. If we are committed to universal education for *all* students in a world of scarce and limited resources, then we must contend with the fact that effort invested in many disabled students may alter the distribution (narrowing it) while having little or no impact on the mean outcomes of schools (Gerber and Semmel 1985; Gerber 1988). This formulation has serious implications for the concept of school effectiveness.

When is a school effective?

The challenge that special education posed to public schooling in the first decade of this century – and still poses – was the insistence that design and deployment of instructional effort within schools could and should be modified to accommodate individual differences rather than expectations for modal students. This insistence implies a value that suggests a non-intuitive definition of school effectiveness. Schools are effective when and if their poorest-performing students demonstrate significant achievement gains.

Very little serious attention has been paid to such an alternative view. Yet, organizational prescriptions drawn from case studies of schools that appear to be effective at the mean (Purkey and Smith 1983, 1985) are not useful for predicting school effectiveness with their disabled students. Schools that rank high on performance of their modal students do not necessarily rank similarly on performance of their disabled students (Semmel and Gerber 1995).

Unlike Coleman and related studies, these findings do not mean that instructional efforts by schools are fruitless, only that they are distributed in such a way so as to make the *average* a poor measure of a school's effectiveness (Brown and Saks 1981). That is, effects of intentionally organizing instructional effort within schools to meet needs of slower-learning, lower-achieving students are not likely to be detected by changes in mean tested achievement. Special education constitutes an institutionalized, explicit pressure for schools to distribute instructional effort in this way.

The next reform

Special education poses difficult technical problems for universal education, but also reveals a challenging view of our real, as opposed to professed, values and commitment to social justice. School effectiveness cannot be meaningfully inferred from an achievement distribution until these values are made explicit. If equality of educational opportunity means equalizing *substantive* opportunity, then school effectiveness can be demonstrated only in one of two ways. Either achievement variance will decrease by increases in achievement in the lower half of the distribution or mean achievement will rise without increases in variance in the higher half of the distribution (i.e. the entire distribution will shift upwards) (Brown and Saks 1981; Gerber and Semmel 1985; Gerber 1988; Bacdayan 1994). To obtain either of these outcomes in the next reform movement will require not only new resources and new technologies of instruction, but also a fundamentally different structure, economy and culture of schooling to permit and support individually variable programs of instruction.

Despite prolific reform rhetoric, the achievement of disabled students as an indicator of school effectiveness has been specifically ignored by blue ribbon panels and commissions (Gerber and Semmel 1995), as well as in state and national assessments of educational progress ('Students excluded from education data' 1991; National Center for Education Statistics 1995). Such a profound silence regarding an aspect of public policy that schools view as intrusive and expensive seems odd and worrisome.

Moreover, the apparent and formal lack of interest in assessing the progress of disabled and other low-achieving students on a national scale prevents the possibility of understanding school effectiveness as explicit, intentional instructional effort. Instead we can only perpetuate discredited concepts of effectiveness, equality and opportunity that represent a tangled, ambiguous mix of socio-economic and instructional effects. More disturbing, though, if such lack of interest is actually a tacit, consensual policy, one that the public silently embraces, then it is reasonable to infer that school authorities, policy-makers and many reformers consciously or unconsciously reject either the value or cost of a truly universal education as well as the kind of social justice that follows from it. The reform of special education currently advocated or supported thus must be viewed with profound scepticism.

References

Averch, H., Carroll, S., Donaldson, T., Kiesling, H. and Pincus, J. (1972) *How Effective is Schooling? a Critical Review and Synthesis of Research Findings.* Santa Monica, CA: Rand Corporation.

Bacdayan, A. W. (1994) Time-denominated achievement cost curves, learning differences and individualized instruction, *Economics of Education Review*, 13: 43–53.

Bartlett, L. (1989) Disciplining handicapped students: legal issues in light of *Honig v. Doe, Exceptional Children*, 55: 357–66.

Biemiller, A. (1993a) Lake Wobegon revisited: on diversity and education, *Educational Researcher*, 22: 7–12.

Biemiller, A. (1993b) Students differ: so address differences effectively, *Educational Researcher*, 22: 14–15.

Bridge, R. G., Judd, C. M. and Moock, P. R. (1979) *The Determinants of Educational Outcomes.* Cambridge, MA: Ballinger.

Brown, B. W. and Saks, D. H. (1981) The microeconomics of schooling, in D. C. Berliner (ed.) *Review of Research in Education*, vol. 9. Washington, DC: American Educational Research Association.

Catlett, S. M. and Osher, T. W. (1994) *What is Inclusion, Anyway? An Analysis of Organizational Position Statements.* Alexandria, VA: National Association of State Directors of Special Education.

Chaikind, S., Danielson, L. C. and Brauen, M. L. (1993) What do we know about the costs of special education? A selected review, *The Journal of Special Education*, 26: 344–70.

Cole, T. (1990) The history of special education: social control or humanitarian progress? *British Journal of Special Education*, 17: 101–7.

Coleman, J. S., Campbell, E. Q., Hobson, C. J., McPartland, J., Mood, A. M., Weinfield, F. D. and York, R. L. (1966) *Equality of Educational Opportunity.* Washington, DC: US Department of Health, Education and Welfare.

Committee on Policy for Racial Justice (1989) *Visions of a Better Way. A Black Appraisal of Public Schooling.* Washington, DC: Joint Center for Political Studies Press.

Dunn, L. M. (1968) Special education for the mildly retarded: is much of it justifiable? *Exceptional Children*, 35: 5–22.

Fuchs, D. and Fuchs, L. S. (1994) Inclusive schools movement and the radicalization of special education reform. *Exceptional Children*, 60: 294–309.

Gamoran, A. (1992) Is ability grouping equitable? *Educational Leadership*, 50: 11–17.

Gartner, A. and Lipsky, D. K. (1987) Beyond special education: toward a quality system for all students, *Harvard Educational Review*, 57: 367–95.

Gerber, M. M. (1988) Tolerance and technology of instruction: implications for special education reform, *Exceptional Children*, 54: 309–14.

Gerber, M. M. (1989) The new 'diversity' and special education: are we going forward or starting again? *Public Schools Forum*, 3: 19–32.

Gerber, M. M. (1994) Postmodernism in special education, *The Journal of Special Education*, 28: 368–78.

Gerber, M. M. (1995) Inclusion at the high-water mark? Some thoughts on Zigmond and Baker's case studies of inclusive educational programs, *The Journal of Special Education*, 29: 181–91.

Gerber, M. M. and Semmel, M. I. (1985) The microeconomics of referral and reintegration: towards a new paradigm of special education evaluation, *Studies in Educational Evaluation*, 11: 13–29.

Gerber, M. M. and Semmel, M. I. (1995) Why do educational reform commissions fail to address special education? in R. Ginsburg and D. N. Plank (eds) *Commissions, Reports, Reforms, and Educational Policy*. Westport, CN: Praeger.

'Governors seek authority to merge IDEA, other money' (1995) *Special Education Report*, 21: 1–2, 9 August.

Hanushek, E. A. (1989) The impact of differential expenditure on school performance, *Educational Researcher*, 18: 45–51, 62.

Hanushek, E. A. (1994) *Money might matter somewhere: a Response to Hedges, Laine and Greenwald, Educational Researcher*, 23(4): 5–8.

Harvard Educational Review (1969) *Equal Educational Opportunity*. Cambridge, MA: Harvard University Press.

Hedges, L. V., Laine, R. D. and Greenwald, R. (1994a) *Does money matter? a meta-analysis of studies of the effects of differential school inputs on student outcomes (an Exchange: Part 1), Educational Researcher*, 23(3): 5–14.

Hedges, L. V., Laine, R. D. and Greenwald, R. (1994b) *Money does matter somewhere: a Reply to Hanushek, Educational Researcher*, 23(4): 9–10.

Heller, K. A., Holtzman, W. H. and Messick, S. (eds) (1982) *Placing Children in Special Education: a Strategy for Equity*. Washington, DC: National Academy Press.

Hendrick, I. G. and MacMillan, D. L. (1989) Selecting children for special education in New York City: William Maxwell, Elizabeth Farrell, and the development of ungraded classes, 1900–1920, *The Journal of Special Education*, 22: 395–417.

Hodgson, G. (1975) Do schools make a difference? in D. M. Levine and M. J. Bane (eds) *The 'Inequality' Controversy: Schooling and Distributive Justice*. New York: Basic Books.

Hoffman, E. (1975) The American public school and the deviant child: the origins of their involvement, *The Journal of Special Education*, 9: 415–23.

'House IDEA draft would lift discipline barrier' (1995) *Special Education Report*, 21: 1–2, 9 August.

Jencks, C. and Brown, M. (1975) The effects of desegregation on student achievement. Some new evidence from the Equality of Educational Opportunity Survey, *Sociology of Education*, 48: 126–40.

Jencks, C., Smith, M., Acland, H., Bane, M. J., Cohen, D. K., Gintis, H., Heyns, B. and Michelson, S. (1972) *Inequality: a Reassessment of the Effect of Family and Schooling in America*. New York: Basic Books.

Kauffman, J. M. (1993) How we might achieve radical reform of special education, *Exceptional Children*, 60: 6–16.

Kauffman, J. M., Gerber, M. M. and Semmel, M. I. (1988) Arguable assumptions underlying the Regular Education Initiative, *Journal of Learning Disabilities*, 21: 6–11.

Kauffman, J. M. and Hallahan, D. P. (eds) (1995) *The Illusion of Full Inclusion*. Austin, TX: Pro-Ed.

Levine, D. M. and Bane, M. J. (eds) (1975) *The 'Inequality' Controversy: Schooling and Distributive Justice*. New York: Basic Books.

Madden, N. A. and Slavin, R. E. (1983) Mainstreaming students with mild handicaps: academic and social outcomes, *Review of Educational Research*, 53: 519–69.

Mosteller, F. and Moynihan, D. P. (eds) (1972) *On Equality of Educational Opportunity*. New York: Vintage Books.

National Association of State Boards of Education (1992) *The Report of the NASBE Study Group on Special Education*. Alexandria, VA: NASBE.

National Center for Education Statistics (1995) *The Condition of Education*. Washington, DC: US Department of Education.

Purkey, S. C. and Smith, M. S. (1983) Effective schools: a review, *Elementary School Journal*, 83: 427–52.

Purkey, S. C. and Smith, M. S. (1985) School reform: the district policy implications of the effective schools literature, *Elementary School Journal*, 85: 353–89.

Ravitch, E. (1974) *The Great School Wars: New York City, 1805–1973*. New York: Basic Books.

Rutter, M. (1983) School effects on pupil progress: research findings and policy implications, *Child Development*, 54: 1–29.

Sarason, S. B. and Doris, J. (1979) *Educational Handicap, Public Policy, and Social History*. New York: The Free Press.

Semmel, M. I. and Gerber, M. M. (1995) *The School Environments Project*, final report. Santa Barbara, CA: Special Education Research Laboratory, University of California.

Skrtic, T. M. (1991) The special education paradox: equity as the way to excellence, *Harvard Educational Review*, 61: 148–205.

Slavin, R. E. (1993) Students differ: so what? *Educational Researcher*, 22: 13–14.

Stainback, W. and Stainback, S. (1984) A rationale for the merger of special and regular education, *Exceptional Children*, 51: 102–11.

'Students excluded from education data' (1991) *Outcomes*, National Center on Educational Outcomes, University of Minnesota, no. 1.

Tomlinson, S. (1982) *A Sociology of Special Education*. London: Routledge and Kegan Paul.

Trent, Jr., J. W. (1994) *Inventing the Feeble Mind*. Berkeley, CA: University of California Press.

Wainer, H. (1993) Does spending money on education help? A reaction to the Heritage Foundation and the *Wall Street Journal*, *Educational Researcher*, 22: 22–4.

Wang, M. C., Reynolds, M. C. and Walberg, H. J. (1988) Integrating the children of the second system, *Phi Delta Kappan*, 70: 248–51.

Whitted, B. R. (1991) Educational benefits after Timothy W.: where do we go from here? *West's Education Law Reporter*, 68: 549–55.

Will, M. (1986) Educating children with learning problems: a shared responsibility, *Exceptional Children*, 52: 411–15.

Conflicts and dilemmas for professionals in special education

In the late twentieth century professionals have been granted unprecedented powers to affect, regulate and control the lives of large numbers of people in modern societies. As Skrtic recently pointed out (1995: 3) professionals base their claims to authority on the practical claim that any modern society needs 'experts' to solve its problems, and on the political claim that they will use their expert knowledge in a disinterested manner for the common good. Every area of social life considered to be problematic is now subject to some kind of professional scrutiny, especially poverty, crime, disease and education – areas which are now unimaginable without the presence of professionals to alleviate, explain, solve or control. Where issues of disability and special education are concerned, a whole range of professionals now earn their living by assessing, diagnosing, discovering, treating and caring for the special and disabled. Almost all these professionals are employed as experts whose knowledge is of use to state bureaucracies. It is the professional status of those involved in assessment processes which legitimates the complex procedures which have been developed to exclude or marginalize young people from mainstream education. It is professional status which rationalizes the interference with the lives of the disabled which is a routine practice. But it is a nineteenth-century assumption that a 'service ideal', implicit in true professionalism, will ensure that the needs of clients take precedence over the needs of state bureaucracies. This assumption rationalizes and softens much of the direction and control exercised by professionals.

This chapter explores some of the conflicts and dilemmas which arise when professionals are employed by educational bureaucracies with the explicit brief of dealing with those regarded as special or disabled. The chapter notes some characteristics and models of professionalism and the expansion of professional influence as more and more young people come to be labelled as 'special'. The bureaucratization of professional–parent relationships and the problems of the 'new' profession of special educational needs coordinator

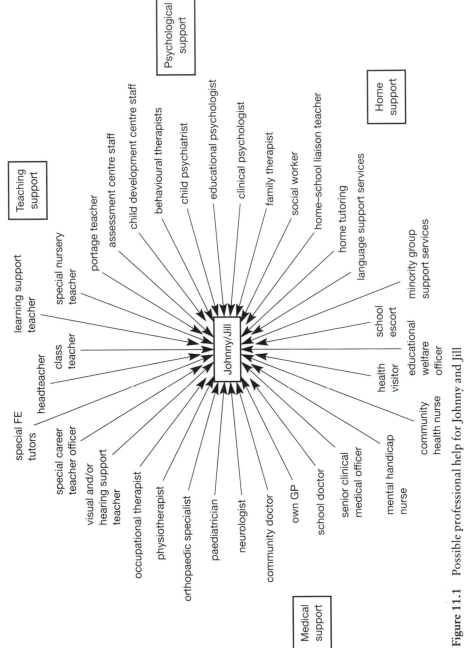

Figure 11.1 Possible professional help for Johnny and Jill

(SENCO), now a required presence in all English and Welsh schools, illustrate some of the conflicts and dilemmas.

The development and characteristics of professionals

Over the past 20 years more and more professionals have joined the older-established professions in claiming a legitimate involvement in special education processes; they constitute what can be, for parents and children, a formidable proliferation of expertise. Indeed, dealing with special educational needs *is* now the province of professionals, almost immune from alternative discourses and views of other groups such as parents and civil rights activists. Figure 11.1 is intended to illustrate the variety of professional services in Britain which could theoretically, be made available to deal with 'Johnny/Jill' should he/she require them. An expanded variety of medical, psychological, teaching support services and home support services are available to deal with special children from pre-school to further education and adult life. It is perhaps unsurprising that in England and Wales in 1990/91 approximately £1.5 billion was spent on provision for special needs pupils.

Each professional group has its own 'culture of professionalism' (Larson 1977), which includes specialized training, its own esoteric language, and its own claims to expert practice. Each professional expects their judgements to be accepted and respected by the clients – children and parents – and by other professionals. An overarching ideology, or generalized belief, that unites all the professionals, is that whatever they do they will be acting 'in the best interests of the child'. This ideology of benevolent humanitarianism (Tomlinson 1982) imbues professionals working with the special and disabled student with a semireligious sanctity, which obscures the reality that professional expertise is being used by governments and state bureaucracies to control particular 'troublesome' social groups. Given that there has been a proliferation of groups claiming professional skills, ideals and status, but who nevertheless are employed by large organizations or state bureaucracies, it is a pertinent question to ask what exactly is a professional. The classic nineteenth-century self-employed professional, typified by the doctor or the lawyer, is not an appropriate way of understanding the modern professional. There are a large number of new professions which share some, if not almost all of the characteristics of other professions, but most professionals now depend to a large extent on employment by the state. Speech therapists and health workers, for example, could sell their skills privately, yet claim to serve the public, just as doctors or lawyers can do, but there is still debate as to how far they are simply an occupational category rather than a profession.

Despite the uncertainty of definition, one of the major aspects of the occupational structure of modern societies is undoubtedly the growth of professionals and professionalization. The American sociologists Faunce and Clellan noted in 1967 that this growth involved:

- more job specification with an increasing proportion of professionals and technicians in the labour force
- a status system in which being a professional and gaining professional recognition is important
- a power structure in which professionals have increasing influence
- a class structure in which class distinctions are increasingly based on access to education and higher level qualifications.

Larson pointed out that professions are not just occupational categories: 'whatever they are, professions are situated in the middle and upper middle levels of the stratification system' (Larson 1977: xvi), and individual professional status is undeniably a middle-class attribute. Since by definition, once a person acquires the education and training required to join a profession, they leave the working class, a relative superiority over (and distance from) the working (and non-working) class is one of the major characteristics of all professions. In special education in all western societies, the majority of the clients dealt with by the various professionals are in the lower socio-economic groups; in the USA, Europe and Australia, where large numbers of ethnic minority pupils are processed into special education, the professional groups are still not only middle class but also predominantly white.

The parents of children being assessed for and placed in special education are likely to have far less education and are more likely to defer to the knowledge and expertise of professionals and to acknowledge their higher social status. This creates an immediate difficulty when professionals are exhorted to 'treat parents as equals' and involve them in decision-making. It is also likely that parents from working-class backgrounds cannot negotiate easily with professionals as they do not have available what Fulcher (1989) has called a 'discourse of democratization' to assert their views and rights.

Professions then, are generally higher status middle-class occupations granted special powers and prestige; although the characteristics of professional groups vary, there is substantial agreement about what makes a profession. These characteristics include having expert esoteric knowledge and techniques, acquired through a specialized training, an esoteric language (or jargon), a claim to autonomy and the right to control the work done, an ethical code and a service ideal. Thus, professionals claim expert knowledge and profess to know better than others what is wrong with their clients. Armed with their expert knowledge, professionals ask to be trusted and do not expect their clients to question their judgements. Professionals not only claim to know better, but also are allowed to define the standards by which their superior competence is judged. 'A profession is an insulated, self-regulating community whose members share an image of the world that is based on strong socialisation and common exposure to the profession's communally-accepted definition of valid knowledge' (Skrtic 1995: 8).

Professional associations insist on a lengthy training through which their particular body of knowledge and techniques are communicated; the training is usually under the control of professional bodies. The creation of a 'professional mystique' is important as professional powers and privileges depend on an ability to create an aura of mystery around the work, and language plays an important role in the creation of the mystique. Habermas (1974) examined in some detail the way those with authority legitimate their actions and the way they use language to dominate and control. In special education, the use of a 'treatment language', carried over from medical discourse, is a powerful tool for professionals. Habermas also pointed out that the use of professional language can be a cover to prevent an open discussion of 'what is really going on'. In special education practices, 'what is really going on' is frequently an attempt by professionals to persuade clients to accept certain judgements without recourse to actual coercion. Special education is an area to which clients seldom come voluntarily, unless there are very clear resource implications, and enforceable procedures – legal sanctions which can force parents to accept special education for their children – have been built into English Education Acts in 1914, 1921, 1944, 1981, 1988 and 1993. The sanction of enforceable procedures has always conflicted with professional claims that assessment and treatment is motivated solely by humanitarian concerns. Professionals seldom mention to parents that coercion can be used if persuasion, fortified by superior knowledge and treatment language, fails to convince. Despite the possibilities of coercion, professionals working in special education share with other professionals the characteristics of the 'service ideal'. They claim a degree of altruism and a disinterestedness from wider social, political and economic considerations.

Models of professionalism

The archetypical nineteenth-century professional groups – notably medicine and the law – were in modern terms, self-employed capitalists who nevertheless presented an anti-market image and distanced themselves from the developing bureaucratic practices of the state. Indeed, professionals regarded themselves, and some still do, as the antithesis of the bureaucratic modes of 'people-processing' which have little regard for individual feelings or interests. But, professionals involved in special education have increasingly been drawn into the service of local and central bureaucracies whose concerns are with the wider education system and with wider social, political and economic considerations.

They are, in Larson's term (1977: 179), 'organizational professionals' who carry out their professional activities within the confines and under the direction of state organizations or publicly funded institutions. Larson has described the way in which groups as varied as college presidents, librarians and social workers can all claim to carry out professional activities while working within state bureaucracies.

Organizational professionals, however, are susceptible to the decisions of those in control of the organization, who may dispense with their services. The expense of employing a variety of professionals to test, observe and interview children and parents, write statements of special educational needs, hold meetings and case conferences, has increased considerably in Britain. Local education authorities, holding limited funds for special educational needs, have attempted to control professional decisions on placements and resources, assessment decisions by professionals being increasingly embedded in the financial needs of local authority bureaucracies. They have for example cut down the numbers of educational psychologists employed to assess children. Ironically, some of these psychologists have returned to the autonomous practice of selling their services as consultants, their reports then being used by parents to claim resources from the local education authorities. Despite working within organizations, most professionals dealing with those regarded as special or disabled have clung on to an image of the professional as a humanitarian agent. Indeed, the overarching model of professional involvement in special education was neatly captured by Kirp in 1983, who, after comparing the situation in the USA and the UK wrote that 'The model of professionalism involved in the UK is essentially a humanitarian welfare model which contemplates professionals and administrators working on behalf of an ever-expanding clientele towards an agreed common goal' (Kirp 1983: 83).

This model, as Kirp pointed out, takes no account of any issues of civil rights, or parental rights backed by the law. Kirp noted that the Warnock Committee, who visited the USA in the 1970s 'came away horrified at the reliance on administrative hearings and litigation . . . in the framework of the Warnock report, rights would war with the idea of efficient service provided by professionals acting to the best of their abilities' (p. 94). Indeed, Mary Warnock herself declared in an interview with Kirp that 'there is something deeply unattractive about the spectacle of someone demanding his own rights' (p. 95).

A 'rights' framework for special education which is overtly political emerged in the USA following the 1964 Civil Rights Act and has been slowly emerging as a possible alternative framework to 'humanitarian bureaucracy' in Western Europe and Australia. As Fulcher has noted, 'the rights discourse is seen as the most progressive and obvious strategy for those excluded from full citizenship in modern welfare states' (Fulcher 1989: 31). The whole way in which professionalism operates in special education has been subjected to a stringent critique by Fulcher. The incorporation of professionals into the bureaucratic practice of control and regulation of large groups of people via welfare state services has, in her view, assisted in the process of marginalizing the disabled and the special, and helped to disempower clients and prevent democratic educational practices which would make assessment for exclusion unnecessary (Fulcher 1989).

There is some evidence that alternative frameworks within which assessment decisions can be made are gradually emerging in Britain, as parents increasingly turn to litigation to clarify the 'right' to particular kinds of provision or levels of resources for their statemented children. As part of an effort to deflect litigation, the 1993 Education Act set up a Special Educational Needs Tribunal, with a president appointed by the Secretary of State for Education, to hear parental appeals against local authority and professional decisions on their children. Some professionals too, may be thinking of themselves in terms of advocates for rights as well as humanitarian bureaucrats.

Professional conflicts

One of the consequences of becoming an organizational professional and working within state bureaucracy is that interprofessional rivalries can be exacerbated and tensions between working on behalf of government and holding to the professional 'service ideal' become more evident. The 'smooth teamwork' envisaged by the Warnock Committee of Enquiry in 1978 (DES 1978) has seldom been a reality. Professionals in special education are as likely as other professionals to experience conflicts over communications, anxiety over status and annoyance at the perceived inadequacies of fellow professionals. In the assessment processes for special education in Britain at the present time some specific conflicts to be noted include:

- a fragmented professionalism;
- the bureaucratization of professional–parent relationships;
- the ambiguous position of professionals within local bureaucracies.

During the 1980s as the assessment process became more bureaucratized under the control of LEA administrators, professional antagonisms appeared to diminish somewhat, but they may have been replaced by what Fulcher (1989) has called a 'fragmented professionalism'. This is the situation where professionals become more reluctant to criticise each other but negotiate to accept or reject a client – 'he's my child not yours' or conversely, 'he's yours, not ours'. A fragmentation of professional responsibilities clearly works against the professional service ideal and a responsibility for the 'whole' child. Professional fragmentation in Britain is currently paralleled by a structural fragmentation, as some schools now seek to deny access to 'difficult' children (Ball *et al.* 1994). The increase in the numbers of children excluded from schools is now well documented (DFE 1994a). Governors at a school in Barnet, London, sent a letter to parents in 1992 urging that the school could 'refuse entry to known troublemakers. Work will be able to proceed faster. Your children will get better results' (Dean 1992: 6).

A second major area of conflict for professionals continues to be with parents. At face value the 1981 Special Education Act formalized a cooperative relationship with parents, parents being ostensibly drawn into the assessment process with legal rights and responsibilities. In practice, the bureaucratization of the professional–parent relationship and of the assessment process has led to a situation in which the primary function of parental involvement is to legitimize professional decisions. In a study of children being assessed as emotionally and behaviourally disturbed (Galloway et al. 1994) many parents felt that their own contribution to assessment was only listened to when they were confirming professional views or decisions and professionals continued to divert or persuade parents towards a seeming consensus. The unique power position, the position of professionals as gatekeepers of crucial information, and the almost foregone conclusion that a child's 'needs' will be subordinate to the perceived 'needs' of schools and teachers negated the notion of parents as equal partners in the assessment process. Ultimately professionals know that in any conflict of interest, they have the sanction of coercion against uncooperative parents.

The ambiguous position of 'organizational professionals' who are in effect 'paid servants of the state' and who carry out their work within the bureaucratic structures of local government is a potential source of conflict between professionals and administrators, and between professionals and their client. It has already been noted that organizations can and do dispense with the services of their professionals. The Government Audit Commission, in its 1992 report on provision made by local education authorities for pupils with special education needs, noted that while

> the educational psychology [sic] service has a pivotal role in deciding with schools and parents whether it is appropriate formally to assess a child, in some LEAs, psychologists have not taken this role either through fear of conflict with the schools, or because the LEA has had no policy on which to base their position.
>
> (Audit Commission 1992: 61)

LEA policy, particularly after 1988 when local management of schools was introduced, has been totally finance-driven as regards assessment for special needs. The 1981 Education Act and a statementing process which required professionals, on behalf of LEAs, to specify provision, was theoretically a blank cheque whereby parents could demand, or professionals recommend, levels of provision which the LEA could not afford. LEAs attempted to use psychologists as gatekeepers to resources, trying to ensure that the wording on statements concerning provision was vague enough to keep costs down, and to delay the completion of statementing. There is evidence that psychologists who refuse to comply with LEA directives on recommendation for provision found their jobs in jeopardy (Pyke 1990). Professions working within bureaucracies are certainly subject to many more conflicts and ambiguities than the old-style self-employed professional.

Case studies of conflict and dilemmas

A study reported in Galloway *et al.* (1994) and funded by the Economic and Social Research Council, was carried out between 1989 and 1991 in three English LEAs and aimed to investigate the views of professionals, parents and children who were involved in the assessment process for possible emotional and behavioural disturbance (EBD). The methodology included observing the key stages of the assessment procedures for 30 children who had been referred by their school as 'having EBD' (which included attending case conferences) and interviewing all the participants in the process, including parents and children at several stages of the assessment. The research aimed to clarify the way professionals defined and used the concept of EBD, and to discover the sources of conflict or agreement between the various professionals involved, between the professionals and the LEA administration, the parents and the other groups (see Armstrong and Galloway 1992; Galloway *et al.* 1994).

The study found evidence of fragmented professionalism, barriers to partnership with parents, and of psychologists being used as gatekeepers to resources. A fragmented professionalism was most evident in the way schools defined their problems. For example, comments were often made such as: 'The headteacher wanted me [a psychologist] to agree that B was not appropriately placed in her school' – that is, B was 'not ours' but someone else's! In another case an LEA inspector challenged a psychologist who was advising teachers because this was 'not his job'. Professionals too, were often 'fragmented' by competing expectations from a variety of sources – parents, LEA officials, other professionals.

Barriers to communication and partnership with parents were also evident during the study. Bureaucratic messages made little impact on parents, who felt uninformed and unsupported, and although often dissatisfied with their child's assessment, felt compelled to agree with professional decisions even when the decisions upset them. In one case a child (John) had been referred for behaviour problems in school. Vague and unsubstantiated allegations of abuse in the home were made and a community nurse who visited the home advised Social Services that 'as professionals we were anxious that we had not managed to engage and intervene within the family and explore deficits in the parenting role' (Armstrong and Galloway 1992: 194). The headteacher in this case reported that 'the parents were only co-operative on the surface' and the whole approach to John's behaviour became defined as a problem within the home and parents. John's mother was demoralized by this process – she thought the headteacher 'was assessing me rather than John, shifting the blame onto me, he used to speak to me like I was a really bad mother, I used to come home in tears' (p. 194). The parents, lacking information and power, had perforce to accept the professionals' view that their deficits as parents had created John's problems, and felt they had no power to determine or influence decisions taken by the local education authority and the professionals who worked within it. In Britain the whole coercive framework of special education continues to make nonsense of a rhetoric of parental involvement and partnership.

If existing professionals working in special education experience conflicts and dilemmas within their organizations, between themselves and with parents, it is to be expected that any 'new' professional entering the areas will experience similar problems. In England and Wales the 1993 Education Act, a long and complex piece of legislation which devoted a whole section (Part 3) to special educational needs, introduced a code of practice on the identification and assessment of special educational needs (DFE 1994b) and the requirement for every mainstream school to appoint a SEN coordinator. Although a majority of schools already had designated teachers working with children with special educational needs, this was the first time that a legal requirement for such a professional, who rapidly acquired the acronym of SENCO, was laid on all schools. The professional tasks of the SENCO include maintaining a SEN register and keeping records of all children with special educational needs, coordinating provision for such children, liaising with parents and external professional agencies, and training and supporting other teachers. The SENCOs are expected to implement the five stages of assessment and provision set out in the code for children considered to 'have SEN', as the quasi-medical terminology adopted in schools has it (see Garner 1995), and to attempt to keep as many children as possible in mainstream schools. The five stages (adapted from DFE 1994b: 3) are as follows:

Stage 1: class or subject teacher identify or register a child's special educational needs and take action in consultation with the SENCO;
Stage 2: the SENCO takes the lead in gathering information and coordinating the child's special educational provision;
Stage 3: the SENCO and teachers are supported by specialists from outside the school;
Stage 4: the local education authority considers the need for statutory assessment and a multidisciplinary assessment;
Stage 5: the local education authority considers the need for a statement of special educational needs and, if appropriate, makes a statement.

The code suggests that SENCOs are responsible for providing an individual education plan (IEP) for children at stage 2, but no advice or guidance on good practice or curriculum for the children is offered and no mention is made of resources. Indeed, a major intention of the code of practice is to ensure that schools deal with as many children identified as having special educational needs as possible, without claiming extra resources and without the statementing process which leads to claims for such resources.

The likely dilemmas for SENCOs include: persuading their colleagues to keep and deal with difficult and 'troublesome' children, at a time when other legislation is requiring that teachers 'raise standards' and get as many pupils as possible to pass public examinations; identifying and working with the large number of professionals and agencies involved in special education; and, since SENCOs have largely been appointed from existing teaching staff in schools, finding time to carry out the newly assigned tasks. As one commentator has already noted, 'This person will carry great responsibilities as well as a greatly increased workload. Without remuneration, training and time free from teaching duties, who would want to undertake this role?' (Simmons 1994: 56). SENCOs appear to be the latest addition to the organizational professionals appointed to solve impossible ideological commitments and wider educational dilemmas.

Conclusions

This chapter has described the expanded organizational professionalism which now characterizes special education in Britain and elsewhere in 'developed' countries. Notions of autonomous professional behaviour and a service ideal have perforce become subordinated to the requirements of state bureaucracies and organizations – notably the financial needs of local education authorities and the needs of schools to have troublesome children removed or dealt with by other professionals. The model of professionalism continues to be that of a humanitarian welfare bureaucrat still heavily influenced by medical practices, with a treatment language and a view of clients (parents and children) as deficient. A variety of new conflicts and dilemmas have been generated by the increased subordination of professionals in special education to the state, including a fragmented professionalism which encourages a division of responsibility for children; conflicts with parents who feel subordinated to professional decisions and insufficiently consulted or informed; and an ambiguity of position as local or central authorities demand professional behaviour and ideals while treating professionals as expendable employees. It remains true, however, that interprofessional conflicts are often themselves the source of a particular construction of children's needs. The 'new' professional of special educational needs coordinator in English schools will be at the centre of dilemmas of definition as teachers continue to want certain children wholly or partially excluded from the mainstream, while local education authorities have a financial interest in unresourced inclusion.

As Skrtic has noted, examining professional practices within special education 'exposes the inconsistencies and contradictions . . . in the knowledge tradition that has justified [special education] practices and discourses in the twentieth century' (Skrtic 1995: 52).

References

Armstrong, D. and Galloway, D. (1992) On being a client: conflicting perspectives or assessment, in T. Booth, W. Swann, M. Masterton and P. Potts (eds) *Learning for All. Policies for Diversity in Education*. London: Routledge.

Audit Commission and Her Majesty's Inspectorate (1992) *Getting in on the Act. Provision for Pupils with Special Educational Needs: the National Picture*. London: HMSO.

Ball, S. J., Bowe, R. and Gewirtz, S. (1994) Market forces and parental choice, in S. Tomlinson (ed.) *Educational Reform and its Consequences*. London: Rivers-Oram Press/IPPR.

Dean, C. (1992) Troublesome pupils cannot be sifted out, *Times Educational Supplement*, 3 July.

Department for Education [DFE] (1994a) *Statistics on School Exclusion*. London: DFE.

Department for Education [DFE] (1994b) *Code of Practice on the Identification and Assessment of Special Educational Needs*. London: DFE.

Department of Education and Science [DES] (1978) *Special Educational Needs*. London: HMSO.

Faunce, W. and Clellan, D. A. (1967) Professionalization and stratification patterns in an industrial community, *American Journal of Sociology*, 72: 341–52.

Fulcher, G. (1989) *Disabling Policies – a Comparative Approach to Educational Policy and Disability*. Lewes: Falmer Press.

Garner, P. (1995) Sense or nonsense? Dilemmas in the SEN code of practice, *Support for Learning*, 10(1): 3–7.

Galloway, D., Armstrong, D. and Tomlinson, S. (1994) *The Assessment of Special Educational Needs – Whose Problem?* London: Longman.

Habermas, J. (1974) *Theory and Practice*. London: Heinemann.

Kirp, D. (1983) Professionalisation as a policy choice: British special education in corporative perspectives, in J. G. Chambers and W. T. Hartman (eds) *Special Education Policies – Their History, Implementation and Finance*. Philadelphia, PA: Temple University Press.

Larson, M. S. (1977) *The Rise of Professionalism – a Sociological Analysis*. Berkeley, CA: University of California Press.

Pyke, N. (1990) Psychologist wins support for sacking, *Times Educational Supplement*, 4 July.

Simmons, K. (1994) Decoding a new message, *British Journal of Special Education*, 21(2): 56–9.

Skrtic, T. M. (ed.) (1995) *Disability and Democracy. Reconstructing (Special) Education for Post-Modernity*. New York: Teachers College Press.

Tomlinson, S. (1982) *A Sociology of Special Education*. London: Routledge.

Index

MARKETS, CHOICE AND EQUITY IN EDUCATION

Sharon Gewirtz, Stephen J. Ball and Richard Bowe

- What has been the impact of parental choice and competition upon schools?
- How do parents choose schools for their children?
- Who are the winners and losers in the education market?

These important and fundamental questions are discussed in this book which draws upon a three year intensive study of market forces in education. The authors carefully examine the complexities of parental choice and school responses to the introduction of market forces in education. Particular attention is paid to issues of opportunity and equity, and patterns of access and involvement related to gender, ethnicity and social class are identified.

This is the first comprehensive study of market dynamics in education and it highlights the specificity and idiosyncrasies of local education markets. However, the book is not confined to descriptions of these markets but also offers a systematic theorization of the education market, its operation and consequences. It will be of particular interest to students on BEd and Masters courses in education, headteachers and senior managers in schools, and policy analysts.

Contents
Researching education markets – Choice and class: parents in the marketplace – An analysis of local market relations – Managers and markets: school organization in transition – Schooling in the marketplace: a semiological analysis – Internal practices: institutional responses to competition – Choice, equity and control – Glossary of terms – References – Index.

224pp   0 335 19369 2 (Paperback)   0 335 19370 6 (Hardback)

MANAGING SPECIAL EDUCATION
CODES, CHARTERS AND COMPETITION

John Fish and Jennifer Evans

How can the educational and other special needs of children and young people with disabilities and/or significant learning difficulties be met by policies which emphasize competition, market forces and short-term financial planning?

This is the key issue which concerns *Managing Special Education*. The book discusses a number of persistent and unresolved issues about the relationship of special education to primary, secondary and further education.

Local management of schools and colleges and increased parental choice has created new and difficult market conditions for special educational provision. Increased choice costs money and the more special the need, the greater the cost. How will responsibilites delegated to schools and colleges ensure that children, young people and adults with disabilities and learning difficulties have reasonable access to quality educational opportunities, given that the market system provides no incentives for schools and colleges to provide higher cost minority provision unless it is self financing?

This book is both topical and forward looking. It concludes with a possible agenda for the future which identifies both issues to be resolved and management tasks from central government to schools and college level.

Contents
Education and individual differences – The new framework – Perspectives in 1993 – Basic issues and policy development – Meeting needs in schools – A range of provision – Post-16 further and continuing education – Funding special education – Major themes revisited – An agenda for the future – Bibliography – Index.

144pp   0 335 19438 9 (Paperback)   0 335 19439 7 (Hardback)